REALISM
IN
EUROPEAN
THEATRE AND DRAMA,
1870-1920

REALISM
IN
EUROPEAN
THEATRE AND DRAMA,
1870-1920
A BIBLIOGRAPHY

Compiled by
Robert D. Boyer

Greenwood Press
Westport, Connecticut • London, England

Library of Congress Cataloging in Publication Data

Boyer, Robert D
  Realism in European theatre and drama, 1870-1920.

  Includes index.
  1. European drama—19th century—Bibliography.
2. European drama—20th century—Bibliography.
3. Realism in literature—Bibliography. 4. Theater—
Europe—Bibliography. I. Title.
Z5784.R27B69 [PN1851] 809.2'9'12   78-19934
ISBN 0-313-20607-4

Library of Congress Catalog Card Number: 78-19934
ISBN: 0-313-20607-4

First published in 1979

Greenwood Press, Inc.
51 Riverside Avenue, Westport, Connecticut 06880

Printed in the United States of America

10 9 8 7 6 5 4 3 2 1

CONTENTS

ACKNOWLEDGMENTS

That this volume was ever completed is due quite significantly to the encouragement and assistance of many friends and colleagues, to whom I offer sincere, if inadequate, thanks.

For generously sharing their considerable expertise in my behalf, as well as for kind words of confidence in the project, I am grateful to Mildred E. Gillars, Frank Rodriguez, Lowanne E. Jones and Clifford Hallam.

More than praise and gratitude are due to Jane M. Ott, who typed the bibliography twice, carefully maneuvering through the pitfalls and potholes of my rough manuscript with competence and experience, and transforming the most difficult copy into attractive, finished text.

The Federal Work/Study Program underwrote the salaries of three undergraduate assistants whose dogged and congenial cooperation considerably unburdened me for many months: David Kizer, Richard Lindgren, and especially Kathleen Shear, who negotiated the musty library stacks with ease, compiled and collated with unfailing good humor, and in sum, more than earned her meager stipend.

At risk of neglecting many other deserving persons, who gave of their time and energy, I gladly name Sandi Bogus, Michael and Jacqueline Hurwitz, Beth Hutchison, Janet Johnsen, Jenny King, Glen Kizer, Lorelei Lanier, and Patricia Wilson.

The OSU College of Humanities (Arthur E. Adams, Dean) supplied two small grants-in-aid which paid for a substantial part of the filing supplies and typing services.

I am particularly indebted to Arthur H. Stickney of Greenwood Press for his unflagging confidence, encouragement, and patience.

Robert D. Boyer

PREFACE

Several years ago, when preparing a new undergraduate course in the Realistic Drama, I became aware of a disturbing paucity of useful reference material. I was determined that the course should go beyond the major playwrights of this genre and offer the students an experience in the many lesser-known writers, who in their own time were both influential and commercially successful. Early on, however, I discovered that locating the widely scattered materials on the second-rank realistic dramatists often involved frustrating and time-consuming effort, with precious little result. When coupled with the remarkable fact that even for the major playwrights the existing bibliographies are outdated or poorly compiled, my discovery regarding the lack of scholarship on lesser writers forcefully demonstrated the need for an extensive, current survey of resources in the realistic school of dramaturgy. If undertaking such a bibliography was to be feasible, I had to make certain decisions regarding the scope of the survey, particularly the period to be covered.

The realistic movement in the European theatre began shortly after the mid-point of the nineteenth century and has endured to the present day, for despite the onslaught of a myriad of anti-realistic styles, Realism continues to flourish (particularly, though superficially, in popular dramatic forms). Moreover, the extensive history of the movement, plus the extraordinary number of playwrights involved, made an unlimited compilation, including over a hundred years of critical materials, unmanageable. Thus, for pragmatic reasons, I chose to limit the work to the fifty-year period from 1870 to 1920, which represents the formative and experimental phase of the movement. It was in that period that Realism became the prevailing style in the European theatre.

Although tentative efforts toward more realistic stagecraft—in dialogue, setting, and even theme—can be discerned before 1870, that year seemed a congenial starting line. Plays such as Otto Ludwig's *The Forester* (1850), Alexandre Dumas *fils' The Illegitimate Son* (1858), and Alexander Ostrovski's *The Thunderstorm* (1860), as well as several of Ivan Turgenev's works for the stage, clearly presage the new movement, but these works were lonely and anomalous experiments, almost unnoticed amid the flood of popular Romantic Drama. Early in the 1870s, the frail, splintered evidence of the realistic impetus in drama began to coalesce and arouse the interest of serious critics, innovative writers and, slightly later, theatre managers.

Alternatively, by the post-World War I period, all of the characteristics and major variations of dramatic Realism had been introduced, the style was firmly established, and its potentials had been fully exploited. Additionally, by the second decade of the twentieth century, reputable critics were widely acknowledging the artistic merits of Realism, and the plays of this genre had become standard fare in the playhouses of Europe and the Americas. The playwrights of the early period were innovators; later realistic playwrights, irrespective of their competence and artistic accomplishment, have been imitators.

Once I had determined a manageable time frame for the volume, I established secondary limitations and specific criteria to give needed focus and consistency to the final compilation. Since the widely recognized function of such a bibliography is to provide, in an efficient manner, useful information for the researcher, every effort has been made to simplify this volume for practical use, especially through providing *complete* entries, without the frustrating abbreviations and other bibliographical shortcuts that often plague such works.

Obviously, a series of rather discrete decisions was involved regarding each entry, and it is unnecessary—indeed it would be pretentious—to attempt to list every criterion on which the final decisions of inclusion and exclusion were made. However, the two primary principles of *accesibility* and *utility*, which characterize my bibliographic guide, may be expressed in the following summary:

1. The bibliographic entries represent works of scholarly interest, concerning the general subject of Realism and the dramaturgy of the individual playwrights in that genre.

2. Only works of potential value to an understanding of the *realistic* dramaturgy of the playwrights, in the period covered, and that dramaturgy's subsequent influence, have been included.

3. Only European playwrights have been selected; Realism made no important impact on American dramaturgy until very late in the period covered.

4. No dramatist, of however great reputation, has been included if his

contribution to Realism was only a minor part of his *oeuvre* (e.g., one play of no particular influence).

5. No playwright has been included on whom no critical articles, theses, or books are available (i.e., one for whom only biographical information and a play list could be offered).

6. In regard to the *major* writers, only a sturdy collection of standard works has been included, though the listing of materials published since 1960 is as comprehensive as possible.

7. The list of selected full-length plays, which precedes the bibliographic section on each dramatist, includes the significant plays of the writer in both realistic and nonrealistic styles for the sake of comprehensiveness and of the usefulness of that section.

8. Dates given for individual plays represent the earliest appearance of the play, in print or in production. Because dates for several of the minor plays are in dispute in reputable sources, I have given the earliest plausible date.

9. No works (books, articles, or theses) devoted to the analysis of a single play have been included.

10. No critiques of a specific production or productions of a play have been included.

11. No published versions of the individual plays or anthologies have been included (unless they contain substantial critical material).

The bibliographic entries contained in this volume represent criticism and other scholarship dating from the 1870s to early in 1978, at which time the search for additional resources was terminated.

Robert D. Boyer
May 1978

THE EMERGENCE OF REALISM IN THE EUROPEAN THEATRE

In 1748, the French encyclopedist Denis Diderot argued that "the perfection of a spectacle consists in the imitation of an action so exact that the spectator, deceived without interruption, imagines himself present at the action itself."[1] Curiously, the eighteenth-century stagecraft with which Diderot was familiar, replete with artifice and spectacular fakery on all levels, exhibited this ideal of imitation so minimally that Diderot's vision can only be seen as a remarkable prophecy of a profound and lasting movement, but one that would not be felt in European theatres for another hundred years.

The history of theatre in Europe may be depicted as a broken series of overlapping, often disorderly, experiments seeking a completely appropriate and fully satisfying rhetoric of imitation by which the entire length and breadth of man's experience—or that portion of it deemed "suitable" by the authorities—can be interpreted by actors for an audience. Each generation has explored anew the potentialities of imitation—inventing, refining, and discarding innumerable rules, formulas, conventions, and other artifices. When the concerted efforts of theatre artists produced a recognizably consistent mode of dramaturgy and stagecraft, lasting at least a few generations, subsequent theatre historians have pronounced its special collection of techniques and principles "a style."

In the middle of the nineteenth century, a few daring playwrights, concerned with the banality that had overwhelmed the popular stages of Europe, began to develop a new style, almost unnoticed. Influenced by the unusual honesty of the prose writers of France and Russia, they began to discern the artistic merit of imitating life, on stage, with greater exactitude, allowing the daily experience of man, in all of its detail, to be the compelling example. The goal of these authors was to reproduce life—that is, to imitate action flawlessly—without the artifices and fakery and without the philosophic and moral prejudices typical of romantic writing. Russian playwrights led their European contemporaries toward this ideal of uncontrived dramaturgy, because, as John Gassner has written, the Russians "thought not of theatrical effect but of life first."[2] The style of dramatic writing that they developed came to be known as Realism, and it would shortly engender an offshoot called Naturalism.

DEFINITION OF TERMS

Both the term "Realism" and the term "Naturalism" had been part of philosophic jargon for some years when they were introduced into the vocabulary of the drama. Their usage in dramatic criticism, however, is little illuminated by their established philosophic usage. Dramatic Realism is most simply defined as the set of artistic strategies designed to achieve verisimilitude on stage, to create the appearance of the life that is, with no discernible artifice, no self-justifying poesy, no pretty illusions, and most importantly, no lies. The subject matter is hard material fact (as opposed to the soft, dreamy illusion of Romanticism), which is crafted into a unique form, carefully disguised. William Gerhardie, in his seminal work on Chekhov, expressed this objective, with special insight, as[3]

> extracting from life . . . its characteristic features—for life outside the form of art is like the sea, blurred, formless and with no design—and the replacing of them in a design calculated to represent, within art's focus, life that is like the sea, blurred, formless and with no design.

Naturalism is an extreme form of Realism in which observation and reproduction of detail often become ends in themselves, and for which the subject matter chosen is typically the seamier side of the human condition. All form or design is denied and traditional ideas of art are held to be inimical to the desired end; thus, art approaches science, and the drama becomes documentary—little more than extremely accurate reportage. Emile Zola, announcing the introduction of Naturalism in his Preface to *Therese Raquin* (1873), made clear that the model was to be life itself, "an immense field where each may study and create as he likes," not corrupted by the artist's imagination, selection or arrangement:[4]

> I am for no school, because I am for human truth, which excludes all sects and all systems. . . . The word *art* displeases me; it contains the idea of . . . necessary arrangement and absolute ideal. To make art, is that not outside of man and of nature?

The impulse, however, is the same for both Realism and Naturalism—Gerhardie neatly described it as the desire "to ressurect the complete illusion of real life, using the things characteristic of real life."[5] The results are clearly comparable, although the techniques vary by degree and occasionally by philosophic justification. Thus, for the sake of convenience, I shall use the term "Realism" as inclusive of Naturalism in the remainder of this essay.

THE REVOLT AGAINST MELODRAMA

To understand the emergence of the realistic urge in the theatre, one must investigate the condition of dramatic art at the time Realism first appeared and attempt to comprehend the prevailing taste of the mid-nineteenth-century audience. Realism was a radical response, an undisguised reaction, to Romanticism in the popular theatre—which meant, for the most part, melodrama. Likewise, it was a rebuke to the value system that lay behind the literary impulse on which that popular genre was based, an impulse described by Hippolyte Taine (writing of English literature specifically) as, "always moral, never psychological, bent on exactly measuring the degree of human honesty, ignorant of the mechanisms of our sentiments and faculties."[6]

Melodrama depicted the irrational, dreamy side of life, and postulated a world of absolute values, governed by a just and omnipotent God, who regularly intervened in the affairs of men. Man himself was seen as a perfectable being, a child of God, especially created by divine plan, and thereby endowed with inherent dignity. The universe was perceived as an innately good and congenial environment for the stalwart and God-fearing. The good man might suffer temporarily, but he would ultimately see justice done, for virtue must inevitably triumph if Nature's God loves virtue; moreover, evil doers would be punished in proportion to their misdeeds.

Since the appeal of melodrama was primarily to the impoverished and downtrodden, particularly to the urban proletariat, the plays provided escapist theatre, turning the playhouse into a never-never land where the reality of vermin-ridden and cheerless slums could be repressed for a few hours of moral uplift, haloed by the almost constant music from which the genre takes its name. Faraway settings, narratives from history, and exotic characters helped the spectator to forget his life in the fetid streets and sweatshops of Paris or Petersburg, London or Glasgow. The theatre provided a lively emotional experience—a "culinary experience," to use Brecht's phrase. The spectator could check his intelligence, along with his coat, at the playhouse door. He would be asked to feel, not to think, to forget, not to confront the realities of nineteenth-century urban existence. The overwhelming evidence that most playwrights were no longer attempting to touch the contemporary condition of man, but were supplying a mindless, amnesic experience in the theatre, struck the early Realists as an abdication of a central commitment of the drama: to present the truth of human experience on the stage. Emile Zola, in the preface to *Therese Raquin*, certainly with more hope than objective evidence, declared that the "despicable melodrama," along with historical drama, was dead in the hearts of the general public.

If Realism grew out of an immediate need to provide an alternative to the primary dramatic style of the popular theatre, its philosophical roots and intellectual impetus came not so much from theatrical tradition as from social conditions and intellectual currents being profoundly felt throughout Europe. No earlier style of dramaturgy can be demonstrated more strongly to be a product of the *Zeitgeist* ("the spirit of the times") in which it flourished as can Realism. From the beginning, its writers and sympathetic critics turned to intellectual ideals, not theatrical effect, as justification for their cause. Although aimed at remedying maladies of the popular, commercial theatre, Realism managed, paradoxically, to cultivate a relatively small *coterie* audience: the literati, plus the sophisticated upper-middle class—an audience, in temperament and education, not unlike the playwrights and critics themselves.

The intellectual currents that intermingled in nineteenth-century Europe, and that gave nerve and justification to the new drama, cannot be discretely segmented, but we can isolate the most important and relate these influences directly to dramatic practice.

INFLUENCE: NEW THEOLOGICAL IDEAS

Across the Continent, new theological ideas were being debated and embraced by serious scholar and dilettante alike. Søren Kierkegaard and Friedrich Nietzsche laid the foundations for modern existentialism. Their emphasis on individual responsibility, their rejection of systematic philosophy, and their refusal to accept the comforting illusions of institutional Christianity—different as their ultimate conclusions were—challenged the world of theology. By daring to question the traditionally accepted "meaning of existence," Nietzsche, Kierkegaard, and their comrades opened the door to greater freedom of decision, but, often, to a greater sense of personal alienation. Atheism found a new, broader audience and a new name: free-thinking. For many serious men and women, like Ibsen's Mrs. Alving, the existence of a benevolent and interventionist God was no longer necessary as a basic axiom of universal truth. Whatever became of the Everlasting Arms? Karl Marx, likewise, argued that religions were merely socially expedient ideologies used by the economic establishment to pacify the working class, which had no hope of social progress or justice in this life, with dreams of rest and happiness in the afterlife. Flaubert, in his short story "A Simple Heart," told of an old woman who believed her stuffed parrot to be the Holy Ghost; were man's religious myths really the product of his own deranged imagination? In the latter part of the century, there was serious debate over the place of Christianity in the modern scientific world. Charles Péguy, a socialist and a Christian mystic, summed up one reasoned position in his novel *Clio* (1910):[7]

> What we wish to say . . . is that the modern world has renounced the system altogether, as well as the mystique. . . . [From now on] there is another world, a modern world, and this modern world is not simply an evil Christian world, a world of bad Christianity . . . but an un-Christian world, absolutely de-Christianized, literally, totally un-Christian. That is what must be said, what must be believed. That is what must be seen. If it were only the old story . . . that sin had once again intruded, that would be noth-

ing. We have become used to that; the world is used to that . . . one more bad Christian century like many others. If people knew history as well as I know it, they would know that it has always been thus, that all of those centuries, those twenty centuries, have always been centuries of miserable Christianity.

What is interesting, what is new, is that there is no longer any Christianity at all. That expresses not only the extent but the type and nature of the disaster.

We have seen instituted before our eyes a world both viable and entirely un-Christian. It is necessary to admit that; those who deny it are wretched.

Péguy, the editor of the prestigious *Cahiers de la Quinzaine*, France's leading journal of literature and ideas, thus gave voice to the religious malaise that had gripped Europe for half a century.

In the serious theatre, this spiritual doubt and religious degeneration were in great part responsible for the repudiation of melodrama, which had postulated its world view on traditional religious foundations and comforts. The realistic writers typically pictured a world without God and without the consoling illusions of religion, often a world of accident and chaos. The portraits they produced of the clergy (like Hauptmann's Pastor Kittelhaus and Ibsen's Pastor Manders) were uncomplimentary, depicting guileful or insipid men dispensing false comforts. Moral judgments, the stock-in-trade of conservative religion, were no longer supplied by playwrights—heroes and villains no longer had to be clearly labeled. What meaning have Vice and Virtue in a godless chaos? Naturalism, especially, carried the pessimistic inference of an indifferent universe, uncaring and uncongenial, operating on the impersonal laws of cause and effect, not by benign intention.

INFLUENCE: THE SCIENTIFIC OUTLOOK

The scientific method, glorified in the late nineteenth century as the salvation of man, implied that truth was a product of experiment and not of revelation. Careful observation and reportage led to empirical truth, and empirical truth could, it was believed, answer all the needs of mankind. Ernest Renan wrote in 1849 that "science alone could ameliorate the unhappy state of man."[8] The chemist Berthelot asserted that "science possesses a moral force capable of aiding society to attain, with but a brief delay, the blessed age of equality and fraternity," and the physicist Laplace conceived of a Being who would know the position and momentum of every particle of the universe, together with the laws governing such particles.[9] The scientific ideal of observation and reportage was assimilated by the realistic playwrights, as was the optimism over the possibilities for improving the human condition. On this theme, Zola wrote, "the experimental and scientific spirit of the century will enter the domain of the drama, and in it lies its only salvation,"[10] and several years later, he added,[11]

We have come to an age of method, of experimental science. We have, above all, the need for precise analysis. We should show little appreciation of the freedom won if we wished to wrap ourselves in a new tradition. The terrain is free; we can return to man and to nature.

The powerful influence of scientific method and discovery on the realistic drama makes it necessary to emphasize the overwhelming spirit of optimism that surrounded scientific activity in this period—particularly since, in the twentieth century, reasonable men have developed serious reservations as to the "moral force" of science and its potential for salvation. Three major writers, credited with popularizing the scientific outlook by writing eloquently of its future horizons, remind us of the excitement and hope. David Masson, in his *Recent British Philosophy* (1869), wrote,[12]

There has been . . . in consequence of the revelations of science . . . some most notable enlargements of our views of physical nature and of history— enlargements even to the breaking down of what had been a wall in the minds of most and the substitution on that side of a sheer vista of open space.

Masson went on to specify some of the problems that lay ahead; they included the battle between empiricism and transcendentalism and the question of the place of man in the natural scheme. Ernest Renan in *L'Avenir de la Science* ("The Future of Science," 1849), intoned,[13]

The true world which science reveals to us is much superior to the fantastic world created by the imagination. . . . Let us say without fear that if the marvels of fiction seemed up to now necessary for poetry, the marvels of nature, when laid bare in all of their splendor, will constitute a poetry a thousand times more sublime, a poetry which will be reality itself, which will be, simultaneously, science and philosophy.

Thirty years later, Emil du Bois-Reymond would match Renan's enthusiasm, in *Natural Science and the History of Culture* (1878), as he concluded that,[14]

scarcely anything in the heights or depths remains a mystery. . . . Only in scientific research and power over nature is there no stagnation: knowledge grows steadily, the creative strength develops unceasingly. Here, alone, each generation stands on the shoulders of the preceding one.

Is it any wonder that the realistic playwrights, determined as they were to improve the condition of human life, would attempt to join a movement of such vigor, confidence, and hope?

INFLUENCE: ADVANCES IN PSYCHOLOGY

European dramaturgy, grounded as it was in traditional Judeo-Christian morality, historically envisioned character motivation in terms of choice, the conscious decision to do good or evil. Man, possessed of a conscience and "free will," could freely pursue options of behavior, and thus was responsible for his actions and their results. Discoveries in the emerging science of psychology brought into question this easy assumption about the underlying sources of behavior, and, in so doing, required a reassessment of the ideas of sin and guilt. Messmer, Freud, Charcot, Janet, and other pioneer psychologists began to investigate the realm of the subconscious, a vague and almost unfathomable world, revealed to be the well-spring of human action. Joseph Breuer, an associate of Freud, in the period 1880-82, stumbled upon the method of approaching mental disturbance by unearthing a blurred memory, often under hypnosis, and having the patient "talk it out," a technique now attributed in popular belief to Freud alone. Breuer's process, much refined and debated, became fashionable psychoanalysis by the end of the century. Psychologists spoke of human behavior—particularly aberrant, antisocial, "unnatural" behavior—in terms of subconscious drives, not conscious choices; the action itself became less important than the motives, conscious and unconscious, that engendered it.

The cardboard, one-dimensional characters of melodrama, and the patent naivete of traditional dramatic motivation, began to look pathetically frail and dishonest to the early realistic playwrights in light of contemporary psychology. Fully dimensioned characters, developed with a recognition of current psychological understandings, became a requirement of the new dramaturgy early on. If a man's actions were truly the product of deep, unconscious, and only vaguely understandable causation, could sin have meaning any longer? Or punishment? Poetic justice—the principle that virtue must triumph, that good must be rewarded and evil punished in perfect proportion—lost its appeal to writers, not only because the principle was incompatible with the new concepts of psychological motivation, but because it quite simply was incompatible with the day-to-day experience of real life. Because psychologists faced, with honesty, the seamier side of human behavior, the distasteful and the abhorrent, playwrights found themselves challenged to portray similar behavior, to force their audiences to confront the unpleasant and ugly in human experience.

As with the depiction of behavior, all themes and subject matter, no matter how lurid or objectionable, were justified. Sexuality, a subject considered so intrinsically private at the time that "decent people" dared not even whisper about it if they valued their reputations, was made stageworthy. Even a partial list of the subjects investigated in the domestic dramas of Ibsen, "the best-hated writer of the nineteenth century," is revealing: the innocence of women, hereditary syphilis, political corruption, euthanasia, incest, suicide, religious hypocrisy. Life, these writers asserted, should be portrayed as it is lived, and to the Naturalist, particularly, the stage should provide an objective *tranche da vie* ("slice of life"), without glossing over the distasteful.

Predictably, the Romanticists, the Sentimentalists, and the Moral Guardians bruited their displeasure, accusing the Realists of gratuitously revealing festering sores to public view. Ibsen responded that he descended into the sewers not to bathe, but to cleanse them. And Chekhov, answering a correspondent's charge that he concentrated on the filth of life at the expense of the "pearls," wrote,[15] Indeed, to think that literature bears the responsibility of digging up the "pearl" from the muck heap would amount to rejecting literature itself. Literature is called artistic because it depicts life as it actually is. . . . Surely a man of letters is not a confectioner, nor a dealer in cosmetics. . . . He is compelled to struggle with his fastidiousness and soil his imagination with the dirt of life . . . [to] realize that dung heaps play a very respectable role in the landscape and that evil passions are as inherent in life as good ones.

Psychology had taught the theatre not only crucial lessons in characterization, but also the artist's responsibility to refuse his audience the Romantic comfort of faraway places and times, in favor of the here and now.

INFLUENCE: NEW THEORIES IN ANTHROPOLOGY

The publication of Charles Darwin's *The Origin of Species*, in which natural selection was credited with the evolution of the lower animals, initiated a wider investigation of the generative past of all animate nature. Darwin's revolutionary study of 1859 was followed by Thomas Huxley's *Man's Place in Nature* (1863) and Darwin's *The Descent of Man* (1871), in which man was firmly placed in the evolutionary process. According to traditional Judeo-Christian teaching, based on the early chapters of Genesis, God had created man as a separate species in His own image. This myth had evolved into a fundamental doctrine of Christianity, Special Creation, which endowed man with dignity and his earthly presence with divine authority. In the popular imagination, the importance of evolutionary theory was that it gave all mankind a simian ancestor. Not Old Adam, but a monkey! Where, it was asked, was man's dignity, if his progenitor was an ape? The dramaturgic result of evolutionary theory (coupled with new understandings in genetics) was the portrayal of man without inherent dignity. Authentic heroes and heroines, a staple feature of melodrama and the popular historical drama, virtually disappear. How could a human being, the product of immutable genetic codes, intrinsically selfish, lacking free will, and surviving by animal instincts, possibly be heroic?

Darwin had also emphasized the adaptation to environment and the survival of the fittest. Realistic, and especially, naturalistic playwrights depicted men attempting to cope with depraved environments and frequently failing. Set designers relished the opportunity to reproduce detailed squalor on stage, whether it was the stinking beef carcasses in the setting for Antoine's production of *The Butcher* in 1888 or the closely observed flophouse conditions that constituted the *mise-en-scène* for the Moscow Art Theatre's original production of Gorky's *The Lower Depths* in 1902. Stock settings, pulled from storage, the weary contrivances of hack scene painters, would no longer do. A character both created, and was created by, his surroundings, "the landscape of his soul." Following social and literary theory, espoused by Taine and Stendhal, among earlier critics, the Naturalists believed that man was inseparable from his environment—indeed, from his "national characteristics" as well. A man's "exterior life," his milieu, leaves imprints on his character, just as surely as a man has an impact on his surroundings.

INFLUENCE: SOCIAL AND POLITICAL FACTORS

The nineteenth century witnessed unparalleled civil disorder and social upheaval. The traditional forms of civil governance, and the economic system that had dominated Europe since the decline of feudalism, were challenged in print by imaginative and influential political theorists and in the streets by charismatic, often violent, revolutionaries. The surviving monarchies, facing the twilight of their epoch, teetered uneasily between ancient arrogance and painful compromise. In England, the Chartist movement, seeking rights for the working class, slowly gained significant victories. The incubating socialist movement met its first rigorous test of strength in the Paris uprising of 1848, an insurrection of workers under Alexandre Herzen. This bloody revolt, brutally put down by the military, pitted the bourgeois French legislature against the fearsome reality of proletarian demands. In the same year, similar uprisings hit other capitals of Europe, as though by contagion.

Moreover, Karl Marx published *The Communist Manifesto* in London in that troubled year, and later *A Contribution to the Critique of Political Economy* (1859), and, with Friedrich Engels, issued *Capital* (1867), the three primers of classic Marxist theory. Marx wrote ominously, "a spector is haunting Europe; it is the spector of Communism." The short-lived revolutionary and egalitarian government of France, established in 1871 and known as the Paris Commune, gave additional evidence of proletarian muscle and potential popular support. Marx outlined the basic lessons of the Commune in an address to the General Council of the First International, later published as *The Civil War in France.* In this speech, he portrayed the "struggle of the producing against the appropriating class," and championed "the economic emancipation of labor."[16] The spreading claims of communism and socialism, coupled with the sordid realities of the industrial revolution, hardened class barriers throughout Europe, and hastened a breakdown in society, in part by denying ancient privilege. Dialectical materialism, the basic Marxist system of reasoning, denied permanence and a priori values, and thus was incompatible with the philosophy that sustained melodrama.

In the Realistic theatre, the results of this social unrest and political debate were numerous. Chekhov wrote, "Everything in this world is relative and approximate."[17] Writers like Gerhart Hauptmann, in *The Weavers,* and Maxim Gorky, in *The Lower Depths,* experimented with the "mass hero"; a number of suffering, alienated workers provide the focus of interest, rather than a single character. The breakdown of class barriers was mirrored seriously in Strindberg's *Miss Julie* and humorously in Bernard Shaw's *Pygmalion,* among other works. Ibsen investigated the corruption of capitalist enterprise in *The Wild Duck* and

An Enemy of the People, and joined other playwrights with similar concerns in portraying the chaos of a fragmented citizenry.

Social concerns, the center of liberal (or, as it was often called in the period, Progressive) thinking, found their greatest theatrical expression in the development of the social problem play (*pièce à thèse*)—that is, a work that takes as its theme a specific blight on society, such as prostitution, infidelity, alcoholism, or unwed motherhood, and dramatically demonstrates its causes and effects, and suggests solutions. De Toqueville generalized in 1840, "no portion of literature is connected closer or with more numerous ties with the present state of society than the drama,"[18] and the writers of social problem plays in the ensuing century would more than justify this claim. These playwrights sought immediate redress for grievous social ills. The intensity of their desire for direct action on the part of the audience is clearly demonstrated by Eugène Brieux's *Damaged Goods*, a dramatic treatise on veneral disease. Before the curtain goes up, the stage manager appears and cautions the audience,[19]

> Ladies and Gentlemen, I beg to inform you, on behalf of the author and the management, that the object of the play is a study of the disease of syphillis and its bearing on marriage.

The play portrays the ravages of "loves mischances" in the life of a young French woman. At the final curtain, the doctor, who has served as a *raisonneur* (or spokesman for the author), addresses M. Loches, a member of the Chamber of Deputies:[20]

> This poor girl is typical. The whole problem is summed up in her: she is at once the product and the cause. We set the ball rolling, and others keep it up and it runs back to bruise our own shins. . . . But if you give a thought or two to what you have just seen when you are sitting in the Chamber, we shall not have wasted our time.

In Bernard Shaw's commentary on his *Widowers' Houses* (1892), an attack on slums and absentee landlords, he boldly informed the reader that the play "deals with a burning social question and is deliberately intended to induce people to vote on the Progressive side in the next City Council election in London."[21]

CONCLUSION

The emergence of realistic dramaturgy in the playhouses of Europe was, demonstrably, a product of the complex mingling of the nontheatrical influences described above. However, much established theatre practice, originally unrelated to realistic production, must also be credited with numerous contributions. The serious domestic drama of T. W. Robertson in England, and the *pièce bien fait* ("the well-made play") in France, the rising popularity of the convincing "box set," the concern for authenticity in the setting and costuming of historical drama, even the technology developed to achieve realistic special effects in melodrama, were appropriated by the new movement. Among other influences, which had nonrealistic origins, were the adaptation of electric lighting for stage use, the construction of more intimate theatres with diminished forestages, the emergence of the director as a unique artist, and the conscious efforts by prominent actor-managers to gain a new respectability for the theatre. The list is seemingly endless, and I have been able, in a paper of intentional brevity, hardly to touch the multifarious ways in which the theories and influences that engendered Realism were translated into stage practice; nor could I treat the important power that Realism exerted in the theatre and cinema of the twentieth century. Thus, the reader is respectfully (and confidently) referred to the bibliography that ensues, and in which he or she will find one hundred years of historical scholarship and dramatic criticism sufficient to illuminate the length and breadth of this awesome and ubiquitous style of dramatic expression.

NOTES

1. Quoted in Houghton, p. 11.
2. Gassner, p. 564.
3. Gerhardie, p. 107.
4. Houghton, p. 14.
5. Gerhardie, p. 104.
6. From *The History of English Literature*, translated by H. Van Laun, quoted in Weinstein, p. 93.
7. Péguy, pp. 305, 307, 308.
8. Renan, p. ix.
9. Barrett, p. 38.
10. Clark, p. 401.
11. Zola, p. 286. Chekhov once wrote that a man of letters "must be as objective as a chemist." (Simmons, p. 131.)
12. Masson, p. 113.
13. Renan, pp. 95-96.
14. Bois-Reymond, pp. 37, 38. For an expansion of this and related ideas, the reader is referred to Stromberg, particularly pp. 25-30, 107-118.
15. Simmons, p. 131.
16. Marx, p. 60-61.
17. Simmons, p. 131.
18. De Toqueville, p. 102.
19. Brieux, p. 12.
20. Brieux, p. 79.
21. Quoted in Bentley, p. 103.

BIBLIOGRAPHY

Barrett, William. *Irrational Man*. Garden City, N.Y.: Doubleday, 1958.

Bentley, Eric. *Bernard Shaw*. New York: New Directions, 1947.

Bois-Reymond, Emil H. du. *Culturgeschichte und Naturwissenschaft*. Leipzig: Veit & Comp., 1878.

Brieux, Eugene. *Damaged Goods*. New York: Brentano's, 1912.

Clark, Barrett H. *European Theories of the Drama*. New York: Crown Publishers, 1918.

De Toqueville, Alexis. *Democracy in America*. Volume 1. Cambridge: Sever and Francis, 1863.

Gassner, John. *Treasury of the Theatre*. Volume 1. New York: Simon and Schuster, 1959.

Gerhardie, William. *Anton Chekov: A Critical Study*. London: Cobden-Sanderson, 1923.

Houghton, Norris, ed. *Seeds of Modern Drama*. New York: Dell Publishing, 1963.

Marx, Karl. *The Civil War in France*. New York: International Publishers, 1940.

Masson, David. *Recent British Philosophy*. London: Macmillan and Co., 1877.

Pequy, Charles P. *Deuxieme Elegie XXX*. Paris: Gallimard, 1955.

Renan, Ernest. *L'Avenir de la Science*. Paris: Calmann Levy, 1849.

Simmons, Ernest J. *Chekhov: A Biography*. Boston: Little, Brown, 1962.

Stromberg, Roland N. *Realism, Naturalism and Symbolism*. New York: Walker & Co., 1968.

Weinstein, Leo. *Hippolyte Taine*. New York: Twayne, 1972.

Zola, Emile. *Oeuvres Completes*. Volume 11. Paris: Cercle du Livres Precieux, 1968.

GENERAL SOURCES FOR
THE BIBLIOGRAPHY

The following general resource books have been employed in the compilation
of this volume. The more specialized bibliographies are listed in the appropriate
"General" sections under the various countries and playwrights.

Allen, Charles, and Felix Pollak, eds. *Comprehensive Index to English-Language
Little Magazines, 1890–1970.* New York: Kraus-Thompson, 1975.

Baker, Blanch M. *Theatre and Allied Arts.* New York: H. W. Wilson, 1952.

Breed, Paul F., and Florence M. Sniderman. *Dramatic Criticism Index.* Detroit:
Gale Research, 1972.

British Museum General Catalogue of Printed Books, The. London: Trustees of
the British Museum, 1965.

British Museum Subject Index, The. London: Trustees of the British Museum,
1881-1977.

British National Bibliography. London: Council of the British National Bibliography, 1950-1977.

Cumulated Dramatic Index, 1909–1949. Two Volumes. Boston: G. K. Hall, 1965.

Dissertation Abstracts International. Ann Arbor, Mich.: University Microfilms,
1938-1977.

Essay and General Literature Index. New York: H. W. Wilson Company, 1900-
1977.

*French XX: Bibliography: Critical and Biographical References for the Study of
French Literature Since 1885.* New York: French Institute-Alliance Francaise,
1976.

Gassner, John, and Edward Quinn. *The Reader's Encyclopedia of World Drama.*
New York: Thomas Y. Crowell, 1969.

Grismer, Raymond L. *Bibliography of the Drama of Spain and Spanish America.* Two Volumes. Minneapolis: Burgess-Beckwith, 1966.

Humanities Index, The (formerly *The International Index* and *The Social Sciences and Humanities Index*). New York: H. W. Wilson Company, 1907-1977.

Library of Congress Catalog—Books: Subjects, The. Ann Arbor, Mich.: Edwards, 1955-1977.

Litto, Fredric M. *American Dissertations on the Drama and the Theatre.* Kent, Ohio: Kent State University Press, 1969.

McGraw-Hill Encyclopedia of World Drama. Four Volumes. New York: McGraw-Hill, 1972.

Mikhail, E. H. *English Drama, 1900–1950: A Guide to Information Sources.* Detroit: Gale Research, 1977.

MLA International Bibliography of Books and Articles on the Modern Languages and Literatures. New York: Modern Languages Association of America, 1921-1975.

National Union Catalog: Pre-1956 Imprints, The. London: Mansell, 1968-1977.

Poole's Index to Periodical Literature, 1802–1906. Six Volumes. Gloucester, Mass.: Peter Smith, 1963.

Povoledo, Elena, et al., eds. *Enciclopedia dello Spettacolo.* Rome: Casa Editrice Le Maschere, 1954-1962.

Rancoeur, René. *Bibliographie de la littérature française du Moyen Age à nos jours.* Paris: Librarie Armand Colin, 1953-1976.

Santa Vicca, Edmund F. *Four French Dramatists: A Bibliography of the Works of Eugène Brieux, François de Curel, Émile Fabre, and Paul Hervieu.* Metuchen, N.J.: Scarecrow Press, 1974.

REALISM
IN
EUROPEAN
THEATRE AND DRAMA,
1870-1920

I GENERAL COMMENTARIES

Books

In English:

1. Adams, William Davenport. Dictionary of the Drama.
Philadelphia: Lippincott, 1904.

2. Adelman, Irving and Rita Dworkin. Modern Drama. A Checklist of Critical Literature on 20th Century Plays. Metuchen,
N.J.: The Scarecrow Press, 1967.

3. Andrews, Charlton. Drama of Today. Philadelphia and
London: Lippincott, 1913.

4. Archer, William. The Old Drama and the New. Boston:
Small, Maynard, 1923.

5. _____. Play Making. London: Chapman and Hall, 1912.

6. Armstrong, Cecil Ferard. Shakespeare to Shaw. London:
Mills and Boon, 1913.

7. Balmforth, Ramsden. Ethical and Religious Values of the
Drama. London: Allen and Unwin, 1925.

8. _____. The Problem-play and Its Influence on Modern
Thought and Life. London: Allen and Unwin, 1928.

9. Baring, Maurice. Punch and Judy & Other Essays. Garden
City, New York: Doubleday, 1924.

10. Bentley, Eric Russell. The Life of the Drama. New York:
Atheneum, 1964.

11. _____. The Modern Theatre. New York: Doubleday,
1955.

12. Bentley, Eric Russell. The Playwright as Thinker: A Study of Drama in Modern Times. New York: Reynal, 1946.

13. _____. In Search of Theatre. London and New York: Vintage Books, 1954.

14. Björkman, Edwin August. Voices of Tomorrow: Critical Studies of the New Spirit in Literature. New York and London: M. Kennerley, 1913.

15. Block, Anita Cahn. Changing World in Plays and Theatre. Boston: Little, 1939.

16. Bogard, Travis and William I. Oliver. Modern Drama: Essays in Criticism. New York: Oxford Press, 1965.

17. Boyd, Alice Katharine. The Interchange of Plays between London and New York, 1910-1939; a Study in Relative Audience Response. New York: King's Crown Press, 1948.

18. Brandes, Georg Morris. Creative Spirits of the Nineteenth Century. New York: Crowell, 1923.

19. _____. Main Currents in Nineteenth Century Literature. London: W. Heinemann, 1901-05.

20. Breed, Paul F. and Florence M. Sniderman. Dramatic Criticism Index: A Bibliography of Commentaries on Playwrights from Ibsen to the Avant-Garde. Detroit: Wayne State University Press, 1972.

21. Brockett, Oscar G. Century of Innovation: A History of European and American Theatre and Drama since 1870. New York: Prentice-Hall, 1973.

22. Brooks, Cleanth and Robert Bechtold Heilman, eds. Understanding Drama. New York: Holt, 1948.

23. Brown, Ivor John Carnegie. Parties of the Play. London: Benn, 1928.

24. Brown, John Mason. Art of Playgoing. New York: Norton, 1936.

25. _____. Modern Thought in Revolt. New York: Norton, 1929.

26. Brustein, Robert. The Theatre of Revolt. Boston: Little, Brown, 1964.

27. Buck, Philo Melvin. Directions in Contemporary Literature. New York and Toronto: Oxford, 1942.

28. Burton, Richard. Literary Likings. Boston: Copeland and Day, 1899.

29.   Carpenter, Bruce. Way of the Drama; a Study of Dramatic Forms and Moods. New York: Prentice Hall, 1929.

30.   Carroll, Sydney Wentworth. Some Dramatic Opinions. London: F. V. White, 1923.

31.   Carter, Huntley. New Spirit in Drama and Art. New York and London: Kennerley, 1913.

32.   _____. New Spirit in the European Theatre, 1914-1924. London: E. Benn, 1925.

33.   Chandler, Frank Wadleigh. Aspects of Modern Drama. New York: Macmillan, 1914.

34.   _____. Modern Continental Playwrights. New York and London: Harper, 1931.

35.   Charques, Richard Denis, ed. Footnotes to the Theatre. London: P. Davies, 1938.

36.   Cheney, Sheldon. Art Theater. New York: Knopf, 1925.

37.   Clapp, John Bouvé. Plays of the Present. New York: Dunlap Society, 1902.

38.   Clark, Barrett H. European Theories of the Drama. New York: Crown Publishing, 1947.

39.   _____, and George Freedley. History of Modern Drama. New York and London: Appleton-Century, 1947.

40.   _____. A Study of the Modern Drama. New York: Appleton, Century, 1938.

41.   Cleaver, James. Theatre through the Ages. London: Harrap, 1946.

42.   Cole, Toby. Playwrights on Playwriting. New York: Hill and Wang, 1965.

43.   Davies, Hugh S. Realism in the Drama. New York: Macmillan, 1934.

44.   Deseo, Lydia May Glover and Hulda Mossberg Phipps. Looking at Life through Drama. New York: Abington, 1931.

45.   Dickinson, Thomas H. Outline of Contemporary Drama. New York: Houghton, 1927.

46.   _____. Theatre in a Changing Europe. New York: H. Holt, 1937.

47.   Dobrée, Bonamy. The Lamp and the Lute. London: Oxford, 1929.

48. Dukes, Ashley. Drama. London: Butterworth, 1936.

49. _____ . Modern Dramatists. London: F. Palmer, 1911.

50. _____ . The Youngest Drama: Studies of Fifty Dramatists. London: Benn, 1923.

51. Eaton, W. P. Drama in English. New York: Scribners Sons, 1930.

52. Ellis, H. H. New Spirit. New York: Boni and Liveright, 1935.

53. Ervine, St. John. How To Write a Play. London: Allen and Unwin, 1928.

54. _____ . Theatre in My Time. New York: Mussey, 1934.

55. Fergusson, Francis. The Idea of a Theater: A Study of Ten Plays: The Art of Drama in Changing Perspective. Princeton, N.J.: Princeton University Press, 1949.

56. Flanagan, Hallie. Shifting Scenes of the Modern European Theatre. New York: Coward-McCann, 1928.

57. Ford, Ford Madox. Portraits from Life. New York: Houghton, 1937.

58. Freedman, Morris. The Moral Impulse: The Drama from Ibsen to the Present. Carbondale, Ill.: University of Southern Illinois Press, 1967.

59. Furst, Lilian R. and Peter N. Skrine. Naturalism. (Volume 18 of "The Critical Idiom Series.") London: Methuen, 1971.

60. Garland, Hamlin. Crumbling Idols. Chicago: Stone and Kimball, 1894.

61. Gaskell, Ronald. Drama and Reality: The European Drama since Ibsen. London: Routledge and K. Paul, 1972.

62. Gassner, John. Form and Idea in the Modern Theatre. New York: Dryden Press, 1956.

63. _____ . Masters of the Drama. New York: Dover Publications, 1945.

64. _____ , and Ralph Allen. Theatre and Drama in the Making. Boston: Houghton Mifflin, 1964.

65. Gilman, Richard. The Making of a Modern Drama: A Study of Büchner, Ibsen, Strindberg, Chekhov, Pirandello, Brecht, Beckett, Handke. New York: Farrar, Straus and Giroux, 1974.

66. Goldberg, I. Drama of Transition: Native and Exotic
Playcraft. Cincinnati: Stewart Kidd Co., 1922.

67. Goldman, Emma. The Social Significance of Modern Drama.
Boston: R. G. Badger, 1914.

68. Gorelik, Mordecai. New Theatres for Old. New York:
French, 1941.

69. Grant, Damion. Realism. (Vol. 9 of "The Critical Idiom
Series.") London: Methuen, 1970.

70. Granville-Barker, Harley. Study of Drama. London: Cambridge University Press, 1934.

71. _____. Use of the Drama. London: Sidgewick, 1946.

72. Gray, James. On Second Thought. Minneapolis: University
of Minnesota Press, 1946.

73. Hale, Edward Everett, Jr. Dramatists of Today. New
York: Holt, 1911.

74. Hamilton, Clayton Meeker. Conversations on Contemporary
Drama. New York: Macmillan, 1924.

75. _____. Seen on the Stage. New York: H. Holt and
Co., 1920.

76. _____. The Theory of Theatre and Other Principles
of Dramatic Criticism. New York: Holt, 1939.

77. Hamilton, Cosmo. People Worth Talking About. New York:
McBride, 1933.

78. Harris, Frank. Contemporary Portraits. Four Volumes.
New York: The Author, 1919.

79. Heller, Otto. Prophets of Dissent. New York: Knopf,
1918.

80. Henderson, Archibald. The Changing Drama: Contributions
and Tendencies. New York: Holt, 1914.

81. _____. European Dramatists. Cincinnati: Stewart
Kidd, Co., 1918.

82. _____. Interpreters of Life and the Modern Spirit.
New York: M. Kennerley, 1911.

83. Henderson, John A. The First Avant-Garde, 1887-1894.
London: Harrap, 1971.

84. Herrmann, Oscar, ed. Living Dramatists. New York:
Brentano, 1905.

85. Howe, Percival P. _Dramatic Portraits_. London: Kennerley, 1913.

86. Hudson, Lynton Alfred. _Twentieth Century Drama_. London: Harrap, 1946.

87. Huneker, James G. _Iconoclasts, a Book of Dramatists_. New York: Scribner, 1905.

88. _____. _Ivory Apes and Peacocks_. New York: Scribner, 1915.

89. _____. _Steeplejack_. New York: Scribner, 1920.

90. Jackson, H. _The Eighteen Nineties: A Review of Art and Ideas at the Close of the 19th Century_. New York: M. Kennerley, 1914.

91. Jameson, Margaret Storm. _Modern Drama in Europe_. London: W. Collins Sons, 1920.

92. Jourdain, Eleanor F. _The Drama in Europe in Theory and Practice_. London: Methuen, 1924.

93. Kraft, Irma. _Plays, Players, Playhouses_. New York: G. Dobsevage, 1928.

94. Krutch, Joseph Wood. _"Modernism" in Modern Drama_. Ithaca: Cornell University Press, 1953.

95. Lamm, Martin. _Modern Drama_. Oxford: Blackwell, 1952.

96. Lancaster, Henry C. _Adventures of a Literary Historian_. Baltimore, Maryland: Johns Hopkins Press, 1942.

97. Lavrin, J. _Aspects of Modernism from Wilde to Pirandello_. Freeport, New York: Books for Libraries Press, 1968.

98. Lewis, Allan. _The Contemporary Theatre_. New York: Crown Publishers, Inc., 1971.

99. Lewisohn, Ludwig. _The Modern Drama: An Essay in Interpretation_. New York: Heubsch, 1915.

100. _____. _The Drama and the Stage_. New York: Harcourt Brace and Co., 1922.

101. Lucas, Frank Lawrence. _The Decline and Fall of the Romantic Ideal_. New York: The Macmillan Company, 1936.

102. Lukács, György. _The Meaning of Contemporary Realism_. London: Merlin Press, 1962.

103. _____. _Realism in Our Time: Literature and Class Struggle_. New York: Harper and Row, 1964.

104. Lukács, György. Studies in European Realism (A Socio-logical Study of the Writings of Balzac, Stendhal, Zola, Tolstoy, Gorki and Others). London: Merlin Press, 1972.

105. Lumley, F. New Trends in Twentieth Century Drama: A Survey since Ibsen and Shaw. New York: Oxford University Press, 1972.

106. Macy, John Albert. Critical Game. New York: Boni and Liveright, 1922.

107. MacIver, R. M., ed. Great Moral Dilemmas in Literature, Past and Present. New York: Institute for Religious and Social Studies, 1956.

108. Mais, Stuart Petre Brodie. Some Modern Authors. New York: Rich Publishing Company, 1923.

109. _____. Some Modern Dramatists. New York: Rich Publishing Company, 1923.

110. Marriot, James William. Modern Drama. London: Nelson, 1934.

111. Matthews, James Brander. Books and Play-books: Essays on Literature and the Drama. London: Osgood, McIlwaine, 1895.

112. _____. Development of the Drama. New York: Scribners, 1903.

113. Metwally, Abdalla A. Studies in Modern Drama. Beirut: Arab University, 1971.

114. Middleton, G. These Things Are Mine: The Autobiography of a Journeyman Playwright. New York: Macmillan Co., 1947.

115. Miller, Anna Irene. Independent Theatre in Europe, 1887 to the Present. New York: Long and Smith, 1931.

116. Miller, J. William. Modern Playwrights at Work. New York: Samuel French, 1968.

117. Miller, Nellie Burget. The Living Drama. New York and London: The Century Company, 1924.

118. Moderwell, Hiram K. The Theatre of Today. New York: John Lane, 1914.

119. Montague, Charles Edward. Dramatic Values, Essays. London: Chatto, 1931.

120. Moore, C. L. Incense and Iconoclasm: Studies in Literature. New York: G. P. Putnam's Son, 1915.

121. Moore, George. Impressions and Opinions. New York: Brentano, 1913.

122. Newmark, Maxim. Otto Brahm: The Man and the Critic. New York: G. E. Stechert and Company, 1938.

123. Nicoll, Allardyce. History of the Late Nineteenth Century Drama, 1850-1900. New York: Macmillan, 1947.

124. _____. The Theatre and Dramatic Theory. London: G. G. Harrap, 1962.

125. _____. The Theory of Drama. New York: B. Blom, 1966.

126. _____. World Drama from Aeschylus to Anouilh. London: Harrap, 1949.

127. Palmer, Helen H. and Anne Jane Dyson. European Drama Criticism. Hamden, Conn.: Shoe String Press, 1968.

128. Palmer, J. L. The Future of the Theatre. London: G. Bell, 1913.

129. Peacock, Ronald. Poet in the Theatre. London: Routledge, 1946.

130. Pearson, Hesketh. A Persian Critic. London: Chapman and Dodd, 1923.

131. Perry, Henry Ten Eyck. Masters of Dramatic Comedy and Their Social Themes. Cambridge: Harvard University Press, 1939.

132. Phelps, William Lyon. Essays on Modern Dramatics. New York: Macmillan, 1921.

133. _____. Twentieth Century Theatre. New York: The Macmillan Company, 1920.

134. Pogson, Rex. Theatre between Wars (1919-1939). Clevedon, England: Triangle Press, 1947.

135. Robertson, John G. Essays and Addresses on Literature. London: Routledge, 1935.

136. Shaw, George Bernard. Major Critical Essays. London: Constable, 1932.

137. _____. Pen Portraits and Reviews. London: Constable, 1932.

138. Sokel, Walter Herbert. The Writer in Extremis. Stanford: Stanford University Press, 1959.

139. Strang, Lewis C. Players and Plays of the Last Quarter Century. Boston: L. C. Page, 1903.

140. Stromberg, Roland N. Realism, Naturalism and Symbolism. New York: Walker, 1968.

141. Stuart, Donald Clive. The Development of Dramatic Art.
New York and London: Appleton-Century, 1928.

142. Sturgis, G. F. The Influence of the Drama. New York:
The Shakespeare Press, 1913.

143. Styan, J. L. The Dark Comedy. New York and London:
Cambridge University Press, 1962.

144. Sutton, Graham. Some Contemporary Dramatists. Port
Washington, New York: Kennikat Press, 1967.

145. Symons, Arthur. Plays, Acting and Music. New York:
E. P. Dutton and Company, 1909.

146. Taylor, John Russell. The Rise and Fall of the Well-
Made Play. New York: Hill and Wang, 1967.

147. Thompson, Alan R. The Anatomy of Drama. Berkeley:
University of California Press, 1946.

148. _____ . The Dry Mock: A Study of Irony in the
Drama. Berkeley: University of California Press, 1948.

149. Valency, Maurice. The Breaking String. New York:
Oxford University Press, 1966.

150. _____ . The Flower and the Castle. New York:
Grosset and Dunlap, 1963.

151. Van Druten, John. The Playwright at Work. New York:
Harper, 1953.

152. Vernon, Frank. Twentieth Century Theatre. London:
Harrap, 1924.

153. Walkley, A. B. Drama and Life. New York: Brentano,
1908.

154. Wellwarth, G. E. The Theatre of Protest and Paradox.
New York: New York University Press, 1964.

155. Williams, Raymond. Drama from Ibsen to Brecht. New
York: Oxford University Press, 1968.

156. _____ . Modern Tragedy. Stanford: Stanford University Press, 1966.

157. Wilson, N. Scarlyn. European Drama. London: Nicholson
and Watson, 1937.

158. _____ . The Shadows of the Stage. New York:
Macmillan, 1895.

159. Winter, William. The Wallet of Time. London: Moffat,
1913.

160. Yeats, William Butler. The Cutting of an Agate. New York: Macmillan, 1912.

161. _____. Essays. London and New York: Macmillan, 1924.

162. _____. Plays and Controversies. New York: The Macmillan Company, 1924.

In German:

163. Arnold, Robert Franz. Das moderne Drama. Strassburg: K. J. Trübner, 1908.

164. Boelsche, Carl Edvard Wilhelm. Die Naturwissenschaftlichen Grundlagen der Poesie. Leipzig: C. Reissner, 1887.

165. Brahm, Otto. Kritiken und Essays. Zurich: Artimis Verlag, 1964.

166. Brandes, Georg Morris. Moderne Geister: literarische Bildnisse aus neunzehnten Jahrhundert. Frankfurt: Rütten und Loening, 1887.

167. Cowen, Roy C. Der Naturalismus: Kommentar zu e. Epoche. Munich: Winkler-Verlag, 1973.

168. Dietrich, Margarete. Europäische Dramaturgie im 19. Jahrhundert. Graz: H. Böhlaus, 1961.

169. Fechter, Paul. Das Europäische Drama: Geist und Kultur im Spiegel des Theaters. Mannheim: Bibliographisches Institut, 1956-8.

170. _____. Geschichte der deutschen Literatur von Naturalismus bis zur Literatur des Unwirklichen. Leipzig: Bibliographisches Institut, 1938.

171. Germann, Klaus. Studien zum Naturalismus im englischen Drama. Stuttgart: R. Bosch, 1967.

172. Hettner, Hermann J. T. Das moderne Drama; aesthetische Untersuchungen. Berlin: B. Behr, 1924.

173. Kerr, Alfred. Das neue Drama. Berlin: S. Fischer, 1912.

174. _____. Technik des realistischen Dramas. Berlin: S. Fischer, 1905.

175. Kindermann, Heinz. Theatergeschichte Europas. Salzburg: O. Müller, 1957.

176. Lothar, Rudolph. Kritische Studien zur Psychologie der Literatur. New York: G. E. Stechert, 1895.

177. Lukács, György. Der russische Realismus in der Welt-
literatur. Berlin: Aufbau-Verlag, 1951.

178. _____. Probleme des Realismus. Berlin: Aufbau-
Verlag, 1955.

179. _____. Zur Soziologie des modernen Dramas.
Tübingen: Archiv für Sozialwissenschaft und Socialpolitik,
1914.

180. Marcuse, Ludwig. Die Welt der Tragödie. Berlin:
F. Schneider, 1923.

181. Münchow, Ursala. Naturalismus, Dramen, Lyrik, Prosa.
Berlin: Aufbau-verlag, 1970.

182. Ruprecht, Erich. Literarische Manifeste des Naturalismus, 1880-1892. Stuttgart: J. B. Metzler, 1962.

183. Schmidt, Günter. Die literarische Rezeption des Darwinismus: das Problem d. Vererbung bei Émile Zola u. im
Drama d. dt. Naturalismus. Berlin: Akademie-Verlag, 1974.

In French:

184. Doumic, René. De Scribe à Ibsen. Paris: Perrin et
cie, 1901.

185. Flat, Paul. Figures du théâtre contemporain. Paris:
E. Sansot, 1912.

186. Knowles, Dorothy. La réaction idéaliste au théâtre
depuis 1890. Paris: E. Droz, 1934.

187. LeMaître, Jules. Impressions de théâtre. Paris:
Société français d'imprimerie et de librarie, 1888.

188. Ruth, Léon. Sur le théâtre d'hier. Liège: Bénard,
1917.

189. Sée, Edmond. Le movement dramatique. Paris: Les Éditions de France, 1930.

In Spanish:

190. Guerrero Zamora, Juan. Historia del teatro contemporáneo. Barcelona: Juan Flors, 1961-1967.

In Italian:

191. Artioli, Umberto. Teoría della scèna dal naturalismo
al surrealísmo. Florence: Sansoni, 1972.

192. Codignola, Luciano. Due moménti della crisi del naturalismo teatràle. Urbino: Librería moderna universitària, 1971.

193. Levi, Cesare. Studi di teàtro. Palermo: R. Sandron, 1923.

194. Tilgher, Adriano. La scèna e la vita. Rome: Librería di sciènza e léttere, 1923.

Theses and Dissertations

195. Barnhart, Thearle A. "Our Greater Realists." M. A. Thesis. The Ohio State University, 1927.

196. Brookbank, Charles D. "The Theme of Boredom in Selected Modern Dramas." Ph.D. Dissertation, University of Minnesota, 1972.

197. Clay, James H. "The Problem of What Is Real in the Drama. An Analysis of Ibsen's Realism and Maeterlinck's Symbolism." Ph.D. Dissertation, University of Illinois, 1957.

198. Covert, Marjorie A. "Realism in the Prose Theatre of France and England, 1890-1910." Ph.D. Dissertation, University of Wisconsin, 1934.

199. Fitch, Girdler B. "A Study of the Dramatic Technique of Six Nineteenth Century Dramatists." Ph.D. Dissertation, The Ohio State University, 1937.

200. Hargrove, Claire A. "Silences in the Realistic Theatre." Ph.D. Dissertation, University of Wisconsin, 1971.

201. Schubert, Leland. "The Realistic Tendency in the Theatre." Ph.D. Dissertation, Cornell University, 1938.

202. Shatzky, Joel L. "Shaw, Barker, and Galworthy: The Development of the Drama of Ideas, 1890-1910." Ph.D. Dissertation, New York University, 1971.

203. Walsh, Dwight Rolfe. "Diety in Drama: The Representation of the Absolute in Some Plays of Ibsen, Strindberg and Hauptmann." Ph.D. Dissertation, Harvard University, 1963.

204. Woodson, Grace Isobel. "A Study of the Conflict between the Old and New Generation in Modern Drama." M.A. Thesis, The Ohio State University, 1928.

Articles

205. Borgerhoff, E. B. O. "Realisme and Kindred Words:
Their Use as Terms of Literary Criticism in the First Half of
the Nineteenth Century." PMLA. Vol. 53 (September, 1938),
pp. 837-43.

206. Capus, Alfred. "The Subjects of Plays." Dramatist.
Vol. 6 (July, 1915), pp. 583-8.

207. Cary, Elizabeth L. "Apostles of the New Drama." Lamp.
Vol. 27 (January, 1904), pp. 593-8.

208. Courtney, William Leonard. "Modern Social Drama as
Influenced by the Novel." Fortnightly Review. Vol. 77,
(1902), pp. 666-74.

209. _____. "Realistic Drama." Fortune. Vol. 98
(May, 1913), pp. 945-62.

210. Dickenson, T. H. "Drama of Intellectualism." Drama.
No. 7 (August, 1912), pp. 148-62.

211. _____. "Dramatic Art as an Expression of Society."
Forum. Vol. 53 (January, 1915), pp. 121-32.

212. Figgis, D. "Reality in Drama." Living Age. Vol. 59
(May 31, 1913), pp. 571-3.

213. Fiske, Minnie Maddern. "Matter of the Play." International Monthly. Vol. 5 (1902), pp. 629-44.

214. Fox, R. M. "The Drama of the Dregs." New Statesman.
Vol. 27 (August 21, 1926), pp. 525-6.

215. George, W. L. "Drama for the Common Man." Fortune.
Vol. 99 (September 1, 1913), pp. 568-78.

216. Grabowski, Simon. "Unreality in the Plays of Ibsen,
Strindberg and Hamsun." Mosaic. Vol. 4 (1970), pp. 63-76.

217. Hamilton, Clayton. "European Dramatists on the American Stage." Bookman. Vol. 31 (1910), pp. 419-20.

218. Irving, L. "The Drama as a Factor in Social Progress."
Fortune. Vol. 101 (August, 1914), pp. 268-74.

219. _____. "The Plight of the Serious Drama." Fortnightly Review. Vol. 95 (April, 1911), pp. 641-7.

220. Jerome, Jerome K. "Problem of the Problem Play."
Harper's Weekly. Vol. 48 (December 10, 1904), pp. 1916-18.

221. Kauffman, R. W. "Drama and Morality." Forum. Vol.
51 (May, 1914), pp. 664-72.

222. Kaplan, D. M. "Character and Theatre: Psychoanalytic
Notes on Modern Realism." Tulane Drama Review. (Summer,
1966), pp. 93-108.

223. Kerr, S. P. "What are Immoral Plays?" Westminster
Review. Vol. 155 (April, 1901), pp. 444-50.

224. Koch, F. H. "Literary Value in the Modern Drama."
Quarterly Journal. Vol. 3 (April, 1913), pp. 249-69.

225. Laidlow, Allan. "Drama on the Downward Grade." Westminster Review. Vol. 153 (March, 1900), pp. 317-23.

226. "Life and the Theatre." Saturday Review. Vol. 117
(June 27, 1914), pp. 826-7.

227. Loomis, R. S. "Defense of Naturalism." International
Journal of Ethics. Vol. 29 (January, 1919), pp. 188-201.

228. MacCarthy, D. "Realism and Music " New Statesman.
Vol. 12 (February 8, 1919), pp. 399-400.

229. MacGowan, Kenneth. "New Plays for Old." New Republic.
Vol. 17 (November 9, 1919), p. 46.

230. Moore, C. L. "The Modern Drama: Should the Plays
Preach?" Dial. Vol. 58 (April 15, 1915), pp. 287-9.

231. Moses, Montrose J. "Modern Drama as a Social Force."
Book News. Vol. 29 (October, 1910), pp. 92-95.

232. Nathan, George Jean. "American Dramatic Criticism."
Dramatic Mirror. Vol. 79 (December 28, 1918), p. 938.

233. Osborne, John. "Naturalism and the Dramaturgy of the
Open Drama." German Life and Letters. Vol. 23 (1970),
pp. 119-28.

234. Palmer, J. "Plays Without Sex." Saturday Review.
Vol. 116 (October 4, 1913), pp. 422-3, and Living Age.
Vol. 279 (November 8, 1913), pp. 380-2.

235. Plowman, Max. "Hopes and Fears for Modern Drama."
Academy. Vol. 80 (March 25, 1911), pp. 365-7.

236. Ranck, E. C. "New vs. Old Drama." Theatre. Vol. 27
(June, 1918), p. 368.

237. Scott, Clement. "Two Dramatic Revolutions." North
American Review. Vol. 157, pp. 476-84.

238. Shanks, E. "Realism in the Theatre." Outlook
(London). Vol. 51 (June 9, 1923), p. 470.

239. Smith, L. W. "The Drift toward Naturalism " South
Atlantic Quarterly. Vol. 22 (October, 1923), pp. 355-69.

240. Viereck, G. S. "Intellectual Drama." International.
Vol. 12 (May, 1918), pp. 154-55.

241. Wedmore, Frederick. "Literature and the Theatre."
Nineteenth Century. Vol. 51 (April, 1902), pp. 568-80.

242. Young, S. "Music and the Poetic and Realistic Styles
in Drama." Drama. No. 3 (August, 1911), pp. 123-35.

II AUSTRIA

General Commentaries

243. Liptzin, S. "Young Vienna." Poet Lore. Vol. 47, no. 4 [1941], pp. 339-40.

244. Mühlher, Robert, ed. Beiträge zur Dramatik Österreichs im 20. Jahrhundert. Vienna: Hirt, 1968.

LUDWIG ANZENGRUBER

(pseudonym for Ludwig Gruber, 1839-1889)

Selected Full-length Plays:

> Der Pfarrer von Kirchfeld (The Parson of
>   Kirchfeld, 1870)
> Der Meineidbauer (The Perjured Farmer,
>   The Farmer Forsworn, 1871)
> Der Kreuzelschreiber (The Cross Markers,
>   1872)
> Das vierte Gebot (The Fourth Commandment,
>   1877)

Books

245. Ferriss, Emery N. Anzengruber's Portrayal of Character. Dayton, Ohio: The Otterbein Press, 1911.

246. Koessler, Louis. Louis Anzengruber, auteur dramatique. Toulouse: Imprimerie Toulousaine, 1943.

Articles

247. Barget, C. W. "Work of Ludwig Anzengruber." Colonnade.
Vol. 9 (January, 1905), pp. 30-8.

248. Bettelheim, A. "Zur Auferstehung von Anzengrubers
viertem Gebot." Deutsche Rundschau. Vol. 223 (April, 1930),
pp. 50-53.

249. Morgan, B. Q. "Music in the Plays of Ludwig Anzengruber." Modern Languages Association. Vol. 35 (September,
1920), pp. 334-57.

Theses and Dissertations

250. Ermish, Karl Wilhelm. "Anzengruber und der Naturalismus." Ph.D. Dissertation. University of Minnesota, 1927.

251. Ernst, Adolphine Bianca. "Frauencharaktere und Frauen-
probleme bei Ludwig Anzengruber." Ph.D. Dissertation. University of Wisconsin, 1912.

252. Ferriss, Emery Nelson. "Anzengruber's Portrayal of
Character." Ph.D. Dissertation. University of Iowa, 1911.

253. Gantkowski, Harry A. "The Social Message in Anzengruber's Dramas." Ph.D. Dissertation. University of Pittsburgh, 1937.

254. O'Brien, George M. "The Ethic Developed in the Works
of Ludwig Anzengruber." Ph.D. Dissertation. University of
Minnesota, 1970.

HERMANN BAHR

(1863-1934)

Selected Full-length Plays:

> Die neuen Menschen (The New Men, 1887)
> Die grosse Sünde (The Great Sin, 1888)
> Die Mutter (The Mother, 1891)
> Die häusliche Frau (The Domestic Woman, 1891)
> Juana (1896)
> Josephine (1897)
> Das Tschaperl (The Simpleton, 1898)
> Der Star (The Star, 1898)
> Der Athlet (The Athlete, 1899)
> Wienerinnen (Viennese Women, 1900)
> Der Krampus (The Bogie Man, The Devil's Emissary,
>   1901)
> Der Franzl (Francis, 1901)
> Der Apostel (The Apostle, 1901)
> Der Meister (The Master, 1903)

Die gelbe Nachtigall (The Yellow
   Nightingale, 1904)
Unter Sich (Among Themselves, 1904)
Sanna (1905)
Die Andere (The Other Woman, 1906)
Das Konzert (The Concert, 1910)
Die Kinder (The Children, 1911)
Das Tänzchen (The Little Dance, 1911)
Das Prinzip (The Principle, 1912)
Das Phantom (1913)
Der Querulant (The Complainer, 1914)
Die Stimme (The Voice, 1916)
Der Augenblick (The Moment, 1917)

Books

255. Bogner, Kurt. Hermann Bahr und das Theaterwesen seiner
Zeit. Vienna: Ohne Press, 1946.

256. Handl, Willi. Hermann Bahr. Berlin: S. Fischer, 1913.

257. Kinderman, Heinz. Hermann Bahr: ein Leben für das europäische Theater. Graz: H. Bohlaus Nachf, 1954.

258. Widder, Erich. Hermann Bahr: Sein Weg zum Glauben.
Linz: Oberösterreichischer Landesverlag, 1963.

Articles

259. Daviau, Donald G. "Dialog vom Marsyas: Hermann Bahr's
Affirmation of Life over Art." Modern Language Quarterly.
Vol. 20 (December, 1959), pp. 360-70.

260. _____. "Hermann Bahr as Director of the Burg-
theater." German Quarterly. Vol. 32 (January, 1959), pp.
11-21.

261. Jahnichen, M. "Hermann Bahr und die Tschechen." In
W. Krauss, et al., eds., Slawischdeutsche Wechselbeziehungen
in Sprache, Literatur und Kultur. Berlin: Akademie-Verlag,
1969, pp. 363-77.

262. Lehner, Friedrich. "Hermann Bahr." Monatshefte. Vol.
39 (1947), pp. 54-62.

263. Rubinstein, H. F. "The Work of Hermann Bahr." Forum.
Vol. 53 (March, 1915), pp. 375-9.

Theses

264. Daviau, Donald G. "The Significance of Hermann Bahr
to Austria." Ph.D. Dissertation. University of California,
1955.

265. Simmons, Robert Edward. "Hermann Bahr as a Literary
Critic, an Analysis and Exposition of His Thought." Ph.D.
Dissertation. Stanford University, 1957.

ARTHUR SCHNITZLER

(1862-1931)

Selected Full-length Plays:

>Alkandis Lied (The Song of Alkandis, 1890)
>Märchen (The Fairy Tale, 1893
>Anatol (The Affairs of Anatol, 1892)
>Liebelei (Light-O'-Love, Playing with Love, 1894)
>Freiwild (Fair Game, Free Game, 1896)
>Das Vermächtnis (The Legacy, 1898)
>Der Grüne Kakadu (The Green Cockatoo, 1898)
>Der Schleier der Beatrice (Beatrice's Veil, The
>   Bridal Veil, 1900)
>Reigen (La Ronde, Hands Around, Round Dance, 1900)
>Literatur (Literature, The Literary Sense, 1902)
>Der Einsame Weg (The Lonely Way, 1903)
>Der Ruf des Lebens (The Call of Life, 1905)
>Zwischenspiel (Intermezzo, 1905)
>Lebendige Stunden (Living Hours, 1906)
>Komtesse Mizzi (Countess Mitzi, 1909)
>Das weite Land (The Wide Country, The Vast Domain,
>   1911)
>Dr. Bernhardi (1912)
>Die Schwestern, oder Casanova in Spa (The Sisters,
>   or Casanova at the Spa; The Return of Casanova,
>   1919)

Books

266. Allen, Richard H. An Annotated Arthur Schnitzler Bibliography. Chapel Hill, North Carolina: University of North Carolina Press, 1966.

267. Baumann, Gerhart. Arthur Schnitzler: Die Welt von Gestern, eines Dichters von Morgen. Frankfurt am Main: Athenäum Verlag, 1965.

268. Bergel, Kurt. Georg Brandes und Arthur Schnitzler: Ein Briefwechsel. Berkeley: University of California Press, 1956.

269. Fritsche, Alfred. Dekadenz im Werk Arthur Schnitzlers. Bern: Lang, 1974.

270. Just, Gottfried. Ironie und Sentimentalität in den erzählenden Dichtungen Arthur Schnitzlers. Berlin: Schmidt, 1968.

271. Kapp, Julius. Arthur Schnitzler. Leipzig: Xenien Verlag, 1912.

272. Körner, Josef. Arthur Schnitzlers Gestalten und Probleme. Zurich and Leipzig: Amalthea-verlag, 1921.

273. Liptzin, Solomon. Arthur Schnitzler. New York: Prentice-Hall, Inc., 1932.

274. Melchinger, Christa. Illusion und Wirklichkeit im dramatischen Werk Arthur Schnitzlers. Heidelberg: Winter, 1968.

275. Nichl, Therese and Heinrich Schnitzler, eds. Arthur Schnitzler, Jugend in Wein: Eine Autobiographie. Vienna: Molden, 1968.

276. Reichert, Herbert William and Herman Salinger. Studies in Arthur Schnitzler. Chapel Hill: University of North Carolina Press, 1963.

277. Reik, Theodor. Arthur Schnitzler als Psycholog. Minden: Bruns, 1913.

278. Rieder, Heinz. Arthur Schnitzler. Vienna: Bergland, 1973.

279. Specht, Richard. Arthur Schnitzler. Der Dichter und Sein Werk. Berlin: S. Fischer, 1922.

280. Swales, Martin. Arthur Schnitzler: a Critical Study. Oxford: Claredon Press, 1971.

281. Urbach, Reinhard. Arthur Schnitzler. Velber bei Hannover: Friedrich, 1968.

282. _____ . Schnitzler-Kommentar zu den erzählenden Schriften und dramatischen Werken. Munich: Winkler, 1974.

Articles

283. Apsler, Alfred. "A Sociological View of Arthur Schnitzler." German Review. Vol. 18 (1943), pp. 90-106.

284. Berharriell, F. "Arthur Schnitzler's Range of Theme." Monatshefte. Vol. 43 (1951), pp. 301-11.

285. _____ . "Schnitzler's Anticipation of Freud's Dream Theory." Monatshefte. Vol. 45 (1953), pp. 81-9.

286. Berlin, Jeffrey B. "Arthur Schnitzler: A Bibliography of Criticism." Modern Austrian Literature. Vol. 4, no. 4 (1971), pp. 7-20.

287. Doppler, Alfred. "Dramatische Formen bei Arthur Schnitzler." In Beiträge zur Dramatik Österreichs im 20. Jahrhundert. Vienna: Hirt, 1968, n. pag.

288. Ende, Amelia von. "The Work of Arthur Schnitzler." Theatre. Vol. 16 (July, 1912), pp. 5-8.

289. Grummann, P. H. "Criticism of the Work of Arthur Schnitzler." Poet Lore. Vol. 23 (January-February, 1912), pp. 25-41.

290. Henderson, Archibald. "Sketch of Arthur Schnitzler." North American Review. Vol. 196 (November, 1912), pp. 635-45.

291. Hill, Claude. "The Stature of Arthur Schnitzler." Modern Drama. Vol. 4 (1961), pp. 8-91.

292. Koehler, Selma. "The Question of Moral Responsibility in the Dramatic Works of Arthur Schnitzler." Journal of English and German Philology. Vol. 22 (1923), pp. 376-411.

293. Korner, J. "Arthur Schnitzlers Spätwerk." Preussische Jahrbücher. Vol. 208 (April-May, 1927), p. 53.

294. Morgan, B. Q. "Sketch of Arthur Schnitzler." Drama. Vol. 7 (August, 1912), pp. 3-13.

295. Politzer, H. "Arthur Schnitzler: The Poetry of Psychology." Modern Languages Notes. Vol. 78 (October, 1963), pp. 353-72.

296. Reiss, H. S. "Problems of Fate and Religion in the Work of Arthur Schnitzler." Modern Language Review. Vol. 40 (October, 1945), pp. 300-8.

297. Samuel, H. B. "Arthur Schnitzler." Fortnightly Review. Vol. 93 (March, 1910), pp. 447-69.

298. Schlein, Rena R. "The Motif of Hypocrisy in the Works of Arthur Schnitzler." Modern Austrian Literature. Vol. 2 no. 1, pp. 28-37.

299. Storer, E. "The Art of Arthur Schnitzler." Academy. Vol. 86 (January 10, 1914), pp. 37-8.

300. Stroka, Anna. "Arthur Schnitzlers Tragikomödien." Germanica Wratislaviensia. Vol. 14 (1971), pp. 55-73.

301. Weiss, Robert O. "Arthur Schnitzler's Notes on Journalistic Criticism." Germanic Review. Vol. 38 (May, 1963), pp. 226-37.

302. _____. "The Psychoses in the Works of Arthur Schnitzler." German Quarterly. Vol. 41 (1968), pp. 377-400.

Theses and Dissertations

303. Allen, Richard Harry. "Arthur Schnitzler's Works and Their Reception: An Annotated Bibliography." Ph.D. Dissertation. University of Michigan, 1964.

304. Alter, Maria Popischill. "The Concepts of Physician in the Writings of Hans Carossa and Arthur Schnitzler." Ph.D. Dissertation. University of Maryland, 1961.

305. Conner, Maurice. "An Investigation of Three Themes Pertaining to Life and Death in the Works of Arthur Schnitzler." Ph.D. Dissertation. University of Nebraska, 1974.

306. Davis, Evan B. "Moral Problems in the Works of Arthur Schnitzler." Ph.D. Dissertation. University of Pennsylvania, 1950.

307. Friedrichsmeyer, Erhard Martin. "Erwartung und Erinnerung in den Werken Arthur Schnitzlers." Ph.D. Dissertation. University of Minnesota, 1964.

308. Green, Jon D. "The Impact of Musical Theme and Structure on the Meaning and Dramatic Unity of Selected Works by Arthur Schnitzler." Ph.D. Dissertation. University of Syracuse, 1972.

309. Ilmer, Frida. "Die Gestalt des Künstlers bei Schnitzler." Ph.D. Dissertation. Johns Hopkins University, 1933.

310. Lederer, Herbert. "The Problem of Ethics in the Works of Arthur Schnitzler." Ph.D. Dissertation. University of Chicago, 1954.

311. Schneider, Gerd K. "Arthur Schnitzler und die Psychologie seiner Zeit, unter besonderer Berücksichtigung der Philosophie Friedrich Nietzsches." Ph.D. Dissertation. University of Washington, 1969.

312. Walton, Saral Luverne. "Arthur Schnitzler on the New York Stage." Ph.D. Dissertation. Indiana University, 1967.

313. Whiton, John Nelson. "The Problem of Marriage in the Works of Arthur Schnitzler." Ph.D. Dissertation. University of Minnesota, 1967.

III BELGIUM AND HOLLAND

CYRIEL BUYSSE

(1859-1932)

Selected Full-length Plays:

> Driekoningenavond (The Three Kings,
>   1903)
> Het Gezin van Paemel (The Van Paemel
>   Family, 1903)

Books

314. Elslander, A. van. Cyriel Buysse: Uit zijn leven en
ijn werk. Anvers: 1960-1961.

315. Puymbroek, Herman van. Cyriel Buysse en zijn land.
Antwerp: Resseler, 1929.

316. Vreckem, P. H. S. van. De invloed van het franse naturalisme in het werk van Cyriel Buysse. Brussels: Tidschrift
van Vrije Univ. te Brussel, 1968.

Articles

317. Bittremieux, C. "Bij een studie over Cyriel Buysse."
Tirade. Vol. 12 (1968), pp. 202-10.

318. Mussche, Achilles. "Cyriel Buysse als Van Nu en Strak-
ser." Nieuw Vlaams Tidjschrift. Vol. 21 (1968), pp. 521-26.

319. Vreckem, Paul van. "Cyrille Buysse, un diciple Flamand
des naturalistes Français." Revue de Littérature Comparée.
Vol. 41 (1967), pp. 54-87.

HERMAN HEIJERMANS

(1864-1924)

Selected Full-length Plays:

> Dora Kremer (1893)
> Nummer Tachtig (Number Eighty, 1898)
> Puntje (The Dot, 1898)
> Het Antwoord (The Answer, 1898)
> Ghetto (1899)
> De Machien (The Machine, 1899)
> Zet Zevende Gebot (The Seventh Commandment, 1899)
> Op Hoop van Zegen (The Good Hope, 1900)
> Het Pantzer (The Suit of Armour, 1901)
> Ora et Labora (Pray and Work, 1902)
> Het Kind (The Child, 1903)
> Schakels (Links, 1903)
> In de Jonge Jan (At the Jon Jange, A Case of
>   Arson, 1903)
> Allerzielen (All Souls, 1904)
> Bloeimaand (Maytime, 1904)
> Saltimbank (1904)
> De Meid (The Maid, 1905)
> Vit Kumst (The Way Out, 1907)
> Feest (Jubilee, 1908)
> Det opgaande zon (The Rising Sun, 1908)
> Vreemde jacht (Strange Chase, 1909)
> Beschuit met Muisjes (Blessed Event, 1910)
> Gluck Auf! (Good Luck!, 1911)
> Eva Bonheur (The Devil to Pay, 1916)
> Dagaraad (Dawn, 1916)
> De Wijze Kater (The Wise Cat, 1918)
> De Vlieaends Hollander of De Goote Widdenschap
>   (The Flying Dutchman, or The Big Bet, 1920)

Books

320. Hulleman, Frans. Heijermans--herinneringen. Laren
(Gooiland): A. G. Schoonderbeck, 1926.

321. Hunningher, Benjamin. Tooneel en werkelijkheid. Rot-
terdam: W. L. & J. Brusse, 1947.

322. Jong, Evert de. Herman Heijermanns en de vernieuwing
van det Europese drama. Groningen: Wolters, 1967.

323. _____. Met waarachtige zorg De toneelschrijver
Herman Heijermans. Leiden: Sijthoff, 1971.

Theses and Dissertations

324. Flaxman, Seymour Lawrence. "Herman Heijermans and his
Dramas." Ph.D. Dissertation. Columbia University, 1950.

Articles

325. Barnouw, A. J. "The Work of Herman Heijermans." Theatre Arts Monthly. Vol. 9 (February, 1925), pp. 109-12.

326. Dukes, Ashley. "The Plays of Herman Heijermans."
Drama. Vol. 2 (November, 1912), pp. 3-15.

327. Flaxman, Seymour L. "Herman Heijermans on the New
York Stage." German Review. Vol. 27 (1952), pp. 131-7.

IV ENGLAND

General Commentaries

Books

328. Agate, James Evershed. A Short View of the English Stage, 1900-1926. London: H. Jenkins, 1926.

329. _____. My Theater Talks. London: A. Barker, 1933.

330. Archer, William. About the Theatre. London: T. F. Unwin, 1886.

331. _____. English Dramatists of To-day. London: W. Low, Marston, 1882.

332. Borsa, Mario. English Stage of Today. London: J. Lane, 1908.

333. Bradbrook, M. C. English Dramatic Form: A History of its Development. London: Chatto & Windus, 1965.

334. Clark, Barrett H. The British and American Drama of Today. New York: H. Holt, 1915.

335. Cunliffe, John William. English Literature During the Last Half-Century. New York: Macmillan, 1919.

336. _____. Modern English Playwrites: A Short History of the English Drama From 1825. New York and London: Harper, 1927.

337. Dark, Sidney. Stage Silhouettes. London: A. Treherne and Co., Ltd., 1901.

338. Dickinson, Thomas H. The Contemporary Drama of England.
Boston: Little Brown, 1917.

339. Dukes, Ashley. The Youngest Drama. Chicago: Charles H.
Sergel, 1924.

340. Ellehauge, Martin O. Striking Figures Among Modern
English Dramatists. London: Williams and Norgate, 1931.

341. Ellis-Fermor, Una Mary. The Frontiers of the Drama.
London: Methuen, 1946.

342. Ellmann, Richard. Edwardians and Late Victorians. New
York: Columbia University Press, 1960.

343. Ervine, St. John. Some Impressions of My Elders. New
York: Macmillan, 1922.

344. Filon, Augustin. The English Stage. London: John
Milne, 1897.

345. Garland, Hamlin. My Friendly Contemporaries. New
York: Macmillan, 1932.

346. Gaw, Allison. Studies in English Drama. New York: D.
Appleton, 1917.

347. Hudson, Lynton. The English Stage, 1850-1950. London:
George G. Harrap & Co., Ltd., 1951.

348. Jones, Henry Arthur. Foundations of a National Drama.
London: Chapman, 1913.

349. _____ . The Renaissance of the English Drama.
New York: Macmillan, 1895.

350. Knight, G. Wilson. The Golden Labyrinth: A Study of
British Drama. London: Phoenix House, 1962.

351. MacCarthy, Sir Desmond. The Court Theatre, 1904-1907:
A Commentary and Criticism. London: A. H. Bullen, 1907.

352. Meier, Erika. Realism and Reality: The Function of
Stage Directions in the New Drama from Thomas William Robertson to Bernard Shaw. (Cooper Monograph on English and American Literature, no. 12.) Bern: A. Francke Verlag, 1967.

353. Moore, George. Impressions and Opinions. London:
David Hutt, 1891.

354. Morgan, Arthur Eustace. Tendencies in Modern English
Drama. London: Constable and Co., 1924.

355. Nicoll, Allardyce. British Drama: An Historical Survey from the Beginning to the Present Time. New York:
Thomas Crowell, 1925.

356. Nicoll, Allardyce. English Drama, 1900-1930: The Beginnings of the Modern Period. London: Cambridge University Press, 1973.

357. Oliver, D. E. The English Stage: Its Origins and Modern Developments. London: J. Ouseley, 1912.

358. Pellizzi, Camillo. English Drama: The Last Great Phase. London: Macmillan, 1935.

359. Rowell, George. The Victorian Theatre: A Survey. Oxford: Oxford University Press, 1956.

360. Roy, Emil. British Drama Since Shaw. Carbondale: Southern Illinois University Press, 1972.

361. Salerno, Henry F., ed. English Drama in Transition, 1880-1920. New York: Pegasus Press, 1968.

362. Schilling, F. E. English Drama. London: J. M. Dent and Sons, Ltd., 1914.

363. Shaw, George Bernard. Our Theatre in the Nineties. Three Volumes. London: Constable, 1932.

364. Sherbo, Arthur. English Sentimental Drama. East Lansing: Michigan State University Press, 1957.

365. Starkie, Enid. From Gautier to Eliot: The Influence of France on English Literature, 1851-1939. London: Hutchinson University Library, 1960.

366. Stokes, John. Resistable Theatres: Enterprise and Experiment in the Late Nineteenth Century. London: Elek, 1972.

367. Sutton, Graham. Some Contemporary Dramatists. New York: G. H. Doran, 1925.

368. Tindall, William York. Forces in Modern British Literature, 1885-1946. New York: Knopf, 1947.

369. Trewin, J. C. The Edwardian Theatre. Oxford: Basil Blackwell, 1976.

370. Walkley, Arthur Bingham. Drama and Life. London: Methuen, 1907.

371. _____. Playhouse Impressions. London: T. F. Unwin, 1892.

372. Weales, Gerald. Edwardian Plays. New York: Hill and Wang, 1962.

373. Wearing, J. P. The London Stage, 1890-1899: A Calendar of Plays and Players. Metuchen, N.J.: Scarecrow Press, 1976.

374. Williams, Harold. Modern English Writers, 1890-1914.
London: Sidgwick and Jackson, 1919.

375. Wilson, Albert E. Edwardian Theatre. London: Barker,
1951.

Theses and Dissertations

376. Covert, Marjorie A. "Realism in the Prose Theatre of
France and England, 1890-1910." Ph.D. Dissertation. University of Wisconsin, 1934.

377. Decker, Clarence Raymond. "The Reaction of English
Literary Criticism of the Late Nineteenth Century to Foreign
Realistic Thought." Ph.D. Dissertation. University of Chi-
cago, 1929.

378. Emerson, Flora Elizabeth. "English Dramatic Critics
of the Nineties and the Acting of the 'New Theatre.'" Ph.D.
Dissertation. Bryn Mawr.

379. Gottlieb, Lois J. "Chekhov and Some Chekhovians in the
English-Speaking Theatre, 1910-1935." Ph.D. Dissertation.
University of Michigan, 1970.

380. Hirsch, Foster L. "The Edwardian Drama of Ideas."
Ph.D. Dissertation. Columbia University, 1971.

381. Kochman, Andrew John, Jr. "Realism in the Early and
Middle Nineteenth Century British Theatre." Ph.D. Dissertation. University of Wisconsin, 1957.

382. Moore, John Brooks. "The Comic and the Realistic in
English Drama." Ph.D. Dissertation. University of Wisconsin,
1923.

383. Osborn, Margaret E. "The Conception of Imagination in
Edwardian Drama." Ph.D. Dissertation. University of Pennsylvania, 1967.

384. Rice, Enid Elva. "Changing Attitudes toward Social
Criticism in the Plays of Robertson, Pinero, Galsworthy and
Maugham." Master's Thesis. University of Maine, 1941.

Articles

385. Beers, Henry A. "English Drama of Today," North American Review. Vol. 180 (May, 1905), pp. 746-57.

386. Cheney, Sheldon. "New English Dramatists," Theatre.
Vol. 19 (February, 1914), pp. 81-4.

387. Cunliffe, John William. "Victorian Drama," in Leaders
of the Victorian Revolution. London: D. Appleton-Century,
1934, pp. 312-22.

388. Decker, C. R. "The Aesthetic Revolt Against Naturalism in Victorian Criticism." PMLA. Vol. 53 (September, 1938), pp. 844-56.

389. Granville-Barker, Harley. "The Theatre: The Next Phase." Forum. Vol. 44 (August, 1910), pp. 159-70.

390. Henderson, Archibald. "The New Drama in England." Forum. Vol. 45 (June, 1911), pp. 707-24.

391. Waugh, Arthur. "London Letter." Critic. Vol. 24 (February 24, 1894), p. 134.

392. Weales, Gerald. "Edwardian Theatre and the Shadow of Shaw," in Richard Ellman, ed., English Institute Essays, 1959. New York: Columbia University Press, 1960, pp. 70-89.

JOHN GALSWORTHY

(1867-1933)

Selected Full-length Plays:

> The Silver Box (1906)
> Joy (1907)
> Strife (1908)
> Justice (1910)
> The Fugitive (1910)
> The Foundations (1911)
> The Little Dream (1911)
> The Eldest Son (1912)
> The Little Man (1913)
> The Mob (1914)
> A Bit o' Love (1914)
> The First and the Last (1918)
> The Sun (1918)
> Windows (1920)
> Loyalties (1922)

Books

393. Barker, Dudley. The Man of Principle: A View of John Galsworthy. New York: London House and Maxwell, 1963.

394. Coats, Robert H. John Galsworthy as a Dramatist Artist. London: Duckworth, 1926.

395. Croman, Natalie. John Galsworthy: A Study in Continuity and Contrast. Cambridge: Harvard University Press, 1933.

396. DuPont, V. John Galsworthy the Dramatic Artist. Paris: H. Didier. 1942.

397. Galsworthy, John. Letters from John Galsworthy, 1900-1932. New York: Scribner, 1934.

398. Guedalla, Phillip A. _A Gallery_. New York: G. P. Putnam's Sons, 1924.

399. Kaye-Smith, Sheila. _John Galsworthy_. London: Nisbet,
1916.

400. Marrot, Harold Vincent. _Bibliography of the Works of
John Galsworthy_. London: E. Matthews, 1928.

401. _____. _Life and Letters of John Galsworthy_. New
York: Charles Scribner's Sons, 1936.

402. Mikhail, E. _John Galsworthy the Dramatist, A Bibliography of Criticism_. Troy, New York: Winston Publishing, 1971.

403. Morris, Margaret. _My Galsworthy Story_. London: Owen,
1967.

404. Ould, Hermon. _John Galsworthy_. London: Chapman and
Hall, Ltd., 1934.

405. Phelps, William. _Essays on Modern Dramatists_. New
York: Macmillan, 1921.

406. Reynolds, Mabel Edith. _Memories of John Galsworthy by
His Sister_. New York: Stokes, 1937.

407. Sauter, Rudolph. _Galsworthy the Man: An Intimate Por-
trait_. London: Owen, 1967.

408. Schalit, Leon. _John Galsworthy: A Survey_. New York:
Charles Scribner's Sons, 1929.

409. Schrey, Kurt. _John Galsworthy und die besitzenden
Klassen Englands_. Marburg: N. G. Elwert, 1917.

Theses and Dissertations

410. Amend, Victor Earl. "The Development of John Galsworthy
as a Social Dramatist." Ph.D. Dissertation. University of
Michigan, 1953.

411. Bartholomew, Raymond Elon. "The Tooth of Time: The
Critical Reputation of John Galsworthy." Ph.D. Dissertation.
Western Reserve University, 1964.

412. Childs, Harold F. "John Galsworthy: A Study in the
Naturalistic Drama." B.A. Thesis. The Ohio State University, 1913.

413. Kent, George E. "Social Criticism in the Novels, Plays
and Representative Short Stories of John Galsworthy." Ph.D.
Dissertation. University of Boston, 1953.

414. Schwab, William. "The Dramatic Art of John Galsworthy."
Ph.D. Dissertation. University of Wisconsin, 1951.

415. Smith, Philip E., II. "John Galsworthy's Plays: The Theory and Practice of Dramatic Realism." Ph.D. Dissertation. Northwestern University, 1970.

416. Stern, Faith, E. B. "John Galsworthy's Dramatic Theory and Practice." Ph.D. Dissertation. Stanford University, 1971.

417. Trumbauer, Walter. "Gerhart Hauptmann and John Galsworthy: A Parallel." Ph.D. Dissertation. University of Pennsylvania, 1917.

418. Wilson, Asher Boldon. "John Galsworthy's Letters to Leon Lion." Ph.D. Dissertation. Stanford University, 1962.

419. Winters, Edna Spring. "A Modern Socrates: John Galsworthy." Ph.D. Dissertation. Cornell University, 1931.

Articles

420. Adcock, St. John. "Critical Sketch of John Galsworthy." Bookman (London). Vol. 42 (June, 1912), pp. 127-8.

421. Alexander, Henry. "Galsworthy as Dramatist." Queen's Quarterly. Vol. 40 (1933), pp. 177-88.

422. Austin, H. D. "John Galsworthy." Dublin Review. Vol. 189 (July, 1931), pp. 95-106.

423. Armstrong, A. "Women of Galsworthy." Saturday Review. Vol. 155 (February 4, 1923), p. 115.

424. Aynard, J. "John Galsworthy." Journal des Débats. Vol. 40 (February 10, 1923), pp. 247-8.

425. Baillon de Wailly, L. "John Galsworthy." Revue Politique et Littéraire. Vol. 71 (July 1, 1933), pp. 408-12.

426. Baughan, Edward Algernon. "John Galsworthy as Dramatist." Fortnightly Review. Vol. 91 (May, 1909), pp. 971-7.

427. Björkman, E. "John Galsworthy: An Interpreter of Modernity." American Monthly Review of Reviews. Vol. 43 May, 1911), pp. 634-6.

428. Boyd, E. "The Novelist as Dramatist." Theatre Arts. Vol. 13 (May, 1929), pp. 334, 337-41.

429. Brash, W. B. "John Galsworthy." London Quarterly Review. Vol. 160 (October, 1935), pp. 460-71.

430. Brown, Ivor. "John Galsworthy, Dramatist." Bookman (London). Vol. 75 (December, 1928), pp. 151-6.

431. Butt, G. B. "Tragedy and Mr. Galsworthy." Living Age. Vol. 315 (November 4, 1922), pp. 287-9.

432.   Canby, H. S.   "An Estimate of John Galsworthy."   Saturday Review of Literature.   Vol. 9 (March 18, 1933), pp. 485-6.

433.   Davis, S. H.   "Galsworthy the Craftsman."   Bookman (London).   Vol. 86 (April, 1934), pp. 12-16.   Also Vol. 87 (October, 1934), pp. 27-31.

434.   Eaker, J. G.   "Galsworthy and the Modern Mind."   Philological Quarterly.   Vol. 29 (January, 1950), pp. 31-48.

435.   Ervine, St. John G.   "The Later Plays of John Galsworthy."   Fortnightly Review.   Vol. 110 (July, 1918).   pp. 83-92.

436.   Ford, Ford M.   "John Galsworthy and George Moore."   English Review.   Vol. 57 (August, 1933), pp. 130-42.

437.   Gallenga, R.   "John Galsworthy."   Nuova Antologia.   Vol. 368 (July 1, 1933), pp. 82-92.

438.   Galsworthy, John.   "Anglo-American Drama and its Future," in Another Sheaf.   New York: Charles Scribner's Sons, 1919, pp. 112-39.

439.   _____.   "Some Platitudes Concerning Drama," in The Inn of Tranquillity.   New York: Charles Scribner's Sons, 1912, pp. 189-202.

440.   Glasgow, G.   "John Galsworthy: Teacher and Prophet."   Contemporary.   No. 926 (February, 1943), pp. 16-19.

441.   Harding, J. N.   "John Galsworthy and the Just Man."   Contemporary Review.   Vol. 199 (April, 1961), pp. 198-203.

442.   Herrick, M. J.   "Current English Usage and the Dramas of Galsworthy."   American Speech.   Vol. 7 (August, 1932), pp. 412-19.

443.   "Later Plays of Mr. John Galsworthy."   Fortnightly Review.   Vol. 10 (July, 1918), pp. 83-92.

444.   MacDermot, T. W. L.   "Galsworthy's Life and Work."   Dalhousie Review.   Vol. 9 (October, 1929), pp. 354-68.

445.   Martin, Dorothy.   "Mr. Galsworthy as Artist and Reformer."   Yale Review.   Vol. 14 (October, 1924), pp. 126-39.

446.   Mencken, Henry Lewis.   "Critical Sketch."   Smart Set.   Vol. 43 (July, 1914), pp. 153-60.

447.   Moses, Montrose J.   "John Galsworthy as Dramatist."   Book News.   Vol. 30 (July, 1912), pp. 771-4.

448.   _____.   "Sketch of John Galsworthy."   Metropolitan Magazine.   Vol. 37 (December, 1912), pp. 31-32.

449. Mottram, R. H. "John Galsworthy." New Statesman and Nation. Vol. 5 (February 4, 1933), pp. 128-9.

450. Ould, Herman. "John Galsworthy: Internationalist." Bookman. Vol. 83 (March, 1933), p. 486.

451. "Satire in John Galsworthy's Plays. Nation. Vol. 97 (October 23, 1913), p. 380.

452. Scott-James, R. A. "John Galsworthy." Spectator. Vol. 150 (February 3, 1933), pp. 145-6.

453. Scrimgeour, Gary J. "Naturalist Drama and Galsworthy." Modern Drama. Vol. 7 (1964), pp. 65-78.

454. Skelton, Isabel. "John Galsworthy, an Appreciation." World Today. Vol. 21 (August, 1911), pp. 995-9.

455. Sparrow, J. "John Galsworthy." London Mercury. Vol. 28 (May, 1933), pp. 50-5.

456. Steinermayr, F. C. "Der Werdegang von John Galsworthy, Weltundkunstansschauung." Anglia. Vol. 49 (May, 1925), n pag.

457. Véron, Jeanne. "John Galsworthy through French Eyes." Cornhill. Vol. 74 (April, 1933), pp. 385-8.

458. White, W. "Houseman on Galsworthy: More Marginalia." Review of English Studies. Vol. 24 (July, 1948), pp. 240-1.

459. Williamson, H. R. "Soames Forsythe: John Galsworthy as a Dramatist." Bookman. Vol. 83 (March, 1933), pp. 473-9.

HARLEY GRANVILLE-BARKER

(1877-1946)

Selected Full-length Plays:

> The Family of Oldroyds (with Berte Thomas, 1895)
> Our Visitor to Work-a-Day (with Berte Thomas,
>   1899)
> The Marrying of Ann Leete (1899)
> Prunella, or Love in a Dutch Oven (with
>   L. Houseman, 1904)
> The Voysey Inheritance (1905)
> Waste (1907)
> The Madras House (1910)
> Souls on Fifth (1916)

Books

460. Howe, Percival Presland. The Repertory Theatre: A Record and A Criticism. New York: Kennerley, 1911.

461. Morgan, Margery Mary. A Drama of Political Man: A
Study in the Plays of Harley Granville-Barker. London: Sidgwick and Jackson, 1961.

462. Purdom, Charles Benjamin. Harley Granville-Barker: Man
of The Theatre, Dramatist, Scholar. London: Rockliff, 1955.

Articles

463. Clayton, N. "The Plays of Granville Barker." Bookman.
Vol. 35 (April, 1912), pp. 195-7.

464. Downer, A. S. "Harley Granville-Barker." Sewanee
Review. Vol. 55 (October, 1947), pp. 627-45.

465. Evans, T. F. "Granville-Barker: Shavian Disciple."
Shaw Bulletin. Vol. 2, No. 5 (1958), pp. 1-19.

466. Farmer, A. J. "Harley Granville-Barker (1877-1946)."
Études Anglaises. Vol. 10 (1958), pp. 304-9.

467. Haskell, Margaret. "Granville-Barker as Dramatist."
Drama. No. 8 (May, 1918), pp. 284-94.

468. Howe, Percival P. "Plays of Harley Granville Barker."
Fortune. Vol. 99 (September 13, 1913), pp. 476-85.

469. Moore, George. "George Moore and Granville Barker."
Dial. Vol. 75 (August, 1923), pp. 135-50.

470. Moses, Montrose J. "What Harley Granville Barker Has
Done for the Art of Theatre." Independent. Vol. 82 (May 3,
1915), pp. 194-97.

471. Nathan, George Jean. "Work of Harley Granville Barker."
Smart Set. Vol. 45 (April, 1913), pp. 428-9.

472. Ritchie, Harry M. "Harley Granville Barker's The
Madras House and the Sexual Revolution." Modern Drama.
Vol. 15, pp. 150-158.

473. Scott, D. "Criticism." Bookman. Vol. 46 (July 14,
1914), pp. 153-62.

474. Storer, E. "The Work of Harley Granville Barker."
Living Age. Vol. 280 (January 24, 1914), pp. 225-9.

Theses and Dissertations

475. Glick, Claris. "An Analysis of Granville Barker's
Criticism Of Shakespeare." Ph.D. Dissertation. University
of Texas, 1956.

476. Smithers, Elizabeth Joan. "The Dramatic Method of
Harley Granville Barker." Ph.D. Dissertation. University
of Pennsylvania, 1961.

ST. JOHN [EMILE CLAVERING] HANKIN

(1869-1909)

Selected Full-length Plays:

> The Two Mr. Weatherbys (1903)
> The Return of the Prodigal (1905)
> The Charity That Began at Home (1906)
> The Cassilis Engagement (1907)
> The Last of the DeMullens (1908)

Books

477. Drinkwater, John. Prose Papers. London: Elkin Matthews, 1918.

478. Hankin, St. John. The Dramatic Works of St. John Hankin. London: M. Secker, 1912.

Articles

479. Evans, T. F. "A Note on Hankin." Shavian. Vol. 4 (1970), pp. 52-53.

480. Henderson, Archibald. "Dramatic Works of St. John Hankin." Dial. Vol. 55 (December, 1913), pp. 474-6.

481. Howe, Percival P. "Estimate of St. John Hankin's Work." North American. Vol. 197 (January, 1913), pp. 78-89.

482. Phillips, William H. "The Individual and Society in the Plays of St. John Hankin." Shavian. Vol. 4 (1972), p. 170.

Theses and Dissertations

483. O'Neil, John D. "The Comedy of St. John Hankin." Ph.D. Dissertation. University of Michigan, 1954.

484. Whelan, Sister M. de Chantal. "St. John Hankin's Dramatic Esthetic: Its Theory and Practice." Ph.D. Dissertation. University of Indiana, 1974.

JEROME K[LAPKA] JEROME

(1859-1927)

Selected Full-length Plays:

>
> Barbara (1886)
> Sunset (1888)
> When Greek Meets Greek (1888)
> New Lamps for Old (1890)
> MacHaggis (1897)
> Miss Hobbs (1900)
> Susan in Search of a Husband (1906)
> Passing of the Third Floor Back (1908)
> They and I (1909)
> The Master and Mrs. Chilvers (1911)
> Anthony John (1923)

Books

485. Faurot, Ruth M. Jerome K. Jerome. New York: Twayne, 1974.

486. Jerome, Jerome Klapka. My Life and Times. London: Hodder, 1926.

Articles

487. Balotă, Nicolae. "Jerome K. Jerome, Umoristul decent." România Literara. Vol. 3 (August, 1973), n pag.

488. McQuilland, L. J. "Jerome Klapka Jerome." Bookman. London: Vol. 70 (September, 1926), pp. 282-4.

489. Pearson, E. "Appreciation of Jerome K. Jerome." Outlook. Vol. 46 (June 29, 1927), pp. 288-9.

HENRY ARTHUR JONES

(1851-1929)

Selected Full-length Plays:

>
> Hearts of Oak (1879)
> A Drive in June (1879)
> A Garden Party (1880)
> Humbug (1881)
> His Wife (1881)
> Home Again (1881)
> Saints and Sinners (1884)
> The Noble Vagabond (1886)
> Hard Hit (1887)
> Wealth (1889)
> Judah (1890)
> The Dancing Girl (1891)

```
The Bauble Shop (1893)
The Rogue's Comedy (1896)
Michael and His Lost Angel (1896)
The Liars (1897)
The Physician (1897)
Carnac Sahib (1899)
Mrs. Dane's Defense (1900)
James the Fogey (1900)
The Lackey's Carnival (1900)
Chance the Idol (1902)
Chrysold (1904)
The Hypocrites (1906)
The Middleman (1907)
The Galilean's Victory (1907)
The Silver King (1907)
We Can't Be As Bad As All That! (1910)
The Ogre (1911)
Lydia Gilmore (1912)
Mary Goes First (1913)
The Divine Gift (1913)
The Lie (1915)
```

Books

490. Cordell, Richard A. Henry Arthur Jones and the Modern Drama. New York: R. R. Smith, 1932.

491. Jones, Doris Arthur. Taking the Curtain Calls: Life and Letters of Henry Arthur Jones. New York: Macmillan, 1930.

492. Jones, Henry Arthur. The Representative Plays of Henry Arthur Jones. Boston: Little Brown, 1925.

Articles

493. Allen, Percy. "Henry Arthur Jones." Fortnightly Review, new series. Vol. 125 (1929), pp. 692-9.

494. Beerbohm, Max. "The Popular Success of Henry Arthur Jones." Saturday Review. Vol. 90 (October 13, 1900), p. 458.

495. Bettany, A. L. "Henry Arthur Jones and the Modern English Drama." Theatre. Vol. 31, p. 203.

496. Brown, W. W. "Interview with Henry Arthur Jones." Theatre. Vol. 15 (April, 1912), pp. 135-6.

497. Bullock, J. M. "Henry Arthur Jones, with Bibliography of His Plays." Bookbuyer. Vol. 16 (April, 1898), p. 225.

498. Henderson, Archibald. "Henry Arthur Jones, Dramatist: Self-revealed." Virginia Quarterly Review. Vol. 1 (October, 1925), pp. 321-37.

499. Henderson, Archibald, and Henry Arthur Jones. "Henry Arthur Jones, Dramatist: Self-Revealed." Nation (London). Vol. 38 (December 5, 1925), p. 349.

500. Howells, William Dean. "The Plays of Henry Arthur Jones." North American Review. Vol. 186 (October, 1907), pp. 205-12.

501. Moses, Montrose J. "Henry Arthur Jones: Dramatist." Book News. Vol. 26 (April, 1908), pp. 437-9.

502. Northend, M. "Henry Arthur Jones and the Development of the Modern English Drama." English Studies. Vol. 18 (October, 1942), pp. 448-63.

503. Pérez Petit, Victor. "Dos dramaturgos ingleses: Henry-Arthur Jones y Arthur W. Pinero." Revista Nacional. Vol. 10 (1965), pp. 321-44; and Vol. 11 (1966), pp. 5-25.

504. Schmidt, K. "The Plays of Henry Arthur Jones." Harpers Weekly. Vol. 60 (February 20, 1915), p. 185.

505. Shelley, H. C. "Henry Arthur Jones." Bookman (London). Vol. 75 (February, 1929), pp. 277-8.

506. Wauchope, George Anthony. "Henry Arthur Jones and the New Social Drama." Sewanee Review. Vol. 29, no. 2 (April, 1921), pp. 147-152.

Theses and Dissertations

507. Goodenough, Aubry Ward. "Henry Arthur Jones: A Study in Dramatic Compromise." Ph.D. Dissertation. University of Iowa, 1920.

D[AVID] H[ERBERT] LAWRENCE

(1885-1930)

Selected Full-length Plays:

>   A Collier's Friday Night (1906-7)
>   Altitude (1912)
>   The Married Man (1912)
>   The Merry-go-round (1912)
>   The Widowing of Mrs. Holyroyd (1913)
>   Touch and Go (1919)

Books

508. Moore, Harry T. The Life and Works of D. H. Lawrence. New York: Twayne Publishers, 1951.

509. Nardi, Piero. La vita di D. H. Lawrence. Milan: A Mondadori, 1947.

510. Slkar, Sylvia. The Plays of D. H. Lawrence. (Critical Studies Series.) New York: Barnes and Noble, 1974.

511. Tedlock, Ernest Warnock. The Frieda Lawrence Collection of D. H. Lawrence Manuscripts. Albuquerque: University of New Mexico Press, 1948.

512. Williams, Raymond. Modern Tragedy. Stanford: Stanford University Press, 1966.

Articles

513. Beards, Richard D. "D. H. Lawrence: Ten Years of Criticism, 1959-1968." D. H. Lawrence Review. Vol. 1 (1968), pp. 245-85.

514. Bramley, J. A. "The Significance of D. H. Lawrence." Contemporary Review. Vol. 195 (May, 1959), pp. 304-7.

515. Cecchetti, G. "Verga and D. H. Lawrence's Translations." Comparative Literature. Vol. 9 (Fall, 1957), pp. 333-44.

516. Gordon, David J. "Two Anti-Puritan Puritans: Bernard Shaw and D. H. Lawrence." Yale Review. Vol. 56 (1967), pp. 76-90.

517. Grein, J. T. "Criticism." Illustrated London News. Vol. 170 (June 4, 1927), p. 1010.

518. Harrison, A. W. "The Philosophy of D. H. Lawrence." Hibbert Journal. Vol. 32 (July, 1934), pp. 554-63.

519. Hepburn, James G. "D. H. Lawrence's Plays: An Annotated Bibliography." Book Collector. Vol. 14 (Spring, 1965), pp. 78-81.

520. Hervey, G. M. "The Genius of Mr. D. H. Lawrence." Nation (London). Vol. 39 (August 21, 1926), pp. 581-2.

521. Jones, S. W. H. "D. H. Lawrence and the Revolt Against Reason." London Quarterly Review. Vol. 173 (January, 1948), pp. 25-31.

522. Mahnken, Harry E. "The Plays of D. H. Lawrence: Addenda." Modern Drama. Vol. 7, no. 4 (February, 1965), pp. 431-32.

523. Moe, Christian. "Playwright Lawrence Takes the Stage in London." The D. H. Lawrence Review. Vol. 2 (1969), pp. 93-97.

524. Neville, D. H. "The Early Days of D. H. Lawrence." London Mercury. Vol. 23 (March, 1931), pp. 477-80.

525. Sagar, Keith. "D. H. Lawrence: Dramatist." The D. H. Lawrence Review. Vol. 4 (1971), pp. 154-82.

526. Sale, R. "D. H. Lawrence, 1912-1916." Massachusetts Review. Vol. 6 (Spring, 1965), pp. 467-80.

527. Warner, R. E. "The Philosophy of D. H. Lawrence." Saturday Review. Vol. 149 (April 26, 1930), pp. 351-2.

528. Waterman, Arthur E. "The Plays of D. H. Lawrence." Modern Drama. Vol. 2, no. 4 (February, 1960), pp. 349-57.

529. Watson, E. L. G. "On Hell and Mr. D. H. Lawrence." English Review. Vol. 38 (March, 1924), pp. 386-92.

530. Williams, Raymond. "Tolstoy, Lawrence and Tragedy." Kenyon Review. Vol. 25 (Autumn, 1963), pp. 633-50.

531. Williamson, H. R. "D. H. Lawrence: The Last of the Puritans." Bookman (London). Vol. 79 (December, 1930), pp. 177-8.

Theses and Dissertations

532. Coniff, Gerald W. "The Plays of D. H. Lawrence." Ph.D. Dissertation. Penn State University, 1974.

533. Fedder, Norman Joseph. "The Influence of D. H. Lawrence on Tennessee Williams." Ph.D. Dissertation. New York University, 1962.

[WILLIAM] SOMERSET MAUGHAM

(1874-1965)

Selected Full-length Plays:

>   A Man of Honour (1899)
>   The Explorer (1899)
>   Lady Frederick (1907)
>   Grace (also played as Landed Gentry, 1910)
>   The Land of Promise (1913)
>   Caroline (1916)
>   Our Betters (1917)
>   Love in a Cottage (1917)
>   Home and Beauty (also played as Too Many
>   Husbands, 1919)
>   The Unknown (1920)
>   The Circle (1921)

Books

534. Aldington, Richard. W. Somerset Maugham: An Appreciation. New York: Doubleday, 1939.

535. Barnes, Donald Edward. The Dramatic Comedy of William Somerset Maugham. The Hague: Mouton, 1968.

536. Brander, Laurence. Somerset Maugham: A Guide. New York: Barnes and Noble, 1963.

537. Brown, Ivor. W. Somerset Maugham. London: International Textbook, 1970.

538. Calder, Robert L. W. Somerset Maugham and the Quest for Freedom. New York: Doubleday, 1973.

539. Cordell, Richard Albert. Somerset Maugham, A Writer for All Seasons. 2nd ed. Bloomington, Indiana: Indiana University Press, 1969.

540. _____. Somerset Maugham: A Bibliography and Critical Study. Bloomington, Indiana: University of Indiana Press, 1969.

541. _____. W. Somerset Maugham. Edinburgh, Toronto and New York: Nelson, 1937.

542. Kanin, Garson. Remembering Mr. Maugham. New York: Atheneum, 1966.

543. McIver, Claude Searcy. William Somerset Maugham: A Study of Technique and Literary Sources. Upper Darby, Pennsylvania: The Author, 1936.

544. Mander, Raymond and Joe Mitchenson. Theatrical Companion to Maugham. London: Rockliff, 1955.

545. Maugham, William Somerset. The Summing Up. New York: Doubleday, Doran & Co., 1938.

546. Naik, M. K. W. Somerset Maugham. Norman: University of Oklahoma Press, 1969.

547. Pfeiffer, Karl Graham. W. Somerset Maugham: A Candid Portrait. New York: W. W. Norton, 1959.

548. Ward, Richard Heron. William Somerset Maugham. London: G. Bles, 1937.

Theses and Dissertations

549. Barnes, Donald Edward, Jr. "The Dramatic Comedy of William Somerset Maugham." Ph.D. Dissertation. Stanford University, 1963.

550. Kuner, Mildred Christophe. "The Development of W. Somerset Maugham." Ph.D. Dissertation. Columbia University, 1951.

551. McIver, Claude Searcy. "William Somerset Maugham: A Study of Technique and Literary Sources." Ph.D. Dissertation. University of Pennsylvania, 1936.

552. Sawyer, Newell Wheeler. "The Comedy of Manners from
Sheridan to Maugham. A Study of the Type as a Dramatic Form
and as a Social Document." Ph.D. Dissertation. University
of Pennsylvania, 1930.

Articles

553. Ervine, St. John Greer. "The Plays of Somerset
Maugham." Life & Letters. Vol. 11, no. 3 (March, 1935),
pp. 640-55.

554. Fielden, John S. "The Ibsenite Maugham." Modern Drama.
Vol. 4 (1961), pp. 138-51.

555. _____ . "Somerset Maugham on the Purpose of Drama."
Educational Theatre Journal. Vol. 10 (October, 1958), pp.
218-22.

556. Gordon, C. "Notes on Chekhov and Maugham." Sewanee
Review. Vol. 57 (July, 1949), pp. 401-10.

557. Mikhail, E. H. "Somerset Maugham and the Theatre."
Bulletin of Bibliography. Vol. 27 (April-June, 1970), pp.
42-48.

558. Montague, C. M. "William Somerset Maugham-Dramatist."
Poet Lore. Vol. 47, no. 1 (1941), pp. 40-55.

559. Spencer, Theodore. "Somerset Maugham." College English. Vol. 2 (1940), pp. 1-10.

560. Stokes, Sewell. "W. Somerset Maugham." Theatre Arts.
February, 1945, pp. 94-100.

561. Wescott, Glenway. "Somerset Maugham and Posterity."
Harper's. Vol. 195 (1947), pp. 302-11.

GEORGE MOORE

(1852-1933)

Selected Full-length Plays:

> The Strike at Arlingford (1893)
> The Bending of the Bough (reworking of
>   E. Martyn's A Tale of a Town, 1900)
> The Apostle (1911)
> Esther Waters (1913)
> Elizabeth Cooper (1913)
> The Coming of Gabrielle (1920)

Books

562. Gilcher, Edwin. A Bibliography of George Moore. De-Kalb: Northern Illinois University Press, 1970.

563. Hone, Joseph Maunsell. The Life of George Moore. London: Gollancz, 1936.

564. Moore, George. Impressions and Opinions. London: David Mutt, 1891.

565. Noël, Jean C. George Moore. L'homme et l'oeuvre, 1852-1933. Paris: Didier, 1966.

Articles

566. Bott, A. "Savagery of Electric Sky-signs: A Conversation with G. Moore." World Today. Vol. 43 (February, 1924), pp. 221-4.

567. Clark, Barrett H. "George Moore At Work." American Mercury. Vol. 4 (February, 1925), pp. 202-9.

568. Collet, G. P. "George Moore et la France." Comparative Literature. Vol. 2 (Spring, 1959). pp. 174-6, and Modern Language Review. Vol. 53 (October, 1958), pp. 573-4.

569. Furst, Lilian G. "George Moore, Zola and the Question of Influence." Canadian Review of Comparative Literature. Vol. 1 (1974), pp. 138-55.

570. McFate, Patricia. "The Bending of the Bow and The Heather Field: Two Portraits of the Artists." Eire-Ireland Vol. 8, no. 1 (1973), pp. 52-61.

571. Moore, George. "George Moore and Granville Barker." Dial. Vol. 75 (August, 1923), pp. 135-50.

572. Ransom, John C. "Man Without a Country." Sewanee Review. Vol. 33 (July, 1925), pp. 301-7.

573. Rosati, S. "George Moore." Nuova Antologia. Vol. 381 (October 16, 1935), pp. 553-4.

574. Yeats, William Butler. "Dramatis Personae, 1896-1902." London Mercury. Vol. 33 (November, 1935-January, 1936), pp. 12-21, 140-150, 280-289.

Theses and Dissertations

575. Adams, Mildred D. "The Appreciation of George Moore. His Response to Cultural Influences." Ph.D. Dissertation. Columbia University, 1960.

576. Armato, Phillip M. "Theory and Practice in George Moore's Major Dramas, 1897-1930." Ph.D. Dissertation. Purdue University, 1970.

577.   Brown, Malcolm J.   "George Moore's Criticism."   Ph.D. Dissertation. University of Washington at Seattle, 1947.

578.   Doherty, William Edward.   "The Philosophy of George Moore."   Ph.D. Dissertation.   Tulane University, 1965.

579.   Ferguson, Walter Dewey.   "The Influence of Flaubert on George Moore."   Ph.D. Dissertation.   University of Pennsylvania, 1932.

580.   Kennedy, Sister Eilleen.   "Circling Back: The Influence of Ireland on George Moore."   Ph.D. Dissertation, 1968.

581.   Sechler, Robert Porter.   "George Moore, a Disciple of Walter Pater."   Ph.D. Dissertation.   University of Pennsylvania, 1931.

582.   Sinfelt, Frederick William.   "The Unconventional Realism of George Moore: His Unique Concepts of Men and Women."   Ph.D. Dissertation.   Pennsylvania State University, 1967.

583.   Stock, J.C.   "The Role of Conscience in the Early Works of George Moore."   Master's Thesis.   Trinity College, Dublin, 1967.

584.   Weaver, Jack W.   "A Story-Teller's Holiday: George Moore's Irish Renaissance, 1897-1911."   Ph.D. Dissertation. Kansas State University, 1966.

[SIR] ARTHUR WING PINERO

(1855-1934)

Selected Full-length Plays:

        Two Can Play at That Game (1877)
        Two Hearts (1878)
        Bygones (1880)
        Imprudence (1881)
        The Squire (1881)
        The Rector (1883)
        Mayfair (1885)
        Lords and Commons (1883)
        Sweet Lavender (1888)
        The Profligate (1889)
        Lady Bountiful (1891)
        The Second Mrs. Tanqueray (1893)
        The Notorious Mrs. Ebbsmith (1895)
        Trelawny of the 'Wells' (1898)
        The Gay Lord Quex (1899)
        Iris (1901)
        Letty (1903)
        Low Water (1905)
        A Wife Without a Smile (1905)

His House in Order (1906)
The Thunderbolt (1908)
Mid-Channel (1909)
Quick Work (1919)

Books

585. Armstrong, Cecil Ferard. Shakespeare to Shaw. London: Mills & Boon, 1913.

586. Boas, Frederick S. From Richardson to Pinero. New York: Columbia University Press, 1937.

587. Dunkel, Wilber D. Sir Arthur Pinero: A Critical Biography with Letters. Chicago: University of Chicago Press, 1941.

588. Fyfe, Henry Hamilton. Arthur Wing Pinero, Playwright: A Study. London: Greening, 1902.

589. _____ . Sir Arthur Pinero's Plays and Players. New York: Macmillan, 1930.

590. Hamilton, Clayton Meeker, ed. The Social Plays of Sir Arthur Wing Pinero. New York: E. P. Dutton, 1917-1918.

591. Küther, Herman Heinrich. Arthur Wing Pinero und sein Verhältnis zu Henrik Ibsen. Bochum-Langendreer: H. Pöppinghaus, 1937.

592. Lazenby, Walter. Arthur Wing Pinero. New York: Twayne, 1970.

593. Pinero, Sir Arthur Wing. The Collected Letters of Sir Arthur Wing Pinero. Minneapolis: University of Minnesota Press, 1974.

Articles

594. Burns, Winifred. "Certain Women Characters in Pinero's Serious Drama." Poet Lore. Vol. 54 (1948), pp. 195-219.

595. Davies, C. W. "Pinero: The Drama of Reputation." English. Vol. 14 (Spring, 1962), pp. 13-17.

596. Hyde, G. M. "Arthur W. Pinero, with a Bibliography of the Plays." Book-buyer. Vol. 17 (November, 1898), pp. 301-5.

597. Leggatt, Alexander. "Pinero: From Farce to Social Drama." Modern Drama. Vol. 17 (1974), pp. 329-44.

598. Kobbe, Gustav. "Plays of Arthur Wing Pinero." Forum. Vol. 26 (September, 1898), pp. 119-28.

599. Kornbloth, Martin L. "Two Fallen Women: Paula Tanqueray and Kitty Warren." Shavian. Vol. 14 (1959), pp. 14-5.

600. Metcalfe, J. S. "New Edition of Pinero's Plays." Life. Vol. 71 (March 14, 1918), pp. 422-3.

601. Pearson, Hesketh. "Pinero and Barrie." Theatre Arts. Vol. 42 (July, 1958), pp. 56-9.

602. Pérez Petit, Victor. "Dos dramaturgos ingleses: Henry-Arthur Jones y Arthur W. Pinero." Revista Nacional. Vol. 10 (1965). pp. 321-44, and Vol. 11 (1966), pp. 5-25.

603. Rideing, William H. "Some Women of Pinero's." North American Review. Vol. 188 (1908), pp. 38-49.

604. Spong, Hilda. "Working with Pinero, Barrie and Shaw." Theatre. Vol. 32 (July-August, 1920), pp. 32, 34.

605. Tucker, S. M. "Work of Sir Arthur Wing Pinero." Colonnade. (June, 1914), pp. 300-9.

606. Wearing, J. P. "Pinero's Letters in the Brotherton Collection of the University of Leeds." Theatre Notebook. Vol. 24 (1969-1970), pp. 74-9.

607. Wedmore, Sir Frederick. "Literature and the Theatre." Nineteenth Century. Vol. 51 (April, 1902), pp. 568-80.

Theses and Dissertations

608. Carb, Nathan R. E., Jr.   "The Social Plays of Sir Arthur Wing Pinero: An Old Answer to a New Question." Ph.D. Dissertation. University of Pennsylvania, 1959.

609. Hatcher, Harlan. "The Plays of Arthur Wing Pinero as a Reflection of the Growth of Modern Drama." M.A. Thesis. The Ohio State University, 1923.

610. Miner, Brother Sylvester E.   "The Individual and Society: The Plays of Arthur Pinero." Ph.D. Dissertation. Notre Dame University, 1969.

611. Ronning, Robert T. "The Development of English Comic Farce in the Plays of Sir Arthur Pinero." Ph.D. Dissertation. Wayne State University, 1973.

612. Stoakes, James Paul. "Arthur Wing Pinero and the Modern English Drama." Ph.D. Dissertation. University of Michigan, 1942.

613. Wellwarth, George Emanuel. "A Critical Study of the Reputation of Sir Arthur Wing Pinero in London and New York." Ph.D. Dissertation. University of Chicago, 1958.

T[HOMAS] W[ILLIAM] ROBERTSON

(1829-1871)

Selected Full-length Plays:

> David Garrick (based on Mélesville's
>   Sullivan, 1864)
> Society (1865)
> Ours (1866)
> Caste (1867)
> For Love (1867)
> Play (1868)
> Home (adaptation of M. Augier's
>   L'aventurière, 1869)
> School (1869)
> My Lady Clara (1869)
> Progress (adaptation of V. Sardou's Les
>   Ganaches, 1869)
> The M. P. (1870)
> Birth (1870)
> War (1871)

Books

614. Bancroft, Lady. Gleanings from On and Off Stage.
London: George Routledge and Sons, Ltd., n.d.

615. Pemberton, Thomas Edgar. The Life and Writings of
T. W. Robertson. London: R. Bentley, 1893.

616. Robins, Edward, Jr. Echoes of the Playhouse. New York:
G. P. Putnam's Sons, 1895.

617. Savin, Maynard. Thomas William Robertson: His Plays
and His Stagecraft. Providence, R.I.: Brown University
Press, 1950.

618. Watson, Ernest Bradley. Sheridan to Robertson: A Study
of the Nineteenth-Century London Stage. Cambridge: Harvard
University Press, 1926.

Theses and Dissertations

619. Galloway, Gresdna Doty. "The Victorian Age as Reflected
in the Dramatic Works of Tom Taylor and Thomas William Robertson." Master's Thesis. University of Florida, 1957.

620. Lorenzen, Richard L. "The Dramaturgy of Thomas William
Robertson: A Study of Six Plays." Master's Thesis. The Ohio
State University, 1965.

621. Philhour, Charles Walter, Jr. "The Contribution of T.
W. Robertson to Directing." Master's Thesis. University of
Iowa, 1947.

622. Rice, Enid Elva. "Changing Attitudes toward Social Criticism in the Plays of Robertson, Pinero, Galsworthy and Maugham." Master's Thesis. University of Maine, 1941.

Articles

623. Dale, Harrison. "Tom Robertson: A Centenary Criticism." Contemporary Review. Vol. 135 (January-June, 1929), pp. 356-61.

624. Durbach, Errol. "Remembering Tom Robertson (1829-1871)." Educational Theatre Journal. Vol. 24 (1972), pp. 284-88.

625. Rahill, F. "A Mid-Victorian Regisseur." Theatre Arts Monthly. Vol. 13 (November, 1929), pp. 838-44.

626. Street, G. S. "Robertson and Some Others." Saturday Review. Vol. 110 (July 16, 1910), pp. 75-6.

627. "Thomas William Robertson and the Modern Theatre." Temple Barr. Vol. 44 (1875), pp. 199-209.

[GEORGE] BERNARD SHAW

(1856-1950)

Selected Full-length Plays:

        Widowers' Houses (1892)
        The Philanderer (1893)
        Arms and the Man (1894)
        Candida (1895)
        The Devil's Disciple (1897)
        You Never Can Tell (1897)
        Caesar and Cleopatra (1898)
        Captain Brassbound's Conversion (1899)
        Mrs. Warren's Profession (1902)
        Man and Superman (1903)
        John Bull's Other Island (1904)
        Major Barbara (1905)
        The Doctor's Dilemma (1906)
        Getting Married (1908)
        The Shewing-up of Blanco Posnet (1909)
        Misalliance (1910)
        Androcles and the Lion (1912)
        Pygmalion (1912)
        Heartbreak House (1919)

Books

628. Armstrong, Cecil Ferand. Shakespeare to Shaw. London: Mills & Boon, 1913.

629. Barr, Alan P. Victorian Stage Pulpiteer: Bernard Shaw's Crusade. Athens, Georgia: University of Georgia Press, 1973.

630. Bentley, Eric R. Bernard Shaw, A Reconsideration. Norfolk, Connecticut: New Directions, 1947.

631. _____. Bernard Shaw Through the Camera. London: B. and H. White, 1948.

632. Berst, Charles A. Bernard Shaw and the Art of Drama. Urbana: University of Illinois Press, 1973.

633. Boxill, Roger. Shaw and the Doctors. New York and London: Basic Books, 1969.

634. Brinser, Ayers. The Respectability of Mr. Bernard Shaw. Cambridge: Harvard University Press, 1931.

635. Burton, Richard. Bernard Shaw: The Man and the Mask. New York: Henry Holt and Co., Inc., 1916.

636. Carpenter, Charles A. Bernard Shaw and the Art of Destroying Ideals. Madison: University of Wisconsin Press, 1969.

637. Chapman, J. J. Memories and Milestones. New York: Moffet, Yard & Co., 1915.

638. Chesterton, Gilbert Keith. George Bernard Shaw. London and New York: Hill and Wang, 1956.

639. _____. George Bernard Shaw. New York: Dodd and Lane, 1910.

640. Chislett, William, Jr. Moderns and Near Moderns. London: Grafton Press, 1928.

641. Colbourne, Maurice. The Real Bernard Shaw. New York: Dodd, Mead and Co., Inc., 1940.

642. Collis, John S. Shaw. New York: Alfred A. Knopf, 1925.

643. Como, Julio Alfredo. Cuatro puntales del teatro moderno. Buenos Aires: Tinglado, 1948.

644. Crompton, Louis. Shaw the Dramatist. Lincoln, Nebraska: University of Nebraska Press, 1969.

645. Deacon, Renée M. Bernard Shaw as Artist-Philosopher: An Exposition of Shavianism. New York: John Lane, 1910.

646. Duffin, Henry C. The Quintessence of Bernard Shaw. London: Allen and Unwin, 1920.

647. Dukore, Bernard F. Bernard Shaw, Director. Seattle, Washington: University of Washington Press, 1971.

648. Ellehauge, Martin. The Position of Bernard Shaw in
European Drama and Philosophy. New York: G. E. Stechert and
Co., 1931.

649. Ervine, St. John. Bernard Shaw: His Life, Work and
Friends. New York: Morrow, 1956.

650. Fechter, Paul. George Bernard Shaw: Vom 19. zum 20.
Jahrhundert. Gütersloh: Bertelsmann, 1951.

651. Fromm, Harold. Bernard Shaw and the Theatre in the
Nineties. Lawrence: University of Kansas, 1967.

652. Gibbs, Anthony Matthews. Shaw. Edinburgh and London:
Oliver and Boyd, 1969.

653. Hackett, J. P. Shaw, George vs. Bernard. London: Sheed
and Ward, 1939.

654. Hamon, Augustin Frédéric. Twentieth Century Molière:
Bernard Shaw. London: Allen and Unwin, 1915.

655. Hardwick, Michael and Mollie. The Bernard Shaw Companion. London: J. Murray, 1973.

656. Henderson, Archibald. Bernard Shaw, Playboy and
Prophet. New York and London: Appleton, 1932.

657. _____. George Bernard Shaw: His Life and Works.
Cincinnati, Ohio: Stewart and Kidd, 1911.

658. _____. Is Bernard Shaw a Dramatist? New York:
Kennerley, 1929.

659. _____. George Bernard Shaw: Man of the Century.
New York: Appleton-Century-Crofts, 1956.

660. Howe, Percival P. Bernard Shaw: A Critical Study. New
York: Dodd, 1915.

661. Hugo, Leon. Bernard Shaw: Playwright and Preacher.
London: Methuen, 1971.

662. Irvine, William. The Universe of G. B. S. New York:
Whittlesey House, 1949.

663. Joad, C. E. M. Shaw. London: Victor Gollancz, Ltd.,
1949.

664. Kaufmann, Ralph J. G. B. Shaw: A Collection of Critical
Essays. Englewood Cliffs, New Jersey: Prentice Hall, 1965.

665. Kaye, Julian B. Bernard Shaw and the Nineteenth Century
Tradition. Norman, Oklahoma: University of Oklahoma Press,
1958.

666. Kennedy, Andrew K. Six Dramatists in Search of a Language: Studies in Dramatic Language. Cambridge: Cambridge University Press, 1975.

667. Kozelka, Paul A. A Glossary to the Plays of Bernard Shaw. New York: Bureau of Publications, Teachers College. Columbia University, 1959.

668. Kronenberger, Louis, ed. George Bernard Shaw: A Critical Survey. New York: The World Publishing Company, 1953.

669. Lindblat, Ishrat. Creative Evolution and Shaw's Dramatic Art: With Special Reference to Man and Superman and Back to Methuselah. Uppsala: University of Uppsala Press, 1971.

670. Lorichs, Sonja. The Unwomanly Woman in Shaw's Drama and the Social and Political Background. Uppsala: University of Uppsala Press, 1973.

671. Lowenstein, Fritz Erwin. The Rehearsal Copies of Bernard Shaw's Plays: A Bibliographical Study. London: Reinhardt and Evans, 1950.

672. McCabe, J. George Bernard Shaw: A Critical Study. London: K. Paul, 1914.

673. McCarthy, Desmond. Shaw. London: MacGibbon and Kee, 1951.

674. _____ . Shaw's Plays in Review. Great Britain: Cheswick Press, 1951.

675. Mander, Raymond and Joe Mitchenson. Theatrical Companion to Shaw: A Pictorial Record of the First Performance of the Plays of George Bernard Shaw. London and New York: Rockliff, 1954.

676. Matthews, John F. George Bernard Shaw. New York: Columbia University Press, 1970.

677. Mayne, Fred. The Wit and Satire of Bernard Shaw. New York: St. Martin's, 1967.

678. Meisel, Martin. Shaw and the Nineteenth-Century Theater. Princeton, New Jersey: Princeton University Press, 1963.

679. Mencken, Henry Louis. George Bernard Shaw: His Plays. London: J. W. Luce, 1905.

680. Mendelsohn, Michael J. Bernard Shaw's Plays. New York: Norton, 1970.

681. Mills, John A. Language and Laughter: Comic Diction in Plays of Bernard Shaw. Tuscon, Arizona: University of Arizona Press, 1969.

682. Minney, Rubeigh J. Recollections of George Bernard Shaw. Englewood Cliffs, New Jersey: Prentice Hall, 1969.

683. Morgan, Margery M. The Shavian Playground: An Exploration of the Art of George Bernard Shaw. London: Methuen, 1972.

684. Nethercot, Arthur H. Men and Supermen: The Shavian Portrait Gallery. New York: Benjamin Blom, 1966.

685. Norwood, Gilbert. Euripides and Shaw with Other Essays. Boston: John W. Luce and Co., 1921.

686. O'Donovan, John. Shaw and the Charlatan Genius: A Memoir. Chester Springs, Pennsylvania: Dufour, 1967.

687. Ohmann, Richard M. Shaw: The Style and the Man. Middleton, Connecticut: Wesleyan University Press, 1962.

688. Palmer, John Leslie. George Bernard Shaw, Harlequin or Patriot? New York: Century, 1915.

689. Pearson, Hesketh. G. B. S.: A Full Length Portrait. New York: Harper and Brothers, 1942.

690. Phelps, William L. Essays on Modern Dramatists. New York: Macmillan, 1921.

691. Rattray, Robert Fleming. Bernard Shaw: A Chronicle. London: Luton, 1951.

692. Rosenblood, Norman, ed. Shaw: Seven Critical Essays. Toronto: University of Toronto Press, 1971.

693. Shaw, George Bernard. Dramatic Opinions and Essays. New York: Brentanos, 1906.

694. _____ . The Intelligent Woman's Guide to Socialism and Capitalism. New York: Brentanos, 1928.

695. _____ . Major Critical Essays. London: Constable and Co., 1948.

696. _____ . Our Theatre in the Nineties. London: Constable and Co., Ltd., 1948.

697. _____ . The Table Talk of G. B. S. New York: Harper, 1925.

698. Shaw, Charles. Bernard's Brethren. With Comments by Bernard Shaw. London: Constable, 1939.

699. Smith, Joseph Percy. The Unrepentant Pilgrim. Boston: Houghton Mifflin, 1965.

700. Smith, Warren S., ed. Shaw on Religion. New York: Dodd Mead, 1967.

701. Tompkins, Peter, ed. Shaw and Molly Tompkins. London: Anthony Blond, 1961.

702. Valency, Maurice. The Cart and the Trumpet: The Plays of George Bernard Shaw. London: Oxford University Press, 1973.

703. Wagenknecht, Edward C. Guide to Bernard Shaw. New York and London: Appleton, 1929.

704. Wall, Vincent. Bernard Shaw: Pygmalion to Many Players. Ann Arbor: University of Michigan Press, 1973.

705. Ward, Alfred C. Bernard Shaw. London: Longmans, Green, 1951.

706. Watson, Barbara B. A Shavian Guide to the Intelligent Woman. New York: Norton, 1972.

707. Weintraub, Stanley. Journey to Heartbreak: The Crucible Years of Bernard Shaw, 1914-1918. New York: Weybright and Talley, 1971.

708. _____, ed. Shaw: An Autobiography, 1856-1898, Selected from His Writings. New York: Weybright and Talley, 1969.

709. Williamson, Audrey. Bernard Shaw: Man and Writer. New York: Crowell-Collier, 1963.

710. Wilson, Edmund. The Triple Thinkers. New York: Harcourt, Brace and Company, 1938.

711. Wilson, Colin. Bernard Shaw: A Reassessment. New York: Atheneum, 1969.

712. Winsten, Stephen. Days with Bernard Shaw. New York, London, Melbourne: Hutchinson, 1948.

713. _____. G. B. S. 90. New York: Dodd, Mead and Co., Inc., 1948.

714. Wisenthal, J. L. The Marriage of Contraries: Bernard Shaw's Middle Plays. Cambridge: Harvard University Press, 1974.

Theses and Dissertations

715. Abbott, Anthony Sternsen. "Shaw and Christianity." Ph.D. Dissertation. Harvard University, 1962.

716. Austin, Don Deforest. "The Comic Structure in Five Plays of Bernard Shaw." Ph.D. Dissertation. University of Washington, 1960.

717. Bader, Earl D. "The Self-Reflexive Language: Uses of Paradox in Wilde, Shaw and Chesterton." Ph.D. Dissertation. University of Indiana, 1970.

718. Barr, Alan Philip. "Bernard Shaw as a Religious Dramatist." Ph.D. Dissertation. University of Rochester, 1964.

719. Bennett, Kenneth Chesholm, Jr. "George Bernard Shaw's Philosophy of Art." Ph.D. Dissertation. University of Indiana, 1962.

720. Bernd, Daniel Walter. "The Dramatic Theory of George Bernard Shaw." Ph.D. Dissertation. University of Nebraska, 1963.

721. Berquist, Gordon N. "War and Peace in the Plays of Bernard Shaw." Ph.D. Dissertation. University of Nebraska, 1972.

722. Berst, Charles Ashton. "Bernard Shaw's Comic Perspective: A View of Self and Reality." Ph.D. Dissertation. University of Washington, 1965.

723. Besant, Lloyd Alfred. "Shaw's Women Characters." Ph.D. Dissertation. University of Wisconsin, 1964.

724. Best, Brian S. "Development of Bernard Shaw's Philosophy of the Responsible Society." Ph.D. Dissertation. University of Wisconsin, 1971.

725. Bond, George Robert. "The Method of Iconoclasm in George Bernard Shaw." Ph.D. Dissertation. University of Michigan, 1959.

726. Boxhill, Roger. "Shaw and the Doctors." Ph.D. Dissertation. Columbia University, 1966.

727. Bringle, Jerald E. "The First Unpleasant Play by Bernard Shaw: An Analysis of the Formation and Evolution of Widowers' Houses." Ph.D. Dissertation. New York University, 1971.

728. Byers, William F. "The Nineteenth Century English Farce and its Influences on Bernard Shaw." Ph.D. Dissertation. Columbia University, 1963.

729. Carpenter, Charles Albert, Jr. "Bernard Shaw's Development as a Dramatist Artist, 1884-1899." Ph.D. Dissertation. Cornell University, 1963.

730. Cathey, Kenneth Clay. "George Bernard Shaw's Drama of Ideas." Ph.D. Dissertation. Vanderbilt University, 1957.

731. Cirillo, Nancy R. "The Poet Armed: Wagner, D'Annunzio, Shaw." Ph.D. Dissertation. New York University, 1969.

732. Clayton, Robert Boree. "The Salvation Myth in the Drama of Ideas." Ph.D. Dissertation. Vanderbilt University, 1957.

733. Costello, Donald P. "George Bernard Shaw and the Motion Picture." Ph.D. Dissertation. Chicago University, 1963.

734. Crane, Gladys M. "The Characterization of the Comic Women of George Bernard Shaw." Ph.D. Dissertation. University of Indiana, 1969.

735. Donaghy, Henry. "A Comparison of the Thought of George Bernard Shaw and G. K. Chesterton." Ph.D. Dissertation. New York University, 1967.

736. Dower, Margaret Winifred. "The Political and Social Thinking of George Bernard Shaw." Ph.D. Dissertation. Boston University, 1957.

737. Dupler, Dorothy. "An Analytical Study of the Use of Rhetorical Devices in Three Selected Plays of George Bernard Shaw." Ph.D. Dissertation. University of Southern California, 1961.

738. Forter, Elizabeth T. "A Study of the Dramatic Technique of Bernard Shaw." Ph.D. Dissertation. University of Wisconsin, 1955.

739. Fromm, Harold. "Bernard Shaw and the Theaters in the Nineties." Ph.D. Dissertation. University of Wisconsin, 1962.

740. Gerould, Daniel Charles. "The Critical Reception of Shaw's Plays in France, 1908-1950." Ph.D. Dissertation. University of Chicago, 1960.

741. Gillespie, Charles Richard. "A Study of Characterization of Selected Disquisitory Plays of Bernard Shaw." Ph.D. Dissertation. University of Iowa, 1961.

742. Goodykoontz, William Francis. "John Bunyan's Influence on George Bernard Shaw." Ph.D. Dissertation. University of North Carolina, 1956.

743. Graham, Philip Bruce. "Bernard Shaw's Dramatic Technique, 1892-1924." Ph.D. Dissertation. Yale University, 1960.

744. Groshong, James Willard. "G. B. S. and Germany: The Major Aspects." Ph.D. Dissertation. Stanford University, 1958.

745. Hatcher, Joe B. "G. B. S. on the Minor Dramatists of the Nineties." Ph.D. Dissertation. University of Kansas, 1969.

746. Herrlin, Virginia T. "Bernard Shaw and Richard Wagner: A Study of Their Intellectual Kinship as Artist Philosophers." Ph.D. Dissertation. University of North Carolina, 1955.

747. Holt, Charles Lloyd. "The Musical Dramaturgy of Bernard Shaw." Ph.D. Dissertation. Wayne State University, 1963.

748. Hornby, Richard. "Bernard Shaw's Dark Comedies." Ph.D. Dissertation. Tulane University, 1967.

749. Hummert, Paul A. "Marxist Elements in the Works of George Bernard Shaw." Ph.D. Dissertation. Northwestern University, 1953.

750. Hutchinson, P. William. "The Critical Reception of the Major Plays of G. Bernard Shaw Performed in New York, 1894-1950." Ph.D. Dissertation. University of South Carolina, 1969.

751. Karr, Harold S. "Samuel Butler: His Influence on Shaw, Forster, and Lawrence." Ph.D. Dissertation. University of Minnesota, 1953.

752. Kaye, Julian Bertram. "Bernard Shaw and the Nineteenth Century Tradition." Ph.D. Dissertation. Columbia University.

753. Kester, Dolores A. "Shaw and the Victorian 'Problem' Genre: The Woman Side." Ph.D. Dissertation. University of Wisconsin-Madison, 1973.

754. Lapan, Maureen Therese. "An Analysis of Selected Plays of Bernard Shaw as Media for the Examination of 'Closed Areas' of Contemporary Society by Secondary School Students." Ph.D. Dissertation. University of Connecticut, 1962.

755. Leary, Daniel James. "The Superman and Structure in George Bernard Shaw's Plays: A Study in Dialectic Action." Ph.D. Dissertation. Syracuse University, 1959.

756. Lynch, Vernon E. "George Bernard Shaw and the Comic." Ph.D. Dissertation. University of Texas, 1951.

757. McCague, Wilma Gallagher. "The Influence of Shaw's Experience as a Director of Plays on His Stage Directions." Ph.D. Dissertation. The Ohio State University, 1937.

758. Meisel, Martin. "Shaw and the Nineteenth-Century Theater." Ph.D. Dissertation. Princeton University, 1961.

759. Mills, John Arvin. "Language and Laughter: A Study of Comic Diction in the Plays of Bernard Shaw." Ph.D. Dissertation. Indiana University, 1962.

760. Mundell, Richard F. "Shaw and Brieux: A Literary Relationship." Ph.D. Dissertation. University of Michigan, 1971.

761. Nelson, Raymond. "Religion and the Plays of Bernard Shaw." Ph.D. Dissertation. University of Nebraska, 1969.

762. Pettet, Edwin Burr. "Shavian Socialism and the Shavian Life Force: An Analysis of the Relationship between the Philosophic and Economic Systems of George Bernard Shaw." Ph.D. Dissertation. New York University, 1951.

763. O'Bolger, Thomas Denis. "George Bernard Shaw's Social Philosophy." Ph.D. Dissertation. University of Pennsylvania, 1913.

764. Paxon, Omar M. "Bernard Shaw's Stage Directions." Ph.D. Dissertation. Northwestern University, 1961.

765. Peters, Sally A. "Shaw: A Formal Analysis of Structural Development Through an Examination of Representative Plays." Ph.D. Dissertation. Florida State University, 1973.

766. Pierce, Glenn Quimby. "Arnold Daly's Productions of Plays by Bernard Shaw." Ph.D. Dissertation. University of Illinois, 1961.

767. Plotinsky, Melvin Lloyd. "The Play of the Mind: A Study of Bernard Shaw's Dramatic Apprenticeship." Ph.D. Dissertation. Harvard University, 1963.

768. Radford, Frederick L. "The Idealistic Iconoclast: Aspects of Platonism in the Works of Bernard Shaw." Ph.D. Dissertation. University of Washington, 1971.

769. Rodriquez-Seda, Asela C. "George Bernard Shaw in the Hispanic World: His Reputation and Influence." Ph.D. Dissertation. University of Illinois (Urbana-Champaign), 1974.

770. Rogers, Richard W. "Didacticism, Plot, and Comedy: Ways in Which George Bernard Shaw Uses Plot to Keep Comic His Didactic Purpose." Ph.D. Dissertation. Indiana University, 1970.

771. Scott, Robert Lee. "Bernard Shaw's Rhetorical Drama: A Study of Rhetoric and Poetic in Selected Plays." Ph.D. Dissertation. University of Illinois, 1956.

772. Sharp, William L. "The Relation of Dramatic Structure to the Comedy in the Plays of George Bernard Shaw." Ph.D. Dissertation. Stanford University, 1954.

773. Shields, Jean Louise. "Shaw's Women Characters, an Analysis and a Survey of Influences from Life." Ph.D. Dissertation. Indiana University, 1958.

774. Sidhu, Charan D. "The Pattern of Tragic Comedy in Bernard Shaw." Ph.D. Dissertation. University of Wisconsin, 1971.

775. Smith, Robert McCaughan. "Modern Dramatic Censorship: George Bernard Shaw." Ph.D. Dissertation. University of Indiana, 1954.

776. Speckhard, Robert Reidel. "Shaw and Aristophanes: A Study of Eiron, Agaon, Alazon, Doctor/Cook and Sacred Marriage in Shavian Comedy." Ph.D. Dissertation. University of Michigan, 1959.

777. Spector, Samuel Hardy. "The Social and Educational Philosophy of George Bernard Shaw." Ph.D. Dissertation. Wayne State University, 1958.

778. Spencer, Terence James. "The Dramatic Principles of George Bernard Shaw." Ph.D. Dissertation. Stanford University, 1958.

779. Stockholder, Fred Edward, Jr. "G. B. Shaw's German Philosophy of History and the Significant Form of His Plays." Ph.D. Dissertation. University of Washington, 1964.

780. Stokes, Elmore E., Jr. "William Morris and Bernard Shaw: A Socialist-Artistic Relationship." Ph.D. Dissertation. University of Texas, 1951.

781. Talley, Jerry B. "Religious Themes in the Dramatic Works of George Bernard Shaw, T. S. Eliot and Paul Claudel." Ph.D. Dissertation. University of Denver, 1964.

782. Tedesco, Joseph S. "The Theory and Practice of Tragicomedy in George Bernard Shaw's Dramaturgy." Ph.D. Dissertation. New York University, 1971.

783. Veilleux, Jere Shanor. "An Analysis of the Rhetorical Situation and Rhetorical Character Types in Selected Plays of George Bernard Shaw." Ph.D. Dissertation. University of Minnesota, 1957.

784. White, Jean Westrum. "Shaw on the New York Stage." Ph.D. Dissertation. New York University, 1965.

785. Zerke, Carl F. "George Bernard Shaw's Ideas on Acting." Ph.D. Dissertation. Florida State University, 1954.

Articles

786. Adams, Elsie. "Feminism and Female Stereotypes in Shaw." Shaw Review. Vol. 17 (1974), pp. 17-22.

787. Adler, J. H. "Ibsen, Shaw and Candida." Journal of English and Germanic Philosophy. Vol. 58 (January, 1962), pp. 50-58.

788. Anzai, Tetsuo. "Mittau no Dramaturgy--Shakespeare, Ibsen, Shaw." English Literature and Language (Tokyo). Vol. 10 (1973), pp. 17-22.

789. Barnicot, Constance. "Mr. Bernard Shaw's Counterfeit Presentment of Women." Fortnightly Review. Vol. 85 (March, 1906), pp. 516-27.

790. Barr, Alan P. "Diabolian Pundit: G. B. S. as Critic."
Shaw Review. Vol. 2 (1968), pp. 26-28.

791. Batson, E. J. "G. B. S.: The Orator and the Man."
English. Vol. 14 (Autumn, 1962), pp. 97-100.

792. Bentley, Eric. "The Making of a Dramatist (1892-1903)."
Tulane Drama Review. Vol. 1 (1960), pp. 3-21.

793. Bjorkman, E. "The Serious Bernard Shaw." American
Monthly Review of Reviews. Vol. 43 (April, 1911), pp. 425-9.

794. Bond, C. J. "Eugenics and Bernard Shaw." Eugenics
Review. Vol. 21 (July, 1929), pp. 159-61.

795. Chapman, J. J. "Shaw and the Modern Drama." Harper's
Weekly. Vol. 57 (April 19, 1913), p. 10.

796. Chilton, C. B. "Shaw Contra Mundum." Independent.
Vol. 60 (March 8, 1906), pp. 550-6.

797. D'Angelo, N. "George Bernard Shaw's Theory of Stage
Representation." The Quarterly Journal of Speech. (June,
1929), pp. 330-49.

798. DeCasseres, B. "Idealism of George Bernard Shaw." International. Vol. 8 (April, 1914), pp. 129-130.

799. Demarey, J. G. "Bernard Shaw and C. E. M. Joad: The
Adventures of Two Puritans in Their Search for God." PMLA.
Vol. 78 (June, 1963), pp. 262-70.

800. Duffin, Henry Charles. "The Bourgeois Moralist in
Shaw." Shavian. Vol. 2, no. 1 (1960), pp. 12-14.

801. Dukes, Ashley. "A Note on Mr. Bernard Shaw at the
Modern English Theatre." Drama. Vol. 7 (August, 1912),
pp. 78-95.

802. Dunkel, W. D. "George Bernard Shaw." Sewanee Review.
Vol. 50 (April, 1942), pp. 255-62.

803. Ervine, St. John. "Is Shaw Dead?" Spectator. Vol. 89
(December 5-12, 1952), p. 657.

804. "Exuberant Anarchist." Times Literary Supplement. Vol.
3128 (February 9, 1962), p. 88.

805. Fergusson, Francis. "The Theatricality of Shaw and
Pirandello." Partisan Review. Vol. 16, no. 6 (June, 1949),
pp. 598-603.

806. Fox, P. H. "Critical Sketch." Colannade. Vol. 7
(March, 1914), pp. 207-12.

807. Ganz, Arthur. "The Ascent to Heaven: A Shavian Pattern
(Early Plays, 1894-1898)." Modern Drama. Vol. 14 (1971),
pp. 253-63.

808. Gordon, David J. "Two Anti-Puritan Puritans: Bernard
Shaw and D. H. Lawrence." Yale Review. Vol. 56 (1967),
pp. 76-90.

809. Henderson, Archibald. "Bernard Shaw Self-Revealed."
Fortnightly Review. Vol. 125 (1926), pp. 433, 610.

810. _____ . "The Real Bernard Shaw." Virginia Quarterly Review. Vol. 3 (April, 1927), pp. 177-89.

811. Hennecke, H. "Bernard Shaws Vermächtnis." Deutsche
Rundschau. Vol. 79 (November, 1953), pp. 1178-83.

812. Hobsbawm, E. J. "Bernard Shaw's Socialism." Science
and Society. Vol. II, no. 4 (1947), pp. 305-26.

813. Hoffsten, Ernest Godfrey. "The Plays of Bernard Shaw."
Sewanee Review. Vol. 2, no. 4 (1947), pp. 305-26.

814. Howe, P. P. "The Dramatic Craftsmanship of George Bernard Shaw." Fortune. Vol. 99 (July, 1913), pp. 132-46.

815. Hoy, Cyrus. "Shaw's Tragicomedy Irony: From Man and
Superman to Heartbreak House." Virginia Quarterly Review.
Vol. 47 (1971), pp. 56-78.

816. Hugo, L. H. "Some Aspects of Bernard Shaw's Philosophy." Unisa English Studies. Vol. 4 (1967), pp. 1-15.

817. Hunningher, B. "Shaw en Brecht: Wegen en grenzen van
socialistesche theater." Forum der Letteren. Vol. 12 (1971),
pp. 174-90.

818. Irvine, W. "George Bernard Shaw and Karl Marx." Journal of Economic History. Vol. 6 (May, 1946), pp. 53-72.

819. _____ . "Shaw, the Fabians and the Utilitarians."
Journal of the History of Ideas. Vol. 8 (April, 1974), pp.
218-31.

820. _____ . "Shaw's Quintessence of Ibsenism." South
Atlantic Quarterly. Vol. 46 (April, 1947), pp. 252-62.

821. Johnson, Maurice. "Charles Surface and Shaw's Heroines." Shaw Review. Vol. 3, No. 2 (1960), pp. 27-8.

822. Jones, A. R. "George Bernard Shaw." Contemporary
Theatre. Vol. 20 (1963), pp. 57-75.

823. Kantororic, I. B. "B. Šou i sovremennaja zarabežnaja
drama." Filologičeskie Nauki. Vol. 10, no. 3 (1967), pp.
76-88.

824. Kaufmann, R. J. "Shaw's Elitist Vision: A Serial Criticism of the First Decade." Komos. Vol. 1 (1967), pp. 97-104.

825. Kelleher, J. V. "Humorist as Agitated Oracle." Saturday Review. Vol. 45 (March 17, 1962), p. 24.

826. Keough, Lawrence C. "Horror and Humor in Shaw." Shavian. Vol. 3, no. 3 (1965), pp. 9-15.

827. _____. "Shaw's Introduction to New York: The Mansfield Productions, 1894-1900." Shavian. Vol. 4 (1969).

828. _____. "The Theme of Violence in Shaw." Shavian. Vol. 3, no. 6 (1966), pp. 12-17.

829. Ketels, Violet B. "Shaw, Snow and the New Men." Person. Vol. 47 (1966), pp. 520-31.

830. Klein, John W. "Shaw and Brieux: an Enigma." Drama. No. 67 (Winter, 1962), pp. 33-35.

831. Kornbluth, Martin L. "Shaw and Restoration Comedy." Shaw Bulletin. Vol. 2, no. 4 (1958), pp. 9-17.

832. Laing, Allan M. "Bernard Shaw and the Businessman." The Independent Shavian. Vol. 7 (1968-9), p. 23.

833. Lauter, Paul. "'Candida' and 'Pygmalion': Shaw's Subversion of Stereotype." Shaw Review. Vol. III, no. 3 (1960), pp. 14-19.

834. Lawrence, Kenneth. "Bernard Shaw: The Career of the Life Force." Modern Drama. Vol. 15, pp. 130-46.

835. Levine, Carl. "Social Criticism in Shaw and Nietzsche." Shaw Review. Vol. 10 (1967), pp. 9-17.

836. Loraine, Robert. "Where Does Shaw Leave You?" Cosmopolitan. Vol. 40 (January 6, 1906), pp. 339-44.

837. McDowell, Frederick P. W. "Another Look at Bernard Shaw: A Reassessment of His Dramatic Theory, His Practice, and His Achievement." Drama Survey. Vol. I, no. 1 (1961), pp. 34-53.

838. Madrid, Louis. "Brieux and Bernard Shaw." The Mask. Vol. 4, no. 1 (July, 1911), pp. 13-16.

839. Martin, K. "Homage to G. B. S." New Statesman and Nation. Vol. 32 (July 27, 1946), pp. 62-3.

840. Mayer, David. "The Case for Harlequin: A Footnote on Shaw's Dramatic Method." Modern Drama. Vol. III (1960), pp. 60-74.

841. Mills, John A. "Acting is Being: Bernard Shaw on the Art of the Actor." Shaw Review. Vol. 13 (1970), pp. 65-76.

842. Morgan, Margery M. "Bernard Shaw on the Tightrope." Modern Drama. Vol. 2 (1959), pp. 343-54.

843. _____. "Shaw, Yeats, Nietzsche and the Religion of Art." Komos. Vol. 1 (1967), pp. 24-34.

844. Mosely, P. E. "Shavian Paradise Lost." Saturday Review. Vol. 47 (July 18, 1964), p. 32.

845. Moses, Montrose J. "Latest Work of George Bernard Shaw." Book News Monthly. Vol. 33 (December, 1914), pp. 193-4.

846. Murray, G. "Early G. B. S." New Statesman and Nation. Vol. 34 (August 16, 1947), p. 128.

847. Nelson, Raymond S. "The Church, the State, and Shaw." Midwest Quarterly. Vol. 2 (1970), pp. 293-308.

848. _____. "Shaw: Turn-of-the-Century Prophet." Arlington Quarterly. Vol. 2, no. 1 (1969), pp. 112-19.

849. Nethercote, Arthur H. "Bernard Shaw and Psychoanalysis." Modern Drama. Vol. 11 (1969), pp. 356-75.

850. _____. "Bernard Shaw, Philosopher." PMLA. Vol. 69 (March, 1954), pp. 57-75.

851. Nickson, Richard. "The Art of Shavian Political Drama." Modern Drama. Vol. 14 (1971), pp. 324-30.

852. Noguchi, Y. "Sketch." Bookman. Vol. 47 (December, 1914), pp. 75-77.

853. O'Donnell, Norbert F. "The Conflict of Wills in Shaw's Tragicomedy." Modern Drama. Vol. 4 (1962), pp. 413-25.

854, Ostergaard, G. "G. B. S.--Anarchist." New Statesman. Vol. 46 (November 21, 1953), p. 628.

855. Peirce, F. L. "Sketch of Bernard Shaw, and His Work." 20th Century. Vol. 4 (April, 1911), pp. 17-23.

856. Rodenbeck, John. "A Continuing Checklist of Shaviana." Shaw Review. Vol. 13 (1970), pp. 43-45, 89-91.

857. _____. "Bernard Shaw's Revolt Against Rationalism." Victorian Studies. Vol. 15, pp. 409-37.

858. _____. "The Irrational Knot: Shaw and the Uses of Ibsen." Shaw Review. Vol. 12 (1969), pp. 66-76.

859. Sawadski, J. A. "Die philosophischen Dramen Shaws und die moderne Theateraesthetik." Kunst und Literatur. Vol. 15 (1967), pp. 482-88.

860. Schlauch, Margaret. "Symbolic Figures and the Symbolic Technique of George Bernard Shaw." Science & Society. Vol. 21 (1957), pp. 210-221.

861. Schöler-Beinhauer, Monica. "George Bernard Shaw und das Wunder." Literatur in Wissenschaft und Unterricht. Vol. 2 (1969), pp. 149-58.

862. Scott, T. "Bernard Shaw: The Realizer of Ideals." Forum. Vol. 45 (March, 1911), pp. 334-54.

863. Semar, J. "Shaw and the Censor." Mask. Vol. 2 (July, 1909), p. 40.

864. Shapiro, N. J. "Shaw In Hackneyed Moments." Theatre. Vol. 27 (May, 1918), p. 300.

865. Silverman, Albert H. "Bernard Shaw's Political Extravaganzas." Drama Survey. Vol. 5 (1967), pp. 213-22.

866. Smith, W. "Bernard Shaw and His Critics, 1892-1938." Poet Lore. Vol. 47, no. 1 (1941), pp. 76-83.

867. _____. "Mystics in the Modern Theatre." Sewanee Review. Vol. 50 (January, 1942), pp. 44-5.

868. Spong, Hilda. "Working with Pinero, Barrie and Shaw." Theatre. Vol. 32 (July-August, 1920), pp. 32, 34.

869. Stanton, Stephen S. "Shaw's Debt to Scribe." PMLA. Vol. 74 (1961), pp. 575-85.

870. Stewart, H. L. "The Puritanism of Bernard Shaw." Royal Society of Canada. Proceedings and Transactions. (1930) pp. 89-100.

871. Storer, E. "Work of George Bernard Shaw." Living Age. Vol. 281 (April 11, 1914), pp. 8895; and British Review. Vol. 5 (February, 1914), pp. 251-64.

872. Sutton, G. "Shaw and the Younger Generation." Bookman. Vol. 67 (December, 1924), pp. 145-50.

873. Torretta, L. "L'originalità di Bernhard Shaw." Nuova Antologia. Vol. 243 (September 1, 1925), pp. 42-53.

874. Turco, Alfred, Jr. "Ibsen, Wagner and Shaw's Changing Views of 'Idealism.'" Shaw Review. Vol. 17 (1974), pp. 78-85.

875. Turner, Justin G. "George Bernard Shaw: Composer." Coranto. Vol. 2, no. 2 (1965), pp. 3-6.

876. Vielleux, Jere. "Shavian Drama: A Dialectical Convention for the Modern Theatre." Twentieth Century Literature. Vol. 3, no. 4 (January, 1958), pp. 170-176.

877. Watson, Barbara B. "The New Woman and the New Comedy." Shaw Review. Vol. 17 (1974), pp. 2-16.

878. Weales, Gerald. "Edwardian Theatre and the Shadow of Shaw," In Richard Ellman, ed., English Institute Essays, 1959. New York: Columbia University Press, 1960 , n. pag.

879. Weintraub, Stanley. "The Making of an Irish Patriot: Bernard Shaw, 1914-1916." Éire. Vol. 5, no. 4, pp. 9-27.

880. Weisart, John J. "Bahr Describes GBS on the Platform." Shaw Review. Vol. 2 (1959), pp. 13-15.

881. _____ . "Recent Shavian Criticism." Éire. Vol. 4, no. 4 (1969), pp. 82-89.

882. Weiss, Aureliu. "G. B. Shaw and Stage Directions." British Journal of Aesthetics. Vol. 8 (1968), pp. 49-53.

883. West, E. J. "Shaw's Criticism of Ibsen: A Reconsideration." University of Colorado Studies, Series in Language and Literature. Vol. 4 (1953), pp. 101-27.

884. West, Rebecca. "Shaw's Diverted Genius." New Republic. Vol. 1 (December 5, 1914), pp. 13-14.

885. Wilson, Colin. "Shaw and Strindberg." Shavian. Vol. 15 (June, 1959), pp. 22-4.

886. _____ . "Shaw's Existentialism." Shavian. Vol. 2, no. 1 (1960), pp. 4-5.

887. Zueblin, C. "Shavian Socialism." 20th Century. Vol. 5 (April, 1912), pp. 509-14.

V FRANCE

General Commentaries

Books

In English:

888. Bacourt, Pierre D. and John William Cunliffe. French
Literature During the Last Half-Century. New York: Macmillan
Company, 1923.

889. Bennett, Arnold. Books and Persons: Being Comments on
a Past Epoch, 1908-1911. London: Chatto and Windus, 1920.

890. Carlson, Marvin. The French Stage in the Nineteenth
Century. Metuchen, N.J.: Scarecrow Press, 1972.

891. Chandler, Frank W. The Contemporary Drama of France.
Boston: Little, 1920.

892. Cheney, Sheldon. The New Movement in the Theater. New
York: M. Kennerley, 1914.

893. Clark, Barrett H. Contemporary French Playwrights.
Cincinnati: Stewart and Kidd, 1915.

894. _____. The Continental Drama of Today. New York:
H. Holt and Co., 1914.

895. _____. Four Plays of the Free Theater. Cincinnati: Stewart & Kidd, 1917.

896. Courtney, William Leonard. Old Saws and Modern In-
stances. New York: E. P. Dutton, 1918.

897. Dawbarn, Charles. Makers of the New France. New York:
J. Pott, 1915.

898. Faquet, Émile. A Literary History of France. New York:
C. Scribner's Sons, 1907.

899. Filon, Pierre M. Modern French Drama. London: Chapman
and Hall, 1898.

900. Fletcher, John. Forces in Modern French Drama: Studies
in Variations on the Permitted Lie. London: University of
London Press, 1972.

901. Henderson, John A. The First Avant-Garde (1887-1894):
Sources of the Modern French Theatre. London: G. G. Harrap
& Co., 1971.

902. Hind, Charles Lewis. More Authors and I. London:
J. Lane, 1922.

903. Jerrold, Lawrence. The Real France. New York: John
Lane, 1911.

904. Knowles, Dorothy. French Drama of the Inter-War Years,
1918-1939. London: Harrap, 1968.

905. Lancaster, Henry Carrington. Adventures of a Literary
Historian. Baltimore: Johns Hopkins Press, 1942.

906. Lenéru, Marie. Journal of Marie Lenéru. New York:
Macmillan Company, 1923.

907. Madsen, Børge Gedsø. Strindberg's Naturalistic Theatre:
Its Relation to French Naturalism. New York: Russell and
Russell, 1973.

908. Mason, Hamilton. French Theater in New York: A List of
Plays, 1899-1939. New York: Columbia University Press, 1940.

909. Matthews, James Brander. French Dramatists of the 19th
Century. New York: C. Scribner and Sons, 1914.

910. Melcher, Edith. Stage Realism in France between Diderot
and Antoine. Bryn Mawr, Pa.: n.p., 1928.

911. Norman, Hilda Laura. Swindlers and Rogues in French
Drama. Chicago: University of Chicago Press, 1928.

912. Saintsbury, George E. Short History of French Literature. Book 5. Oxford: Claredon Press, 1882.

913. Santa Vicca, Edmund F. Four French Dramatists: A
Bibliography of Criticism of the Works of Eugène Brieux,
François de Curel, Émile Fabre, Paul Hervieu. Metuchen, New
Jersey: Scarecrow Press, 1974.

914. Saurat, Denis. Modern French Literature, 1870-1940.
New York: Putnam, 1946.

915. Scheifley, William H. Essays on French Literature. Los Angeles: Wetzel Publishing, 1930.

916. Smith, Hugh A. Main Currents of Modern French Drama. New York: Holt, 1925.

917. Swerling, Anthony. Strindberg's Impact on France, 1920-1960. Cambridge, Eng.: Trinity Lane Press, 1971.

918. Walkley, Arthur Bingham. Drama and Life. London: Methuen, 1907.

919. Waxman, Samuel Montefiore. Antoine and the Théâtre Libre. New York: B. Blom, 1964.

In French

920. Abram, Paul. Notes de critique, littéraire et dramatique. Paris: E. Sansot, 1913.

921. Acker, Paul. Petites confessions. Visites et portraits. Paris: A Fontemoing, 1904.

922. Albalat, Antoine. Souvenirs de la vie littéraire. Paris: A. Fayard, 1920.

923. Antoine, André. Le Théâtre par Antoine. Paris: Les Éditions de France, 1932.

924. _____. Mes Souvenirs sur le Théâtre-Libre. Paris: A. Fayard, 1921.

925. _____. Mes Souvenirs sur le Théâtre Antoine et sur l'Odéon. Paris: B. Grasset, 1928.

926. Baty, Gaston and René Chavance. La Vie et l'art théâtral, des origines à nos jours. Paris: Plon, 1932.

927. Bédier, Joseph and Paul Hazard, eds. Histoire de la littérature française illustrée. Paris: Larousse, 1924.

928. Benoist, Antoine. Le théâtre d'aujourd'hui. Paris: Société Française d'Imprimerie et de Librairie, 1911.

929. _____. Le théâtre de Brieux. Toulouse: E. Privat, 1907.

930. Béraud, Henri. Retours à pied, impressions de théâtre (1921-1924). Paris: G. Crés, 1925.

931. Bertaut, Jules. Les Grandes Époques du Théâtre Contemporain. Paris: Cercle de la Librairie, 1925.

932. _____. L'Évolution du théâtre contemporain. Paris: Éditions du Mercure de France, 1908.

933. Bertrand, Louis. Idées et portraits. Paris: Plon, 1927.

934. Bidou, Henri. L'Année dramatique (1911-1913). 2 vols. Paris: Hachette, 1913-1914.

935. Billotey, Pierre. Les Grands Hommes en Liberté. Paris: Les Marges, 1923.

936. Bissel, Clifford H. Les conventions du théâtre bourgeois contemporain en France, 1887-1914. Paris: Presses Universitaires de France, 1930.

937. Bloch, Jean Richard. Carnaval est mort. Paris: Editions de la Nouvelle Revue Française, 1920.

938. Blum, Léon. Au théâtre, réflexions critiques. Paris: P. Ollendorff, 1909.

939. Bonnefon, Daniel. Les Écrivains modernes de la France. Paris: A. Fayard, 1927.

940. Bordeaux, Henry. Pèlerinages littéraires. Paris: Fontemoing, 1906.

941. _____. Portraits d'hommes. Paris: Plon-Nourrit, 1924.

942. _____. La vie au théâtre. Paris: Plon Nourrit et cie, 1910.

943. Bourgeois, René, and Jean Mallion. Le Théâtre au XIXe siècle. Paris: Masson et cie., 1971.

944. Braunschvig, Marcel. La Littérature française contemporaine étudiée dans les textes (de 1850 à nos jours). Paris: A. Colin, 1946.

945. Brisson, Adolphe. Les Prophètes. Paris: J. Tallandier, 1903.

946. _____. Pointes sèches, physionomies littéraires. Paris: A. Colin, 1898.

947. _____. Le Théâtre. Paris: E. Flammarion, 1907-1918.

948. _____. Le Théâtre et les moeurs. Paris: Ernest Flammarion, 1907-1913.

949. _____. Le Théâtre pendant la guerre. Paris: Hachette, 1918.

950. Brulat, Paul. Lumières et grandes ombres: souvenirs et confidences. Paris: Grasset, 1930.

951. Brunetière, Ferdinand. Essai sur la littérature contemporaine. Paris: Calmann-Levy, 1913.

952. _____. Conférences de l'Odéon: Les Époques du
théâtre français. Paris: Hachette, 1925.

953. Casella, George and Ernest Gaubert. La Nouvelle Littérature, 1895-1905. Paris: E. Sansot, 1906.

954. Chadeyras, C. T. La Morale vécue. Paris: C. Delagrave,
1910.

955. Champion, Pierre Honoré Jean Baptiste. Marcel Schwob
et son temps. Paris: B. Grasset, 1927.

956. Chardonne, Jacques. Le Ciel dans la fenêtre. Paris:
A. Michel, 1959.

957. Chevalier, Adrien. Études littéraires. Paris: Sansot
& cie, 1911.

958. _____. Humbles Essais. Paris: Bibliothèque de
l'Association, 1905.

959. Copeau, Jacques. Études d'art dramatique: Critiques
d'un autre temps. Paris: Nouvelle revue française, 1923.

960. Curel, François de. L'idée pathétique et vivante.
Paris: E. Sansot, 1912.

961. Curinier, C. Dictionnaire national des contemporains.
Paris: Office Général d'édition, 1906.

962. Daudet, Léon. Au temps de Judas. Paris: Nouvelle
Librairie Nationale, 1920.

963. _____. Écrivains et artistes. Paris: Éditions
du Capitole, 1929.

964. _____. Paris vécu. Paris: Éditions de la Nouvelle
Revue Française, 1929-1930.

965. _____. Fantômes et vivants. Paris: Nouvelle
Librairie Nationale, 1917.

966. _____. Une Campagne d'action française. Paris:
Nouvelle Librairie Nationale, 1910.

967. Delaporte, Louis. Quelques-uns. Paris: A. Fontemoing,
1901.

968. Delpit, L. Théâtre contemporain. Paris: E. Champion,
1925.

969. Deschamps, Gaston. La Vie et les livres. Paris: Armand
Colin, 1896.

970. Doisy, Marcel. Le Théâtre français contemporain. Brussels: La Boétie, 1947.

971. Doumic, René. La défense de l'esprit français, par René Doumic. Paris: Bloud et Gay, 1916.

972. _____. Écrivains d'aujourd'hui. Paris: Perrin, 1903.

973. _____. Éléments d'histoire littéraire. Paris: Librairie classique P. Delaplane, 1890.

974. _____. Essais sur le théâtre contemporain. Paris: Perrin, 1905.

975. _____. Études sur la littérature française. Paris: Perrin, 1905-16.

976. _____. Histoire de la littérature française. Paris: Editions Mellottee, 1947.

977. _____. Les Jeunes, études et portraits. Paris: Perrin, 1913.

978. _____. Portraits d'écrivains. Paris: Perrin et Cie, 1914.

979. _____. Le Théâtre nouveau. Paris: Perrin, 1908.

980. Dubech, Lucien. Histoire générale illustrée du théâtre. Paris: Librairie de France, 1931-1934.

981. _____. Le Théâtre, 1918-1923. Paris: Plon, 1924.

982. Ehrhard, Auguste. Henrik Ibsen et le théâtre contemporain. Paris: Lecène, Oudin, 1895.

983. Ernest-Charles, Jean. Essais critiques. Paris: Ollendorff, 1914.

984. _____. La Littérature française d'aujourd' hui. Paris: Perrin, 1902.

985. Faquet, Émile. Drame ancien; drame moderne. Paris: A. Colin, 1898.

986. _____. Études littéraires. Paris: Boivin et Cie, 1949.

987. _____. Histoire de la littérature française. Paris: Plon-Nourrit et Cie, 1913-1916.

988. _____. Notes sur le théâtre contemporain. Paris: Librairie H. Lecène et H. Oudin, 1891.

989. _____. Notices littéraires sur les auteurs français. Paris: H. Lecène et H. Oudin, 1888.

990. Faquet, Émile. Petite histoire de la littérature française. Paris: J. M. Dent, 1925, and New York: E. P. Dutton
& Co., 1925.

991. _____. À Propos de théâtre. Paris: Société française d'imprimerie et de librairie, 1903-1910.

992. Fejes, André. Le théâtre naturaliste en France. Anne-
masse: Soc. d'imprimerie, 1925.

993. Filon, Pierre and Marie Augustin. De Dumas à Rostand,
Paris: A. Colin, 1911.

994. Flandresy, Jeanne de. Essai sur la femme et l'amour
dans la littérature française du 19e siècle. Paris: Librairie
des Annales, 1908.

995. Flat, Paul. Figures et questions de ce temps. Paris:
Sansot, 1914.

996. _____. Figures du théâtre contemporain. Paris:
Sansot, 1922.

997. Fleury, Jules. Le Réalisme par Champfleury. Paris:
Michel Lévy, 1857.

998. France, Anatole. La Vie littéraire. Paris: Calmann-
Levy, 1949.

999. Frédérix, Gustave. Trente ans de critique. Paris: J.
Hetzel, 1900.

1000. Gahier, Joseph. Le Théâtre Libre. M.François de Curel.
Nantes: Biroche et Dantais, 1899.

1001. Gaillard de Champris, H. Anniversaires et pèlerinages.
Quebec: L'Action Sociale, 1922.

1002. Gaultier, Paul. Les Maîtres de la pensée française.
Paris: Payot, 1921.

1003. Ginisty, Paul. L'Année littéraire, 1888. Paris: Charpentier, 1889.

1004. _____. Souvenirs de journalisme et de théâtre.
Paris: Editions de France, 1930.

1005. Gregh, Fernand. La Fenêtre ouverte. Paris: F. Fasquelle, 1901.

1006. Guiches, Gustave. Au banquet de la vie. Paris: Editions Spes, 1925.

1007. Hanoteau, Guillaume. Ces nuits qui ont fait Paris: Un
demi-siècle de théâtre d'Ubu roi à Huit clos. Paris: Fayard,
1971.

1008. Héritier, Jean. Essais de critique contemporaine. Paris: Sansot, 1923.

1009. Hermant, Abel. Essais de critique. Paris: Bernard Grasset, 1912.

1010. Huret, Jules. Enquête sur l'évolution littéraire. Paris: Charpentier, 1891.

1011. Jaloux, Edmond. De Pascal à Barrès. Paris: Plon, 1927.

1012. _____. L'esprit des livres. Paris: Plon-Nourrit, 1923.

1013. Jullien, Jean. Le Théâtre vivant. Paris: Charpentier et Fasquelle, 1892-1896.

1014. Kahn, Armand. Le Théâtre social en France, de 1870's à nos jours. Laudanne: A Fatio, 1907.

1015. La Jeunesse, Ernest. Les Nuits, les ennuis et les âmes de nos plus notoires contemporains. Paris: Perrin, 1896.

1016. Lalou, René. Histoire de la littérature française contemporaine. Paris: Presses Universitaires, 1941.

1017. _____. Le théâtre en France depuis 1900. Paris: Presses universitaires de France, 1951.

1018. Lanson, Gustave. Histoire illustrée de la littérature française. Paris and London: Hachette, 1923.

1019. Larroumet, Gustave. Études de critiques dramatique. Paris: Hachette, 1906.

1020. _____. Études de littérature et d'art. Paris: Hachette, 1896.

1021. _____. Nouvelles études d'histoire et de critique dramatique. Paris: Hachette, 1899.

1022. Lazare, Bernard. Figures contemporains, ceux d'aujourd'hui, ceux de demain. Paris: Perrin, 1895.

1023. Lebey, André. Disques et pellicules. Paris: Librairie Valois, 1929.

1024. Le Cardonnel, Georges. La Littérature contemporaine. Paris: Éditions du Mercure de France, 1905.

1025. Le Goffic, Charles. La Littérature française au XIXe et au XXe siècle. Paris: Larousse, 1919.

1026. LeMaître, Jules. Impressions de théâtre. Paris: Lecène-Oudin, 1888-1920.

1027. Lencou, Hippolyte. Le Théâtre nouveau. Paris: Savine,
1896.

1028. Lenéru, Marie. Journal de Marie Lenéru. Paris: B.
Grasset, 1945.

1029. Levrault, Léon. Le Théâtre, des origins à nos jours.
Paris: Mellottée, 1932.

1030. Lugné-Poë, Aurélien. Sous les étoiles. Souvenirs du
théâtre, 1902-1912. Paris: Gallimard, 1933.

1031. Marsan, Jules. Théâtre d'hier et d'aujourd'hui.
Paris: Éditions des Cahiers Libres, 1926.

1032. Martin, Jules. Nos auteurs et compositeurs drama-
tiques. Paris: Flammarion, 1897.

1033. Martino, Pierre. Le naturalisme français (1870-1895).
Paris: Libr. Armand Colin, 1969.

1034. Maynial, Édouard. Précis de littérature française
moderne et contemporaine (1715-1925). Paris: Delagrave, 1926.

1035. Mendès, Catulle. L'Art au théâtre. Paris: Fasquelle,
1897-1900.

1036. Meyer, Arthur. Ce que je peux dire. Paris: Plon,
1912.

1037. Mirbeau, Octave. Gens de théâtre. Paris: Flammarion,
1924.

1038. _____. Les Écrivains. Paris: Flammarion, 1925-
1926.

1039. Montfort, Eugene, ed. Vingt-cinq ans de littérature
française. Paris: Librairie de France, 1923-1925.

1040. Mornet, Daniel. Histoire de la littérature et de la
pensée contemporaines. Paris: Larousse, 1927.

1041. Morsier, Edouard de. Silhouettes d'hommes célèbres.
Geneva: Éditions du Mont-Blanc, 1947.

1042. Parmentier, Florian. Histoire contemporaine des
lettres françaises. Paris: E. Figuiere, 1914.

1043. Pellissier, Georges. Anthologies du théâtre français
contemporain. Paris: Delagrave, 1925.

1044. _____, ed. Nouveaux Essais de littérature contemporaine. Paris: Lecène-Oudin, 1895.

1045. _____. Le Movement littéraire contemporain.
Paris: Plon, 1901.

1046. _____. Études de littérature contemporaine. Paris: Perrin, 1898-1901.

1047. Pruner, Francis. Les Luttes d'Antoine. Paris: Lettres modernes, 1964.

1048. Nordau, Max Simon. Vues de dehors. Paris: F. Alcan, 1903.

1049. Petit de Julleville, Louis. Histoire de la langue et de la littérature françaises. Paris: Colin, 1913.

1050. Pouquet, Jeanne Simone. Le Salon de Mme Arman de Caillavet. Paris: Hachette, 1926.

1051. Prévost, Marcel. Marcel Prévost et ses contemporains. Paris: Éditions de France, 1943.

1052. Rageot, Gaston. Le Succès: Auteurs et Public. Paris: Alcan, 1906.

1053. Renard, George F. Critique de combat. Paris: Dentu, 1894.

1054. Saint-Auban, Emile de. L'Idée sociale au théâtre. Paris: Stock, 1901.

1055. Saix, Guillot de and Bernard Lecache. Le Théâtre de demain. Paris: Éditions de la France, 1915.

1056. Sanders, James B. Aux sources de la vérité du théâtre moderne. Paris: Minard, 1974.

1057. Sarcey, Francisque. Quarante ans de théâtre. Paris: Bibliothèque des "Annales politiques et littéraires," 1900-1902.

1058. Scheffer, Robert. Plumes d'oies et plumes d'aigles, figures littéraires. Paris: Éditions de Pan, 1918.

1059. Séché, Alphonse and Jules Bertaut. L'Evolution du théâtre contemporain. Paris: Éditions du Mercure de France, 1908.

1060. Sée, Edmond. Ce soir, notes et impressions drama-tiques. Paris: Renaissance du Livre, 1923.

1061. _____. Le Théâtre des autres. Paris: Ollendorff, 1913-1915.

1062. _____. Le théâtre français contemporain. Paris: A. Colin, 1928.

1063. Silvain, Jean. Tel était Silvain. Paris: Deneöl et Steele, 1934.

1064. Sorel, Albert-Émile. Essais de psychologie dramatique.
Paris: Sansot, 1911.

1065. Soubies, Albert. Almanach des spectacles. Paris:
Librairie des Bibliophiles, 1875-1915.

1066. Stoullig, Edmond. Annales du théâtre et de la musique.
Paris: Ollendorff, 1912.

1067. Suarès, Andre. Essais. Paris: Éditions de la Nouvelle
Revue française, 1913.

1068. Talvart, Hector and Joseph Place. Bibliographies des
auteurs modernes de la langue française. Paris: Éditions de
la Chronique de lettres françaises, 1928.

1069. Tenarq, Paul. Nos bons auteurs et nos mechants critiques. Paris: Chamuel, 1898.

1070. Theime, Hugo P. Bibliographie de la littérature française de 1800 à 1930. Paris: Droz, 1933.

1071. Thomas, Louis. Vingt portraits. A. Messein, 1911.

1072. Vandérem, Fernand. Gens de qualité. Paris: Plon,
1938.

1073. Versini, Georges. Le théâtre français depuis 1900.
Paris: Presses Universitaires, 1970.

1074. Veuillot, François. Les Prédicateurs de la scène.
Paris: Rétaux, 1904.

1075. Wissant, André de. Théâtre d'ombres. Paris: Nouvelles
Editions Debresse, 1968.

In Other Languages:

1076. Banner, Max. Das französische Theater der Gegenwart.
Leipzig: Renger, 1898.

1077. Coenen-Mennemeier, Brigitta. Einsamkeit und Revolte:
Französische Dramen des 20. Jahrhunderts. Dortmund: Lensing,
1966.

1078. Curtius, Ernst-Robert. Die literarischen Wegbereiter
des neuen Frankreichs. Potsdam: G. Kiepenheuer, 1919.

1079. Eloesser, Arthur. Literarische Porträts aus dem
modernen Frankreich. Berlin: Fischer Verlag, 1904.

1080. Erichsen, Svend. Realismens gennembrud i parisisk
teater i det Nittende arhundrede. Copenhagen: Gad, 1972.

1081. Fuimi, Lionello. Lì ho vedúto a Parigi. Milan:
Ghelfi, 1960.

1082. Kemp, Robert and Lucio Chiavarelli. Commedie francesi
fin de siècle. Roma: G. Casini, 1967.

1083. Levi, Cesare. Autori drammatici francesi. Florence:
Le Monnier, 1923.

1084. _____. Il divòrzio nel teàtro francese contemporàneo. Naples: Detken and Rocholl, 1901.

1085. Manfanella, Renato. Le òpere e gli uomini. Rome:
Roux et Varengo, 1904.

1086. Mueller, Karl. Das naturalistische Theater in Frankreich. Munich: M. Hueber, 1930.

1087. Neubert, Fritz. Französische Literaturprobleme.
Gesammelte Aufsätze. Berlin: Duncker & Humblot, 1962.

1088. Pabst, Walter. Das moderne französische Drama. Berlin: E. Schmidt, 1971.

Articles

1089. Baron, Phillipe. "Puskin, Griboedov, Aleksey K. Tolstoj, Gogol sur la scène française en 1877 et 1879." Revue
de Littérature Comparée. January-March, 1973, pp. 138-156.

1090. Benda, Julien. "Le théâtre d'idées." Figaro. January 29, 1920, p. 1.

1091. Catrice, Paul. "L'antisemitisme social français au
miroir de la littérature des XIXe et XXe siècles." Revue de
psychologie des peuples. Vol. 3 (1967), n. pag.

1092. Dargan, E. P. "The Range of French Realism." Nation.
Vol. 110 (February 14, 1920), p. 201.

1093. Deffoux, L. and P. Dufay. "Du Pastiche et des Influences littéraires avant le Naturalisme." Mercure de France.
Vol. 173 (August 1, 1924), pp. 656-74.

1094. Fierson, W. C. "The Impact of French Naturalism on
American Critical Opinion, 1877-1892." PMLA. Vol. 63 (September, 1948), pp. 1007-16.

1095. Granges, Ch. M. des. "La Femme française dans la
comédie contemporaine." Le Correspondant. Vol. 213 (December 10, 1903), pp. 905-36.

1096. _____. "Les Conventions du théâtre naturaliste
en France." Le Correspondant, May 25, 1904, pp. 485-505.

1097. Greenwall, H. J. "Decline of French Drama." Theatre.
Vol. 18 (October, 1913), n pag.

1098. Hatzfeld, H. A. "Discussion sur le Naturalisme Français." Studies in Philology. Vol. 39 (October, 1942), pp.
696-726.

1099. Lerner, Michael G. "Edouard Rod and the Introduction
of Ibsen into France." Revue de Littérature Comparée. Vol.
43 (1969), pp. 69-82.

1100. Lievre, P. "Les écrivains que la Comédie-Française
jouait il y a trente ans." Mercure de France. Vol. 281
(January 15, 1938), pp. 365-8.

1101. MacDonald, John F. "French Life and the French Stage."
Fortnightly Review. Vol. LXXVII (1905), pp. 327-40.

1102. Ogden, P. "A Phase of the Modern French Drama."
Sewanee Review. Vol. 28 (January, 1920), pp. 1-18.

Theses and Dissertations

1103. Berk, Atilay. "Les Précurseurs du théâtre d'idées,
E. Augier et A. Dumas, fils." Thesis. University Poitiers
(Lettres), 1968.

1104. Boe, Lois M. "The Conception of the French Naturalistic Tragedy." Ph.D. Dissertation. University of Wisconsin,
1936.

1105. Bracco, Pierre-Paul. "Le Théâtre populaire en 1900,
étude du théâtre populaire en France de 1895 à 1905." Thesis.
University of Nice (Lettres), 1970.

1106. Carter, Boyd G. "The French Realists and the Theatre.
Gustave Flaubert, the Goncourt Brothers and Alphonse Daudet."
Ph.D. Dissertation. University of Illinois, 1937.

1107. Covert, Margorie A. "Realism in the Prose Theatre of
France and England, 1890-1910." Ph.D. Dissertation. University of Wisconsin, 1934.

1108. Crowder, Robert D. "French Theatre in New York City,
1917-1939." Ph.D. Dissertation. Vanderbilt University, 1967.

1109. Lichty, Elizabeth E. "The Realistic Treatment of Love
in the French Drama." Ph.D. Dissertation. University of
Wisconsin, 1939.

1110. Melchor, Edith. "Stage Realism in France between
Diderot and Antoine." Ph.D. Dissertation. Bryn Mawr: 1928.

HENRY BATAILLE

(pseudonym for Heinrich Kampf, 1872-1922)

Selected Full-length Plays:

> La Lépruse (The Leper, 1896)
> Ton Sang (Your Blood, 1897)
> L'Enchantment (Enchantment, 1900)
> Résurrection (1902)
> Le Masque (The Mask, 1902)
> La Déclaration (1902)
> Madame Calibri (1904)
> La Marche nuptiale (The Wedding March, 1905)
> La Femme de Nue (The Cloud Woman, Dame Nature, 1906)
> Le Scandale (The Scandal, 1909)
> Le Songe d'un soir d'amour (Dream of a Night of Love, 1910)
> La Vierge Folle (The Foolish Virgin, 1910)
> L'Enfant de l'Amour (The Child of Love, 1911)
> Les Flambeaux (The Torches, 1912)
> La Phalène (The Moth, 1913)
> L'Amazone (The Amazon, 1916)
> L'Homme à la rose (Man with the Rose, 1920)
> L'Animateur (The Moving Spirit, 1920)
> La Tendresse (Affection, 1921)

Books

1111. Amiel, Denys. Henry Bataille. Paris: E. Sansot, 1909.

1112. Besançon, Jacques Bernard. Essai sur le théâtre d'Henry Bataille. The Hague: J. B. Wolters, 1928.

1113. Blanchart, Paul. Henry Bataille: Son oeuvre, portrait et autographe. Paris: Carnet-critique, 1922.

1114. Catalogne, Gérard de. Henry Bataille, ou le romantisme de l'instinct. Paris: Ed. de la pensée latine, 1925.

1115. Porche, Simone. Ce qui restait à dire. Paris: Gallimard, 1967.

Articles

1116. Bidou, H. "L'enfance d'Henry Bataille." Journal des Débats. Vol. 36 (February 15, 1929), pp. 284-6.

1117. Scheifley, W. H. "A Predestined Dramatist." North American Review. Vol. 225 (June, 1928), pp. 742-7.

1118. Seillière, Baron E. "L'évolution morale dans le théâtre d'Henry Bataille." Seances et Travaux de l'Académie des Sciences Morales et Politiques, 1936 , n. pag.

HENRY [-FRANÇOIS] BECQUE

(1837-1899)

Selected Full-length Plays:

Michel Pauper (1970)
L'Enlevèment (The Abduction, 1871
La Navette (The Shuttle, 1879)
Les Honnêtes Femmes (The Honest Women, The
    Virtuous Women, 1880)
Les Corbeaux (The Vultures, The Crows, 1882)
La Parisienne (The Woman of Paris, A Woman
    of This World, 1885)

Books

1119. Arnautovich, Aleksander. Henry Becque: devant ses contemporains et devant la postérité. Presses Universitaires de France, 1927.

1120. Becque, Henry. Souvenirs d'un auteur dramatique. Paris: Bibliothèque Artistique et littéraire, 1895.

1121. Blanchart, Paul. Henry Becque, son oeuvre, portrait et autographe. Paris: Éditions de Nouvelle Revue Critique, 1930.

1122. Capuana, Luigi. Libri e teàtro. Catania: N. Giannotta, 1892.

1123. Daudet, Léon. Souvenirs littéraires. Paris: Édit. Bernard Grasset, 1968.

1124. Dubois, Fritz. Henry Becque, l'homme, le critique, l'auteur dramatique. Paris: Dupret, 1888.

1125. Dussane, Beatrix. J'étais dans la salle. Paris: Mercure de France, 1963.

1126. Got, Ambroise. Henry Becque, sa vie et son oeuvre. Paris: Éditions George Crès, 1920.

1127. Guerrero Zamora, Juan. Historia del teatro contemporaneo. Vol. 14. Barcelona: Juan Flors, 1967.

1128. Hyslop, Lois Boe. Henry Becque. New York: Twayne Publishers, 1972.

1129. Jamati, Georges. La conquête de soi, Méditations sur l'art. Paris: Flammarion, 1961.

1130. Jouvet, Louis. Tragédie classique et le théâtre du XIXe siècle. Paris: Gallimard, 1968.

1131. Le Maître, Jules. Theatrical Impressions. Port Washington, N.Y.: Kenneket Press, 1970.

1132. Treich, Léon. L'esprit d'Henry Becque. Paris: Galli-mard: 1927.

Theses and Dissertations

1133. Möller, Gunter. "Henry Becque und Eugène Brieux; Das Naturalistische und das Thesedrama, eine Untersuchung über ihr Wesen und ihr Verhältnis zueinander." Ph.D. Dissertation. University of Halle, 1938.

Articles

1134. Carlson, Marvin. "Henry Becque and André Antoine," in The French Stage in the Nineteenth Century. Metuchen, N.J.: Scarecrow Press, 1972, pp. 177-91.

1135. Corsi, M. "Becque e il suo teàtro." Nuova Antologia. Vol. 258 (April 16, 1928), pp. 471-88.

1136. "Henry Becque et la Comédie-Française." Journal des Débats. Vol. 32 (February 13, 1925), pp. 283-6.

1137. Mazzucco, Roberto. "Becque autóre permalóso." Tempo Presente. Vol. 13, no. 11-12 (1968), pp. 108-9.

1138. Papot, B. "Sketch." Drama. No. 5 (February, 1912), pp. 3-13.

1139. "Portrait of Henry Becque." Theatre Arts Monthly. Vol. 9 (March, 1925), p. 195.

1140. "The Work of Henry Becque." Nation. Vol. 98 (May 28, 1914), pp. 644-5.

HENRY [LEON GUSTAVE CHARLES] BERNSTEIN

(1876-1953)

Selected Full-length Plays:

> Le Bercail (The Fold, 1904)
> La Rafale (The Squall, Baccarat, The
>   Whirlwind, 1905)
> La Griffe (The Claw, 1906)
> Le Voleur (The Thief, 1907)
> Samson (1907)
> Israël (1908)
> Après Moi (After Me, 1911)
> L'Assaut (The Assault, The Attack, 1912)
> Le Secret (1913)
> L'Élévation (1917)

Books

1141. Bathille, Pierre. Henry Bernstein, son oeuvre. Paris: Éditions de La Nouvelle Revue Critique, 1932.

1142. Dort, Bernard. Théâtre publique (1953-1966). Paris: Édit. du Seuil, 1967.

1143. Lins, Alvaro. Teoria literaria. Rio De Janeiro: Edicoes de Ouro, 1967.

1144. Porche, Simone. Ce qui restait à dire. Paris: Galli-mard, 1967.

1145. Renoir, Jean. Écrits, 1926-1971. Paris: Pierre Bel-fond, 1974.

Articles

1146. Harrop, John. "A Constructive Promise: Jacques Copeau in New York, 1917-1919." Theatre Survey. Vol. 12, no. 2 (November, 1971), pp. 104-18.

1147. Lacour, L. "Le théâtre d' Henri Bernstein." Revue de Paris. Vol. 17 (1901), n. pag.

1148. Manet, Edouard. "Henry Bernstein As a Young Man." Decision. Vol. 1, no. 1 (1941), p. 17.

1149. "Obituary." Illustrated London News. Vol. 223 (Decem-ber 5, 1953), p. 935.

1150. Palmer, J. "The Progress of M. Bernstein." Saturday Review. Vol. 143 (April 30, 1927), pp. 659-60.

1151. "Théâtre: un vie sur les stocks." Esprit. Vol. 17, no. 150 (November, 1948), pp. 700-705.

Theses and Dissertations

1152. Goding, Stowell Goolidge. "Henry Bernstein: The Evo-lution of a Playwright." Ph.D. Dissertation. University of Wiscon, 1943.

1153. Knott, Helen M. "Henry Bernstein." M.A. Thesis. The Ohio State University, 1923.

PAUL [CHARLES JOSEPH] BOURGET

(1852-1935)

Selected Full-length Plays:

    Mensonges (Lies, written with Léopold Lacour
        1889)
    Un Divorce (A Divorce, 1908)
    La Barricade (1910)
    Un Cas de conscience (A Case of Conscience,
        written with Serge Basset, 1910)
    Le Tribun (The Trial, 1911)
    Monique (1920)

Books

1154. Feuillerat, Albert. Paul Bourget: histoire d'un
esprit sous la troisième république. Paris: Plon, 1937.

1155. Giraud, Victor. Paul Bourget: essai de psychologie
contemporaine. Paris: Librairie Bloud et Gay, 1934.

1156. Rivasso, R. de. L'unité d'une pensée, essai sur
l'oeuvre de Paul Bourget. Paris: Plon-Nourrit, 1914.

1157. Saueracken, J. Bourget und der Naturalismus. Breslau:
Priebatsch, 1936.

1158. Wissant, André de. Théâtre d'ombres. Paris: Debresse,
1970.

Articles

1159. Cahuet, A. "Un Grand Devil des Lettres françaises."
Illustration. Vol. 193 (January 4, 1936), pp. 1-3.

1160. Charpentier, J. "Paul Bourget, Critique et Romancier
Moraliste." Mercure de France. Vol. 265 (January 15, 1936),
pp. 230-54.

1161. Giraud, V. "L'oeuvre de Paul Bourget." Review des
Deux Mondes. Vol. 31 (January 15, 1936), pp. 436-47.

1162. Jones, E. A. "Paul Bourget: Apologist for Tradition-
alism in France." South Atlantic Quarterly. Vol. 45 (October, 1946), pp. 504-10.

1163. Martin du Gard, Maurice. "Monsieur Paul Bourget."
Revue des Deux Mondes. (April, 1915), pp. 512-15.

1164. Mondelli, Rudolph J. "The Church, Society and Paul
Bourget." Renascence. Vol. 10, no. 2 (Winter, 1958), pp.
77-83.

1165. Pascal, F. "Paul Bourget et les écrivains de son temps." Revue des Deux Mondes. Vol. 39 (June 15, 1937). pp. 915-25.

1166. Sanborn, A. F. "Work of Paul Bourget." Book News. Vol. 31 (October, 1912), pp. 83-6.

1167. Sanvoisin, G. "Le cinquantenaire d'une grande amitié littéraire." Revue des Deux Mondes. Vol. 44 (April 15, 1928), pp. 942-9.

1168. Valeri, D. "Vitalità dell'opera di Bourget." Nuova Antologia. Vol. 383 (January 16, 1936), pp. 153-8.

1169. Vallette, A. "Paul Bourget." Mercure de France. Vol. 296 (February, 1940), pp. 490-2.

Theses and Dissertations

1170. Ross, Flora Emma. "Goethe in France, with Special Reference to Barrès, Bourget, and Gide." Ph.D. Dissertation. University of Illinois, 1932.

EUGÈNE BRIEUX

(1858-1932)

Selected Full-length Plays:

> Ménage d'artistes (Artists' Household,
>   Artists' Families, 1890)
> Blanchette (1892)
> Monsieur de Réboval (1892)
> La couvée (The Nest, 1893)
> L'engrenage (The Machine, Cogwheels, 1894)
> La Rose Bleue (The Blue Rose, 1895)
> L'évasion (The Escape, 1896)
> Les Bienfaiteurs (The Philanthropists, 1896)
> Les Trois Filles de M. Dupont (The Three
>   Daughters of Mr. Dupont, 1897
> Le Résultat des courses (The Consequences of
>   Racing, The Evils of Racetrack Betting,
>   1898)
> Le Berceau (The Cradle, 1898)
> La Robe Rouge (The Red Dress, The Letter of
>   the Law, 1900)
> Les remplaçantes (The Substitutes, 1901)
> La petite amie (The Girl Friend), 1902)
> Les avaries (Damaged Goods, 1902)
> Maternité (Maternity, 1903)
> La Déserteuse (The Woman Deserter, 1904)
> La Française (The French Woman, 1907)
> Les Hannetons (The June Bugs, The Incubus,
>   The Affinity, 1907)

Simone (1908)
Suzette (1909)
La Foi (Faith, Religion, False Gods, 1909)
La Femme seule (Woman Alone, Woman on Her
    Own (The Lone Woman, 1913)
Le Bourgeois aux champs (The City Man in
    the Country, 1914)
Les Américans chez nous (The Americans in
    France, 1920)

Books

1171. Benoist, Antoine. Le théâtre d'aujourd'hui. Paris: Société française d'imprimerie, 1911-1912.

1172. _____. Le Théâtre de Brieux. Toulouse: E. Privat, 1907.

1173. Bertrand, Adrien. Eugène Brieux, biographie critique. Paris: E. Sansot, 1910.

1174. Brisson, Adolphe. Portraits intimes. Paris: A. Colin, 1901.

1175. Byrnes, Malcolm P. Eugène Brieux: Humanitaire et patriote réconnu. London: Editora Continental, Ltd., 1971.

1176. Le Maître, Jules. Theatrical Impressions. Port Washington, N.Y.: Kenneket Press, 1970.

1177. Shaw, George Bernard. Three Plays by Brieux. New York: Brentano's, 1910.

1178. Scheifley, William. Brieux and Contemporary French Society. London: G. Putnam's Sons, 1917.

1179. Thomas, Penrhy Vaughn. Handbook of Brieux's Plays. Boston: J. Luce, 1915.

1180. _____. The Plays of Eugène Brieux. Boston: Luce, 1915.

1181. Westland, Cora. Eugène Brieux. The Hague: Weldt, 1915.

Articles

1182. Baker, George Pierce. "The Plays of Eugène Brieux." Atlantic Monthly. Vol. 90 (July, 1902), pp. 79-86.

1183. "Brieux and the Drama as an Instrument of Reform." Dial. Vol. 58 (February 1, 1913), p. 73.

1184. Clark, Barrett H. "Later Work of Eugène Brieux." Drama. No. 11 (August, 1913), pp. 138-43.

1185. Collins, C. W. "Work of Eugène Brieux." Green Book. Vol. 10 (August, 1913), pp. 1006-12, 138-43.

1186. Courtney, W. L. "Eugène Brieux, Moralist." Fortnightly Review. Vol. 109 (April, 1908), pp. 560-75.

1187. DePratz, Claire. "Brieux and His Works." Contemporary Review. Vol. 81 (March, 1902), pp. 343-357.

1188. Donnay, Maurice. "Eugène Brieux." Revue de France. Vol. I (1936), pp. 167-174.

1189. Harrop, John. "A Constructive Promise: Jacques Copeau in New York, 1917-1919." Theatre Survey. Vol. 12, no. 2 (November, 1971), pp. 104-118.

1190. Irving, Laurence. "Eugène Brieux." Forum. Vol. 43 (June, 1910), pp. 628-632.

1191. Klein, John W. "Shaw and Brieux--An Enigma." Drama. No. 67 (Winter, 1962), pp. 33-5.

1192. Madrid, Louis. "Bernard Shaw and Brieux." Mask. Vol. 4 (July, 1911), pp. 13-16.

1193. Malpy, Phillippe. "Portraits contemporains. M. Brieux." Revue Bleue. (September 4, 1897), pp. 290-293.

1194. Morsier, Edouard de. "Brieux et le théâtre social." Revue Bleue. Vol. 71 (July 1, 1933), pp. 399-401.

1195. Pratz, Claire de. "M. Brieux and His Works." Contemporary Review. Vol. 81 (March, 1902), pp. 343-357.

1196. Reid, L. R. "Interview." New York Dramatic Mirror. Vol. 72 (December 9, 1914), p. 3.

1197. Slosson, E. E. "A Dramatist Who Means Something." Independent. Vol. 74 (April 3, 1913), pp. 749-52.

1198. Sorel, Albert-Émile. "M. Eugène Brieux." Grande Revue. Vol. 29 (February 15, 1904), pp. 277-89.

1199. Steel, W. "Work of Eugène Brieux." Theatre. Vol. 21 (January, 1918), pp. 24-26.

1200. Stock, P. V. "Mémorandum d'un éditeur: Brieux anecdotique." Mercure de France. Vol. 293 (July 15, 1939), pp. 306-50.

1201. "Telling the Truth in the Theatre." Harper's Bazaar. Vol. 49 (December, 1914); and Pall Mall Magazine. Vol. 54 (September, 1914), pp. 84-88.

1202. Van Eerde, John. "Brieux's Realism." College Language Association Journal. Vol. 2 (December, 1958), pp. 111-127.

Theses and Dissertations

1203. Byrnes, Malcon Porter. "The Life and Works of Eugène Brieux." Ph.D. Dissertation. Queen Mary College (London), 1952-53.

1204. Davies, E. G. "Social Ideas of Brieux as Expressed in his Dramatic Works." M.A. Thesis. University of Wales, 1938.

1205. Ferrand, Lucy Margaret. "La Revendication des femmes chez Brieux." M.A. Thesis. McGill University, 1929.

1206. Goode, Luella S. "Hervieu Versus Brieux." M.A. Thesis. The Ohio State University, 1917.

1207. Hankinson, William Chipman. "Le Théâtre à thèses et Brieux." M.A. Thesis. Acadia, 1933.

1208. Möller, Gunter. "Henry Becque und Eugène Brieux. Das Naturalistische und das Thesedrama, eine Untersuchung über ihr Wesen und ihr Verhältnis zueinander." Ph.D. Dissertation. University of Halle, 1938.

1209. Moore, Robert O. "The Last Plays of Brieux." Ph.D. Dissertation. Johns Hopkins University, 1953.

1210. Mundell, Richard F. "Shaw and Brieux: A Literary Relationship." Ph.D. Dissertation. University of Michigan, 1971.

1211. Santa Vicca, Edmund F. "Le Feminisme de Brieux dans son théâtre." M.A. Essay. Wayne State University, 1970.

[VINCENT MARIE] ALFRED CAPUS

(1858-1922)

Selected Full-length Plays:

>   Brignol et sa Fille (Brignol and His Daughter, 1895)
>   Rosine (1897)
>   La Bourse ou la vie (The Purse or Life, 1900)
>   La Veine (Luck, 1901)
>   Les Deux Écoles (The Two Schools, 1902)
>   Les Maris de Léontine (Leontine's Husbands, 1903)
>   Le Petit Fonctionnaire (The Little Functionary, 1902)
>   Monsieur Piégois (1905)
>   Les Passagères (The Transients, The Passersby, 1906)
>   L'Attentat (The Outrage, written with L. Descaves, 1906)

L'Oiseau blessé (The Wounded Bird, 1908)
Un Ange (An Angel, 1909)
Hélène Ardouin (1913)
La Traversée (The Crossing, 1920)

Books

1212. Flat, Paul. Figures et questions de ce temps. Paris: Sansot et cie, 1914.

1213. Quet, Édouard. Alfred Capus. Paris: E. Sansot, 1904.

1214. Vandérem, Fernand. Gens de qualité. Paris: Plon, 1938.

Theses and Dissertations

1215. Bussell, Helen Katherine. "Alfred Capus and the Realistic French Theatre." Ph.D. Dissertation. University of Indiana, 1933.

1216. Noyes, Claire Jackson. "Alfred Capus et son oeuvre dramatique." D.M.L. Middlebury University, 1941.

Articles

1217. Capus, Alfred. "The Subjects of Plays." Dramatist. Vol. 6 (July, 1915), pp. 583-8.

1218. Ogden, P. "A Phase of the Modern French Drama." Sewanee Review. Vol. 28 (January, 1920), pp. 1-18.

1219. Papot, B. "Sketch." Drama. No. 16 (November, 1914), pp. 517-27.

FRANÇOIS [VICOMTE] DE CUREL

(1854-1928)

Selected Full-length Plays:

L'envers d'une sainte (The Opposite of a
    Saint, False Saints, A False Saint,
    The Dark Saint, 1892)
Les Fossiles (The Fossils, 1892)
L'Invitée (The Invited, 1893)
La Figurante (The Supernumerary, The
    Dancer, 1896)
Le Repas du lion (The Lion's Feast, 1897)
La Nouvelle Idole (The New Idol, 1899)
La Fille sauvage (The Wild Girl, 1902)
Le Coup d'aile (The Beat of the Wing, 1906)

La Danse devant le miroir (Dance Before the
    Mirror, 1914, reworking of Sauvé des eaux,
    1889, also played as L'Amour brode, 1893)
L'Âme en folie (A Soul Gone Mad, 1920)

Books

1220. Blanchart, Paul. François de Curel: son oeuvre, portrait et autographe. Paris: Éditions de la Nouvelle revue
critique, 1924.

1221. Braunstein, Edith. François de Curel et le théâtre
d'idées. Geneva: Droz, 1962.

1222. Chambers, G. C. The Religious Sentiment in the Theatre of François de Curel. Talosa: Pailles et Chataigner,
1938.

1223. Conrardy, Joseph. François de Curel. Liège: H.
Dessain, Collège Saint-Servais, 1938.

1224. Guerrero Zamora, Juan. Historia del teatro contemporaneo. Vol. 4. Barcelona: Juan Flors, 1967.

1225. Gilbert de Voisins, Auguste. François de Curel.
Paris: Alcan, 1931.

1226. Hansen, Joseph. Les Idées sociales de François de
Curel. Luxemburg: Éditions des "Cahiers luxembourgeoix,"
1934.

1227. Le Brun, Roger. François de Curel. Paris: E. Sansot, 1905.

1228. Poizat, Alfred. Les Maîtres du théâtre, d'Eschyle à
Curel. Paris: Renaissance du Livre, 1923.

1229. Pronier, Ernest. La Vie et l'Oeuvre de François de
Curel. Paris: Éditions de la Nouvelle revue critique, 1935.

1230. Richter, Kurt. François de Curel, Ein Beitrag zur
französischen dramatischen Literatur um die Jahrhundertwende.
Grimma: Buchdruckerei Frde. Bode, 1934.

1231. Weller, C. François de Curel, Ein moderner Dramatiker.
Langensalza: Beyer & Sohne, 1921.

Theses and Dissertations

1232. Barret, Doris P. "La Pensée religieuse dans le théâtre de François de Curel." M.A. Thesis. McGill, 1942.

1233. Cox, Mary D. "Les Idées dans le théâtre de François
Curel." M.A. Thesis. McGill University, 1935.

1234. Davies, S. D. "A Critical Study of the Drama of François de Curel." Ph.D. Dissertation. Queen Mary's College
(London), 1951-52.

1235. Dowson, F. C. "La psychologie et les idées dans le
théâtre de François de Curel." M.A. Thesis. University of
Birmingham, 1929.

1236. Gaucher-Shultz, Jeanine Solange. "La nature dans le
théâtre de François de Curel." Ph.D. Dissertation. University of Southern California, 1965.

1237. James, W. "The Ideas of François de Curel as Expressed
in his Dramatic Works." M.A. Thesis. University of Wales,
1931.

1238. Mastronie, Joseph Andrew. "Religion in the Plays of
François de Curel." Ph.D. Dissertation. University of
Pittsburg, 1942.

1239. Peza Velázquez, Bertha. "François de Curel y su teatro
de ideas." Ph.D. Dissertation. University of Mexico, 1948.

1240. Ponticello, Eva E. "Les Idées dans les préfaces de
François de Curel." M.A. Thesis. McGill University, 1942.

1241. Price, Walterenne. "The Autobiographical Elements in
the Plays of François de Curel." M.A. Thesis. University
of Southern California, 1939.

1242. Rivola, Glennys. "The Treatment of Nature in the
Theatre of François de Curel." M.A. Thesis. University of
Chicago, 1932.

1243. Schuyler, William Moorhouse. "François de Curel."
Ph.D. Dissertation. University of Chicago, 1938.

1244. Tucker, A. K. "François de Curel, Dramatist and
Philosopher." Ph.D. Dissertation. University of London,
1931.

Articles

1245. Antoine, A. L. "Quelques souvenirs sur François de
Curel." Annales Politiques et Littéraires. Vol. 90 (May
15, 1928), pp. 467-9.

1246. Bidou, H. "François de Curel." Journal des Débats.
Vol. 35 (May 4, 1928), pp. 748-9.

1247. Boyd, Ernest A. "Work of François de Curel." Forum.
Vol. 53 (February, 1915), pp. 258-68.

1248. _____. An Unacademic Academician: François de
Curel." Part I, Egoist. Vol. 5, no. 9 (October, 1918,
pp. 121-2

1249. Boyd, Ernest A. "An Unacademic Academician: François de Curel." Part II, Egoist. Vol. 5, no. 10 (November-December, 1918), pp. 137-8.

1250. _____. "The Work of François de Curel." Forum. Vol. 53 (February, 1915), pp. 258-68.

1251. Fite, Alexander G. "A New Voice in the Contemporary Drama in France. The Plays of François de Curel and their Influence." University Chronicle. (January, 1927), pp. 53-78.

1252. Leveque, A. "François de Curel: Observations sur la creation dramatique." Modern Language Association. Vol. 52 (June, 1937), pp. 550-80.

1253. Malphy, Phillippe. "François de Curel." Revue d'Art Dramatique. (March 1, 1899), pp. 413-23.

1254. Moumet, Louis-Richard. "Théâtre complet de François de Curel." Mercure de France. (August 1, 1921), pp. 741-44.

1255. Pratz, Claire de. "M. de Curel and His Work." Contemporary Review. Vol. 84 (August, 1903), pp. 209-23.

1256. Praviel, Armand. "Théâtre complet de François de Curel." Polybion. Vol. 42 (1921), pp. 16-18.

1257. Scheifley, W. H. "A Worthy Addition to the Forty Immortals." Nation. Vol. 108 (April 19, 1919), pp. 607-8.

1258. Schuyler, W. M. "François de Curel and the Problem of Instinct: Reply to A. Lévèque." PMLA. Vol. 54 (June, 1939), pp. 620-4.

1259. Talamon, René. "Curel et Rostand." Modern Language Notes. Vol. 61 (February, 1946), pp. 121-23.

1260. Vries, Jan van de. "François de Curel." Edda. Vol. 22 (1924), pp. 169-92.

1261. Willotte, M. A. "François de Curel chez lui." Revue Politique et Littéraire. Vol. 74 (September 5, 1936), pp. 600-01.

MAURICE [CHARLES] DONNAY

(1859-1945)

Selected Full-length Plays:

Pension de famille (The Residential Hotel,
    1894)
Amants (Lovers, 1895)
Georgette Lemeurnier (1898)
L'affranchie (The Emancipated Woman, The
    Free Woman, 1898)
La Clairière (The Clearing, 1900)
Éducation de prince (The Education of a
    Prince, 1900)
La Bascule (The Scale, 1901)
L'Autre Danger (The Other Danger, 1902)
Le Retour de Jérusalem (The Return from
    Jerusalem, 1903)
Oiseaux de passage (Bird of Passage,
    written with L. Decaves, 1904)
Paraître (To Appear, 1906)
La Patronne (The Proprietor, 1908)
Les Éclaireuses (The Girl Scouts, 1913)
La Chasse à l'homme (The Manhunt, 1919)

Books

1262. Bathille, Pierre. Maurice Donnay: son oeuvre. Paris:
Éditions de La Nouvelle révue critique, 1932.

1263. Donnay, Maurice. J'ai vécu 1900. Paris: A. Fayard,
1950.

1264. Doumic, René. Essais sur le théâtre contemporain.
Paris: Perrin et cie, 1905.

1265. _____. Le théâtre nouveau. Paris: Perrin et cie,
1905.

1266. Drake, William A. Contemporary European Writers. New
York: John Daay, 1928.

1267. Duvernois, Henri. Maurice Donnay. Paris: G. Servant,
1928.

1268. Labracherie, Pierre. Maurice Donnay, son oeuvre, portrait et autographe. Paris: Éditions de la Nouvelle revue
critique, 1931.

1269. Lauwick, Herve. D'Alphonse Allais à Sacha Guitry.
Paris: Plon, 1963.

1270. Oulmont, Charles. Noces d'or avec mon passé. Paris:
Crepin-LeBlond, 1964.

1271. Treich, Leon. L'esprit de Maurice Donnay. Paris: Gallimard, 1926.

Theses and Dissertations

1272. Werthein, Roy Jacob. "The Mistress in the Plays of Maurice Donnay." M.A. Thesis. The Ohio State University, 1932.

ÉMILE FABRE

(1869-1955)

Selected Full-length Plays:

> Le Devoir conjugal (The Marriage Vow, 1890)
> Comme ils sont tous (As They All Are, 1894)
> Le Lendemain (The Results, 1895)
> L'Argent (Money, 1895)
> Le Bien d'autrui (The Good of Others, 1897)
> L'Impérissable (The Imperishable, 1898)
> Timon d'Athens (1899)
> La Proie et l'ombre (The Prey and the
>   Shadow, 1901)
> La Vie Politique (Political Life, 1901)
> La Vie Publique (Public Life, 1902)
> Les Ventres dorés (Gilded Stomachs, 1905)
> La Maison d'argile (The House of Clay, 1907)
> Les Vainqueurs (The Victors, 1909)
> César Birotteau (written with Balzac, 1911)
> Les Sauterelles (The Grasshoppers, The
>   Locusts, 1911)
> Les Cadeaux de Noël (The Christmas Gifts,
>   1916)
> La Maison sous l'orage (The House Bestormed,
>   1920)

Books

1273. Wissant, André de. Théâtre d'ombres. Paris: Debresse, 1970.

Articles

1274. Abram, Paul. "Le Théâtre de M. Émile Fabre." Revue du Temps Present. (December 2, 1910), n. pag.

1275. Decaves, Pierre. "Le 'Journal de 1900' de Maurice Donnay." La Revue de Caire. Vol. 13, no. 133 (October, 1950), pp. 393-98.

1276. _____. "Maurice Donnay et son secret," in Memoires de ma memoire. Paris: Wesmael-Charlier, 1960, pp. 45-53.

1277. Doumic, René. "Anatole France d'Émile Fabre, etc."
Revue des Deux Mondes. Vol. 48 (1908), pp. 916-922.

1278. Dubeux, Albert. "Celui qui fut toujours drôle sans
jamais être méchant." Le Figaro Littéraire. October 10,
1959, pp. 7-8.

1279. Harrop, John. "A Constructive Promise: Jacques Copeau
in New York, 1917-1919." Theatre Survey. Vol. 12, no. 2
(November, 1971), pp. 104-118.

1280. Lang, A. "Émile Fabre." Les Annales Politiques et
Littéraires. Vol. 83 (August 10, 1924), p. 147.

1281. Leminier, Georges. "Un ton boulevardier, doux-amer,
un peu cruel." Cahiers Littéraires. Vol. 7, no. 2 (October
11-24, 1968), pp. 21-2.

1282. Touchard, Pierre-Aimé. "Coup d'oeil d'ensemble sur
un demisiècle de théâtre français." Europe. April-May,
1962, pp. 3-10.

Theses and Dissertations

1283. Beck, Hans. "Die sozialen Dramen Émile Fabres." Ph.D.
Dissertation. University of Erlangen, 1937.

1284. Radus, Robert. "Émile Fabre: A Life in the Theatre."
Ph.D. Dissertation. Columbia University, 1972.

PAUL HERVIEU

(1857-1915)

Selected Full-length Plays:

>   Les Paroles restent (The Words Remain,
>   1892)
>   Point de lendemain (The Beginning of
>   the Morrow, 1893)
>   Les Tenailles (The Pincers, The Nippers,
>   In Chains, Enchained, 1895)
>   La Loi de l'Homme (The Law of Man, 1897)
>   La Course du Flambeau (The Trail of the
>   Torch, The Passing of the Torch, The
>   Torch Race, 1901)
>   L'Énigme (The Enigma, Caesar's Wife,
>   1901)
>   Le Dédale (Dedalus, The Labyrinth, 1903)
>   L'Armature (The Framework, written with
>   Brieux, 1905)
>   Le Réveil (The Awakening, 1909)
>   Le Destin est maître (Destiny is the
>   Master, 1914)

Books

1285. Aimery de Pierrebourg, Marguerite. Paul Hervieu.
Paris: A. Fayard, 1916.

1286. Barberot, Étienee. Le Chemin de Dumas. Critique des
oeuvres dramatiques de Paul Hervieu au point de vue législatif
et juridique. Paris: A. Rousseau, 1901.

1287. Burkhardt, Helene. Studien zu Paul Hervieu als Romancier und als Dramatiker. Zurich: Orell Fussli, 1917.

1288. Cook, Hulet H. Paul Hervieu and French Classicism.
Bloomington, Indiana: Indiana University Press, 1945.

1289. Estève, Edmond. Paul Hervieu, conteur, moraliste et
dramaturge. Paris: Berger-Levrault, 1917.

1290. Fahmy, Sabri. Paul Hervieu, sa vie et son oeuvre.
Marseilles: Impr. du Sémaphore, 1942.

1291. Guyot, Henri. Paul Hervieu: Son oeuvre dramatique.
Brussels: L'Imprimerie, 1913.

1292. Malherbe, Henry. Paul Hervieu, biographie-critique.
Paris: Sansot, 1912.

Articles

1293. Bell, A. "Interview with Paul Hervieu." Theatre.
Vol. 7 (October, 1907), p. 271.

1294. Cook, H. H. "The Tragic Naturalism of Paul Hervieu."
Modern Language Association. Vol. 56 (September, 1941),
pp. 861-73.

1295. Dargan, E. P. "Work of Paul Hervieu." Nation. Vol.
101 (November 25, 1915), pp. 644-45.

1296. Malpy, Philippe. "Paul Hervieu." Revue d'Art Dramatique. Vol. 40 (1896), pp. 61-67.

1297. Matthews, Brander. "Note on Paul Hervieu. Bookman.
Vol. 42 (January, 1916), pp. 563-65.

1298. Ogden, Phillip. "The Drama of Paul Hervieu." Sewanee
Review. Vol. 18 (April, 1910), pp. 208-22.

1299. Rod, Édouard. "The Dramas of Paul Hervieu." International Quarterly. Vol. 7 (June, 1903), pp. 265-80.

Theses and Dissertations

1300. Goode, Luella S. "Hervieu Versus Brieux." M.A.
Thesis. The Ohio State University, 1917.

1301. Wegener, Luise. "Die Darstellung der Frau in den
Dramen von Paul Hervieu." Ph.D. Dissertation. Münster, 1939.

1302. Williams, Sarah D. W. "A Critical Study of the Drama
of Paul Hervieu." M.A. Thesis. University of Wales, 1935.

[FRANÇOIS ÉLIE] JULES LEMAÎTRE

(1853-1914)

Selected Full-length Plays:

> La revoltée (Woman in Revolt, 1889)
> Le député Leveau (Deputy Leveau, 1890)
> Le mariage blanc (The White Wedding, 1891)
> Flipote (1893)
> Le pardon (The Pardon, Forgiveness, 1895)
> L'âge difficile (The Difficult Age, 1895)
> La bonne Hélène (Good Helen, 1896)
> L'aînée (The Eldest Daughter, 1898)
> La massière (The Studio Assistant, Poor
>   Little Thing, 1905)
> Bertrode (1905)
> La Princesse de Clèves (1908)
> Le Mariage de Télèmaque (The Marriage of
>   Telemachus, 1910)
> Kismet (1912)

Books

1303. Le Maître, Jules. Theatrical Impressions. Port Washington, N.Y.: Kenneket Press, 1970.

1304. Morice, Henri. Jules Le Maître. Paris: Perrin et cie,
1924.

1305. Seillière, Ernest A. Jules Le Maître, historien de
l'évolution naturaliste. Paris: Éditions de la Nouvelle
revue critique, 1935.

Articles

1306. Billy, André. "Août 1914. Mort de Jules LeMaître."
Le Soir (Brussels). August 13, 1964, n. pag.

1307. Harry, M. "L'enfance de Jules LeMaître: documents
inédits." Annales Politiques et Littéraires. Vol. 83 (August 24, 1924), pp. 203-4.

1308. Joseph, Roger. "Le poète Jules LeMaitre à cinquante
années de la mort." Points et contrepoints. December, 1964,
pp. 18-22.

1309. Poulet, Robert. "Le Souvenir de Jules LeMaître."
Rivarol. May 8, 1959, n. pag.

1310. Richard, P. J. "La muse bachique de Jules LeMaître."
Le Cerf-volant. No. 39 (July, 1962), pp. 52-3.

1311. Tremblay, N. J. "The Reconstruction of Myth and Legend
in Jules LeMaître and John Erskine." Revue de Littérature
Comparée. Vol. 29, no. 3 (July-September, 1955), pp. 364-9.

Theses and Dissertations

1312. Alexander, V. Charles. "Jules LeMaître and the Langue
de la Patrie Française." Ph.D. Dissertation. Indiana University, 1975.

1313. Bishop, Morris Gilbert. "The Plays of Jules LeMaître."
Ph.D. Dissertation. Cornell University, 1926.

1314. Dooling, Margaret Frances. "The Classicism of Jules
LeMaître." Ph.D. Dissertation. University of Toronto, 1945.

1315. Parsell, Jack R. "L'Esthétique de Jules LeMaître."
Ph.D. Dissertation. University of Wisconsin, 1938.

OCTAVE MIRBEAU

(1848-1917)

Selected Full-length Plays:

>   Les mauvais bergers (The Evil Shepherds,
>   1897)
>   L'Épidémie (The Epidemic, 1898)
>   Le Portefeuille (The Portfolio, 1902)
>   Les Affaires sont les Affaires (Business
>   is Business, 1903)
>   Scrupules (1904)
>   Interview (1904)
>   Le Foyer (1909)

Books

1316. Aimery de Pierrebourg, Marguerite. La Jeunesse de
Mirbeau. Paris: Les Oeuvres Libres, 1936.

1317. Schwartz, Martin. Octave Mirbeau: Vie et oeuvre. The
Hague: Mouton, 1966.

Articles

1318. Cahuet, A. "La résurrection d'Octave Mirbeau." Illustration. Vol. 195 (November 7, 1946), pp. 302-3.

1319. Dubeux, Albert. "Le féroce Mirbeau." Revue des Deux
Mondes. (March 15, 1968), pp. 211-25.

1320. Dupeyron, Georges. "Sur deux pièces d'Octave Mirbeau." Europe. Vol. 458 (1967), pp. 186-91.

1321. Fournier, Albert. "Parterres et chateaux de Mirbeau." Europe. Vol. 458 (1967), pp. 191-212.

1322. Psichari, Henriette. "Une première au théâtre français." Europe. Vol. 458 (1967), pp. 182-86.

1323. Talva, François. "Octave Mirbeau, juge sûr, lutteur passionné, et fidèle." Europe. Vol. 458 (1967), pp. 173-82.

1324. Truffier, J. "L'affaire Mirbeau: le dénigrement et l'apologie des comédiens." Mercure de France. Vol. 289 (January 15, 1939), pp. 325-48.

Theses and Dissertations

1325. Schwartz, Martin. "Octave Mirbeau. Vie et Oeuvre." Ph.D. Dissertation. University of Wisconsin, 1963.

1326. Shoemaker, Richard L. "Octave Mirbeau. The Man and his Dramatic Works." Ph.D. Dissertation. University of Virginia, 1947.

GEORGES DE PORTO-RICHE

(1849-1930)

Selected Full-length Plays:

> Le vertige (Vertigo, 1874)
> Un Drame sous Phillipe II (A Play of Phillip
>   II, 1875)
> Les Deux Fautes (The Two Mistakes, 1878)
> Don Juan (1878)
> Vanina (1879)
> La Chance de Françoise (Françoise's Luck,
>   Lovers' Luck, 1882)
> L'Infidèle (The Unfaithful, 1890)
> Amoureuse (A Loving Wife, A Woman in Love,
>   The Tyranny of Love, 1891)
> Le Passé (The Past, 1897)
> Les Malefilâtre (1904)
> Le Vieil Homme (The Old Man, 1911)
> Choses vues (Things Seen, 1912)
> Zubiri (1912)
> Le Marchand d'estampes (The Print Merchant,
>   1917)
> Les Vrais Drieux (The True Drieux, 1929)

Books

1327. Brugmans, Hendrick. Georges de Porto-Riche, sa vie, son oeuvre. Paris: E. Droz, 1934.

1328. Leutaud, Paul. Le théâtre de Maurice Boissard. Paris: Gallimard, 1926.

1329. Muller, Walter. Georges de Porto-Riche (1849-1930): l'homme, le poète, le dramaturge. Paris: J. Vrin, 1934.

1330. Oulmont, Charles. Noces d'or avec mon passé. Paris: Crepin-LeBlond, 1964.

1331. Sée, Edmond. Porto-Riche. Paris: Frimin-Didot, 1932.

Articles

1332. Antoine, André. "Georges de Porto-Riche et son oeuvre." L'Illustration. Vol. 88 (September 13, 1930), pp. 30-2.

1333. Bauer, G. "Georges de Porto-Riche." Annales Politiques et Littéraires. Vol. 95 (September 15, 1930), pp. 251-2.

1334. Bibou, H. "Georges de Porto-Riche." Journal des Débats. Vol. 37 (September 12, 1930), pp. 444-6.

1335. Rouveyre, A. "Les pièces de M. Georges de Porto-Riche." Mercure de France. Vol. 223 (October 1, 1930), pp. 160-5.

1336. Sarcey, Y. "Souvenirs." Annales Politiques et Littéraires. Vol. 95 (September 15, 1930), pp. 250.

1337. Talamon, R. "Porto-Riche et Rostand." Modern Language Notes. Vol. 50 (November, 1935), pp. 446-51.

ÉMILE [EDOUARD CHARLES ANTOINE] ZOLA

(1840-1902)

Selected Full-length Plays:

> La Laide (The Ugly Woman, 1865)
> Madeleine (1865)
> Thérèse Raquin (also played as Guilty, 1873)
> Les Héritiers Rabourdin (The Rabourdin Heirs, 1874)
> Le bouton de rose (The Rosebud, 1878)
> Renée (adaptation of his novel La Curée, 1879)

Books

1338. Angeli, N., et al. Présence de Zola. Paris: Pasquelle, 1953.

1339. Brulat, Paul. Zola. Paris: Cercle de la librairie, 1922-1923.

1340. Carter, Lawson A. Zola and the Theatre. New Haven: Yale University Press, 1963.

1341. Céard, R. Lettres inédites à Émile Zola. Paris: Librairie Nizel, 1958.

1342. Croce, Benedetto. Poesía e non poesía. Bari: G. Laterza, 1923.

1343. Euvrard, Michel. Zola. Paris: Eds. Univers., 1967.

1344. Faquet, Émile. Zola. Paris: Imp. A. Eyméoud, 1903.

1345. Grant, Elliot Mansfield. Émile Zola. New York: Twayne Publishers, 1966.

1346. Hemmings, Frederick W. J. Émile Zola. London: Oxford University Press, 1970.

1347. Josephson, Matthew. Zola and His Time. New York: Russell and Russell, 1929.

1348. Kuhn, Gottfried. Zola als Dramatiker. Strasbourg: Imprimerie alsacienne, 1926.

1349. Menichelli, Gian Carlo. Bibliographie de Zola en Italie. Florence: Institut Français de Florence, 1960

1350. Schmidt, Gunther. Die literarische Rezeption des Darwinismus: das Problem d. Vererbung bei Émile Zola u. im Drama d. dt. Naturalismus. Berlin: Akademie-Verlag, 1974.

1351. Sherard, Robert Harborough. Émile Zola, a Biographical and Critical Study. London: Chatto and Unwin, 1893.

1352. Vizetelly, Ernest A. Émile Zola, Novelist and Reformer. London: J. Lane, 1904.

1353. Walker, Phillip. Émile Zola. London: Routledge and K. Paul, 1968.

1354. Zola, Émile. Le naturalisme au théâtre, les théories et les examples. Paris: Pasquelle, 1923.

Articles

1355. Baschet, Robert. "La Critique d'art d'Émile Zola." Revue des Deux Mondes. (December 1, 1966), pp. 360-70.

1356. Benneton, N. A. "Social Thought in Émile Zola."
Sociology and Social Research. Vol. 13 (March, 1929), pp.
366-76.

1357. Bertaux, F. "L'influence de Zola en Allemagne." Revue
de Littérature Comparée. Vol. 4 (January, 1924), pp. 73-91.

1358. Dahlström, Carl E. W. L. "Theomachy: Zola, Strindberg,
Andreyev." Scandinavian Studies. Vol. 17 (November, 1942),
pp. 121-32.

1359. Gahide, Françoise. "'Le naturalisme au théâtre' de
Zola ou l'ouverture de la crise du théâtre." Théâtre Populaire. No. 31 (September, 1958), pp. 1-11.

1360. Gauthier, E. P. "Zola on Naturalism in Art and History." Modern Language Notes. Vol. 70 (November, 1955),
pp. 514-17.

1361. Gouraige, Ghislain. "Le naturalisme et l'amour."
Cahiers Naturalistes. Vol. 44 (1972), p. 188-200.

1362. Guedj, Aimé. "Diderot et Zola: essai de redéfinition
du naturalisme." Europe. April-May, 1968, pp. 287-324.

1363. Hartley, K. H. "Giovanni Verga and Zola." Journal
of the Australian Universities Language and Literature Association. May 1962, pp. 7-76.

1364. Hell, Victor. "Die Ehe im Zeitalter des Naturalismus:
Ihre Soziologie und aesthetic Funktion im Werk von Zola,
Ibsen und G. Hauptmann." Recherches germaniques. Vol. 3
(1973), pp. 125-34.

1365. Hemmings, F. W. "Zola and l'éducation sentimentale."
Roman Review. Vol. 50 (February, 1959), pp. 35-50.

1366. Jones, M. B. "Translations of Zola in the United
States Prior to 1900." Modern Language Notes. Vol. 55 (November, 1940), pp. 520-4.

1367. Kanes, Martin. "Zola and Busnach: the Temptations of
the Stage." PMLA. Vol. 77 (March, 1962), pp. 109-15.

1368. Lapp, J. C. "Watcher Betrayed and the Fatal Woman:
Some Recurring Patterns in Zola." PMLA. Vol. 74 (June,
1959), pp. 276-84.

1369. LeBlond, M. "Zola et les Goncourts." Revue Politique
et Littéraire. Vol. 66 (March 17, 1928), pp. 164-66.

1370. Matthews, J. H. "Les deux Zola: science et personalité
dans l'expression." Modern Language Notes. Vol. 73 (April,
1958), pp. 316-17.

1371. Montreynaud, Florence. "Les Relations de Zola et de Tourguéniev: Documents inédits." Cahiers Naturalistes. Vol. 43 (1972), pp. 55-82.

1372. Osborne, John. "Zola, Ibsen and the Development of the Naturalist Movement in Germany." Zeitschrift für vergleichende Literaturwissenschaft. No. 2 (1968), pp. 196-203.

1373. Pryme, Eileen E. "Zola's Plays in England, 1870-1900." French Studies. Vol. 13 (January, 1959), pp. 28-38.

1374. Sanders, James B. "Antoine, Zola et le théâtre." Les Cahiers naturalistes. No. 42 (1972), pp. 51-60.

1375. Souriau, Etienne. "Sur une novelle formule de réalisme au théâtre." La Revue d'Esthétique. Vol. 27 (1974), pp. 107-19.

1376. Vicaire, G. "L'esthétique d'Émile Zola." Revue de Deux Mondes. Vol. 21 (June 15, 1924), pp. 810-31.

1377. Walker, Phillip. "Zola, Myth and the Birth of the Modern World." Symposium. Summer, 1971, pp. 209-220.

1378. Weinberg, Henry H. "Zola: Some Early Critical Concepts." Modern Language Quarterly. Vol. 28 (1967), pp. 207-12.

1379. White, Lucien W. "Moral Aspects of Zola's Naturalism Judged by His Contemporaries and by Himself." Modern Language Quarterly. Vol. 23 (December, 1962), pp. 360-72.

1380. Zola, Émile. "Le Naturalisme au théâtre," in Toby Cole, Playwrights on Playwriting. New York: Hill and Wang, 1960, pp. 5-14.

Theses and Dissertations

1381. Carter, Lawson A. "Zola and the Theatre." Ph.D. Dissertation. Yale University, 1951.

1382. Colburn, William Elliot. "Zola in England, 1883-1903." Ph.D. Dissertation. University of Illinois (Urbana-Champaign), 1952.

1383. Root, Winthrop Hegeman. "German Criticism of Zola, 1875-1893, with Special Reference to the Rougan-Macquart Cycle and the Roman Experimental." Ph.D. Dissertation. Columbia University, 1931.

1384. Sondel, Bess S. "Zola's Naturalistic Theory with Particular Reference to the Drama." Ph.D. Dissertation. University of Chicago, 1938.

VI GERMANY

General Commentaries

Books

1385. Ackerman, Walter. Die zeitgenössische Kritik an die deutschen naturalistischen Dramen. Munich: Schon, 1965.

1386. Arnold, William Franz. Das deutsche Drama. Munich: Beck, 1925.

1387. Bahr, Herman. Zur überwindung des Naturalismus: theoretische Schriften, 1887-1904. Stuttgart: W. Kohlhammer, 1968.

1388. Brahm, Otto. Kritische Schriften über Drama und Theater. Berlin: S. Fischer, 1913-15.

1389. Brauneck, Manfred. Literatur und Öffentlichkeit im ausgehenden 19.Jahrhundert: Studien zur Rezeption des naturalistischen Theaters in Deutschland. Stuttgart: J. B. Metzler, 1974.

1390. Eller, William Henri. Ibsen in Germany, 1870-1900. Boston: R. G. Badger, 1918.

1391. Eloesser, Arthur. Modern German Literature. New York: Knopf, 1933.

1392. Fechter, Paul. Geschichte der deutschen Literatur von Naturalismus bis zur Literatur des Unwirklichen. Leipzig: Bibliographisches Institut, 1938.

1393. Francke, Kuno. History of German Literature as Determined by Social Forces. New York: Holt, 1931.

1394. Garten, Hugh Frederick. Modern German Drama. London: Methuen, 1959.

1395. Grimm, Reinhold, ed. Deutsche Dramentheorien: Beiträge zu einer historischen Poetik des Dramas in Deutschland. Frankfurt: Athenaum, 1971.

1396. Hayman, Ronald, ed. The German Theatre: A Symposium. New York: Harper, Row, 1975.

1397. Heller, Otto. Studies in Modern German Literature. Boston and New York: Ginn, 1905.

1398. Hoefert, Sigfrid. Das Drama des Naturalismus. Stuttgart: Metzler, 1968.

1399. Kerr, Alfred. Das neue Drama. Berlin: Fischer, 1909.

1400. _____. Die Welt in Drama. Cologne: Kiepenheuer & Witsch, 1964.

1401. Kienze, Camillo von. From Goethe to Hauptmann. New York: Biblo and Tannen, 1966.

1402. Kennartz, Franz. Die Dichter unserer Zeit. Stuttgart: A. Kroner, 1941.

1403. Lessing, Otto E. Masters in Modern German Literature. Dresden: C. Reissner, 1912.

1404. Lothar, Rudolph. Das deutsche Drama der Gegenwart. Munich and Leipzig: G. Müller, 1905.

1405. Lukács, György. Essays über Realismus. Berlin: Aufbau-Verlag, 1948.

1406. _____. Deutsche Realisten des 19. Jahrhunderts. Berlin: Aufbau-Verlag, 1951.

1407. Martini, F. Deutsche Literatur im bürgerlichen Realismus. Stuttgart: J. B. Metzler, 1962.

1408. Maurer, Warren R. The Naturalist Image of German Literature. Munich: W. Fink, 1972.

1409. Mennemeier, Franz N. Modernes deutsches Drama: Kritiken und Charakteristiken I: 1910-1933. Munich: Fink, 1973.

1410. Neudecker, Norbert. Der "Weg" als strukturbildendes Element in Drama. Meisenheim: Hain, 1972.

1411. Osborne, John. The Naturalist Drama in Germany. Manchester: Manchester University Press, 1971.

1412. Pollard, Percival. Masks and Minstrels of New Germany. Boston: J. W. Luce, 1911.

1413. Robertson, John G. A History of German Literature.
New York: Putnam, 1931.

1414. Rose, William. Men, Myths and Movements in German
Literature. London: Allen and Unwin, 1931.

1415. Rosenbaum, Uwe. Die Gestalt des Schauspielers auf dem
deutschen Theater des 19. Jahrhunderts mit der besonderen
Berücksichtigung der dramatischen Werke von Hermann Bahr,
Arthur Schnitzler und Heinrich Mann. Cologne: Selbstverlag,
1970.

1416. Ruden, Peter von. Sozialdemokratisches Arbeiter-
theater (1848-1914): Ein Betrag zur Geschichte des politischen
Theaters. Frankfurt: Athenaum, 1973.

1417. Schlag, H. Das drama: Wesen, Theorie und Technik des
Dramas. Essen: Fredebeul und Koenen, 1909.

1418. Schlenther, Paul. Theater im 19. Jahrhundert. Berlin:
Selbstverlag der Gesellschaft für Theatergeschichte, 1930.

1419. Wiese, Benno von, ed. Deutsche Dramaturgie von Naturalismus bis zur Gegenwart. Tübingen: Niemeyer, 1970.

1420. Wildenbruch, Ernest von. Das deutsche Drama, seine
Entwicklung und sein gegenwärtiger Stand. Leipzig: Verlag
für Literatur, Kunst und Musik, 1906.

1421. Witkowski, Georg. German Drama of the Nineteenth
Century. London: G. Bell, 1909.

Articles

1422. Coar, J. Firman. "Three Contemporary German Dramatists." Atlantic Monthly. Vol. 81 (January, 1898), pp. 71-
80.

1423. Davies, Cecil W. "The Volksbühne: A Descriptive
Chronology." Theatre Quarterly. Vol. 11, no. 5 (Jan.-March,
1972), pp. 57-64.

1424. Döblin, Alfred. "Der Geist des naturalistischen
Zeitalters," in Aufsätze zur Literatur. Breisgau: Walter-
Verlag, 1963, pp. 62-84.

1425. Ende, Amelia von. "Modern German Dramatists."
Theatre. Vol. 16 (July, 1912), pp. 5-8.

1426. _____. "Notes on German Drama." Nation. Vol.
96 (January 2, 1913), pp. 17-18.

1427. Freund, F. E. "Modern German Drama." Drama. Vol. 8
(November, 1912), pp. 124-52.

1428. Lee, Elizabeth. "The German Drama of Today." Living
Age. Vol. 234 (1902), pp. 156-66.

1429. Lewisohn, Ludwig. "The German Theatre of Today." Nation. Vol. 101 (May 15, 1920), pp. 663-4.

1430. McInnes, Edward. "Die naturalistische Dramentheorie und die dramaturgische Tradition." Zeitschrift für deutsche Philologie. Vol. 93 (1974), pp. 161-86.

1431. Osborne, John. "Zola, Ibsen and the Development of the Naturalistic Movement in Germany." Zeitschrift für vergleichende Literatur-Wissenschaft. Vol. 2 (1968), pp. 196-203.

1432. "The New Revolutionary Drama Springing Up in Germany and Austria." Current Opinion. Vol. 66 (June, 1919), p. 368.

1433. Scholz, K. "Bibliography of English Renditions of Modern German Dramas." German-American Annals. Vol. 15 (1917), pp. 3-28.

1434. Schulz, Gerhard. "Zur Theorie des Dramas im deutschen Naturalismus." In Reinhold Grimm. Deutsche Dramentheorien. Frankfurt: Athenäum, 1971, pp. 394-428.

1435. Smith, G. "The Contemporary German Drama." Quarterly Review. Vol. 220 (January, 1914), pp. 69-95.

1436. Soissons, Count de. "The Recent Dramatic Movement in Germany." Contemporary Review. Vol. 105 (February, 1914), pp. 236-43.

Theses and Dissertations

1437. Bauland, Peter Max. "German Drama on the American Stage, 1894-1961." Ph.D. Dissertation. University of Pennsylvania, 1964.

1438. Carlson, Harold Gottfried. "The Motiv of Heredity in Modern German Literature with Particular Reference to the Drama." Ph.D. Dissertation. Cornell University, 1932.

1439. Helinski, Maureen M. "The Image of America in German Drama, 1890-1930." Ph.D. Dissertation. Johns Hopkins University, 1971.

1440. Novak, Sigrid G. "Images of Womanhood in the Works of German Female Dramatists: 1892-1918." Ph.D. Dissertation. Johns Hopkins University, 1974.

1441. Stoecklus, Alfred. "Naturalism in Recent German Drama with Special Reference to Hauptmann." Ph.D. Dissertation. Columbia University, 1903.

MAX HALBE

(1865-1944)

Selected Full-length Plays:

>   Freie Liebe (Free Love, 1890)
>   Der Eisgang (The Ice-drift, The Ice Floe,
>   1892)
>   Jugend (Youth, Youth and Love, 1893)
>   Mutter Erde (Mother Earth, 1897)
>   Die Heimatlosen (The Homeless, 1899)
>   Haus Rosenhagens (The Rosenhagens, The
>   Rosenhagen House, 1901)
>   Der Strom (The Stream, The River, 1904)
>   Das wahre Gesicht (The True Face, 1905)
>   Blaue Berge (Blue Mountains, 1908)
>   Der Ring des Gauklers (The Circle of
>   Gauklers, 1912)
>   Freiheit (Freedom, 1913)
>   Schloss Zeitvorbei (The Castle of Bygone
>   Time, 1917)
>   Hortense Ruland (1919)

Books

1442. Kindermann, Heinz. Max Halbe und der deutsche Osten.
Danzig: P. Rosenberg, 1942.

1443. Kleine, Werner. Max Halbes Stellung zum Naturalismus,
1887-1900. Zeulenroda: B. Sporn, 1937.

1444. Zillmann, Friedrich. Max Halbe, Wesen und Werk.
Würzburg: Holzner-Verlag, 1959.

Articles

1445. "Appreciation." Deutsche Rundschau. Vol. 265 (October, 1940), p. 21.

1446. Ende, Amelia von. "The Work of Max Halbe." Theatre.
Vol. 16 (July, 1912), pp. 5-8.

1447. Grummann, P. H. "Criticism of Max Halbe." Poet Lore.
Vol. 23 (March-April, 1912), pp. 125-38.

1448. Hoefert, Sigfrid. "E. T. A. Hoffmann und Max Halbe:
Ein Beitrag zur Wirkungsgeschichte des ostpreussischen
Romantikers." Mitteilungen der E. T. A. Hoffman-Gesellschaft.
Vol. 13 (1967), pp. 12-19.

1449. "Sketch." Modern Language Notes. Vol. 28 (January,
1913), pp. 169-70.

Theses and Dissertations

1450. Silzer, Edwin. "Max Halbes naturalistische Dramen."
Ph.D. Dissertation. University of Vienna, 1949.

GERHART [JOHAN ROBERT] HAUPTMANN

(1862-1946)

Selected Full-length Plays:

> Vor Sonnenaufgang (Before Dawn, Before
> Sunrise, 1889)
> Das Friedensfest (The Festival of Peace,
> The Coming of Peace, The Reconcil-
> iation, 1890)
> Einsame Menschen (Lonely Lives, 1891)
> Die Weber (The Weavers, 1892)
> Kollege Crampton (Colleague Crampton,
> 1892)
> Der Biberpelz (The Beaver Coat, The Beaver
> Skin, The Thieves' Comedy, 1893)
> Hanneles Himmelfahrt (Hannele's Ascension,
> 1893)
> Florian Geyer (1896)
> Die versunkene Glocke (The Sunken Bell,
> 1896)
> Fuhrmann Henschel (Drayman Henschel,
> 1898)
> Michael Kramer (1900)
> Der Rote Hahn (The Red Rooster, The
> Conflagration, 1901)
> Der Arme Heinrich (Henry of Auë, Poor
> Henry, 1902)
> Rose Bernd (1903)
> Elga (1905)
> Und Pippa Tanzt (And Pippa Dances, 1906)
> Die Jungfern vom Bischofsberg (The
> Maidens of the Mount, 1907)
> Keiser Karl Geisel (1908)
> Griselda (1909)
> Die Ratten (The Rats, 1911)
> Gabriel Shillings Flucht (The Flight of
> Gabriel Shilling, 1912)
> Das Hirtenlied (The Shepherd's Song,
> 1913)

Books

In English:

1451. Behl, Carl Friedrich W. Gerhart Hauptmann: His Life
and Work. Würzburg: Holzner-Verlag, 1956.

1452. Buck, Philo, ed. Directions in Contemporary Literature. New York: Oxford University Press, 1942.

1453. Buck, Shirley. The Origins of Middle-class Serious Drama in Germany. Columbus, Ohio: The Ohio State University Press, 1937.

1454. Chandler, Frank W. Modern Continental Playwrites. New York and London: Harper and Brothers, 1931.

1455. Collins, Ralph A. The Artist in Modern German Drama. Ann Arbor, Michigan: Edwards Brothers, Inc., 1940.

1456. Garten, Hugh Frederick. Gerhart Hauptmann. New Haven: Yale University Press, 1954.

1457. Gruenberg, Elsa. Daemon and Eros in Some Plays of Gerhart Hauptmann. Parkville, Mo.: Park College Press, 1960.

1458. Holl, Karl. Gerhart Hauptmann: His Life and His Work, 1862-1912. Chicago: McClurg, 1914.

1459. Knight, Kenneth Graham and Frederick Norman, eds. Hauptmann Centenary Lectures. London: University of London Press, 1964.

1460. Lewisohn, Ludwig, ed. The Dramatic Works of Gerhart Hauptmann. New York: B. W. Huebsch, 1912.

1461. Marble, Annie. Nobel Prize Winners in Literature, 1901-1931. New York and London: 1925.

1462. Maurer, Warren R. The Naturalistic Image of German Literature. Berlin: Wilhelm Fink Verlag, 1972.

1463. Muller, Siegfried H. Gerhart Hauptman and Goethe. New York: King's Crown Press, 1949.

1464. Osborne, John. The Naturalist Drama in Germany. Manchester: Manchester University Press, 1971.

1465. Pascal, Roy. From Naturalism to Expressionism: German Literature and Society. London: Weidenfeld and Nicolson, 1973.

1466. Quimby, Mary A. The Nature Background in the Dramas of Gerhart Hauptmann. Philadelphia: International Printing Company, 1918.

1467. Rempel, Margareta. Leo Tolstoy, Gerhart Hauptmann and Maxim Gorky: A Comparative Study. Ames, Iowa: University of Iowa Press, 1959.

1468. Seibel, George. Hauptmann and Sudermann. Girard, Kansas: Haldeman-Julius Co., 1925.

1469. Shaw, Leroy R. The Playwright and Historical Change: Dramatic Strategies in Brecht, Hauptmann, Kaiser, Wedekind. Madison: University of Wisconsin Press, 1970.

1470. _____ . Witness of Deceit: Gerhart Hauptmann as Critic of Society. Berkeley: University of California Press, 1958.

1471. Sinden, Margaret J. Gerhart Hauptmann: The Prose Plays. Toronto: University of Toronto Press, 1957.

1472. Von Klenze, Camillo. From Goethe to Hauptmann: Studies in a Changing Culture. New York: Bildo and Tannen, 1966.

1473. Weisert, John Jacob. The Dream in Gerhart Hauptmann. New York: King's Crown Press, 1949.

In German:

1474. Alexander, Neville E. Studien zum Stilwandel in dramatischen Werk Gerhart Hauptmanns. Stuttgart: J. B. Metzler, 1970.

1475. Behl, Carl Friedrich Wilhelm. Gerhart Hauptmann, eine Studie. Berlin: Borngraber, 1913.

1476. _____ . Gerhart Hauptmanns Leben, Chronik und Bild. Berlin: Suhrkamp-Verlag, 1942.

1477. _____ . Gerhart Hauptmann: Überblick über Leben und Werk. Würzburg-Main: Holzner-Verlag, 1952.

1478. _____ . Gerhart Hauptmann zu seinem 50. Berlin: R. Schmidt, 1912.

1479. _____ . Wege zu Gerhart Hauptmann. Goslar: Deutsche Volkbücherei, 1948.

1480. _____ . Zwiesprache mit Gerhart Hauptmann. Munich: X. Desch, 1948.

1481. Brahm, Otto. Kritische Schriften über Drama und Theater. Berlin: S. Fischer, 1913-15.

1482. Bytkowsky, Sigmund. Gerhart Hauptmanns Naturalismus und das Drama. Hamburg and Leipzig: L. Voss, 1908.

1483. Chung, Charles T. Zur Problematic des Gesellsschaftsbildes im Drama Gerhart Hauptmanns: Eine sozio-literaturwissenschaftliche Betrachtung. Cologne: Selbstverlag, 1969.

1484. Fechter, Paul. Gerhart Hauptmann. Gütersloh: S. Mohn, 1961.

1485. Hering, Gerhard Friedrich. Gerhart Hauptmann. Düsseldorf: W. Giradet, 1956.

1486. Herrmann, Christian G. Die Weltanschauung Gerhart Hauptmanns in seinen Werken. Berlin: Gebr. Paetel, 1926.

1487. Hilscher, Eberhard. Gerhart Hauptmann. Berlin: Verlag der Nation, 1974.

1488. Hoefert, Sigfrid. Gerhart Hauptmann. Stuttgart: J. B. Metzler, 1974.

1489. Hülsen, Hans von. Gerhart Hauptmann, Umriss seiner Gestalt. Leipzig: P. Reclay, 1927.

1490. Kersten, Gerhard. Gerhart Hauptmann und Lev Nikolajevic Tolstoj: Studien zur Wirkungsgeschichte von L. N. Tolstoj im Deutschland, 1885-1910. Wiesbaden: Harrassowitz, 1966.

1491. Landsberg, Hans. Los von Hauptmann. Berlin: Walther, 1900.

1492. Marcuse, Ludwig. Gerhart Hauptmann und sein Werk. Berlin: F. Schneider, 1922.

1493. Milch, Werner. Humor um Gerhart Hauptmann. Berlin: Joachim Goldstein Verlag, 1932.

1494. _____. Gerhart Hauptmann: Vielheit und Einheit. Breslau: Priebatsch, 1932.

1495. Reichart, Walter A. Gerhart Hauptmann--Bibliographie. Bad Homburg: Gehlen, 1969.

1496. Requardt, Walter. Gerhart Hauptman. Bibliographie. Three Volumes. Berlin: Selbstverlag von W. Requardt, 1931.

1497. _____. Gerhart Hauptmann. Werk von ihm und über ihn in den Jahren 1922-1930. Berlin: Selbstverlag von W. Requardt, 1930.

1498. Rohmer, Rolf. Gerhart Hauptmann. Leipzig: VEB Bibliog. Inst., 1974.

1499. Schlentner, Paul. Gerhart Hauptmann: Leben und Werke. Berlin: S. Fischer, 1922.

1500. _____. Gerhart Hauptmann: sein Lebensgang und seine Dichtung. Berlin: S. Fischer, 1898.

1501. Schröder, Rudolph Alexander. Gerhart Hauptmann. Mainz: Eggebrecht-Presse, 1953.

1502. Spiero, Heinrich. Gerhart Hauptmann. Bielefeld: Velhagen und Klasing, 1922.

1503. Sternberg, Kurt. Gerhart Hauptmann: der Entwicklungsgang seiner Dichtung. Berlin: Borngraber, 1910.

1504. Sulger-Gebing, Emil. Gerhart Hauptmann. Leipzig:
B. G. Teubner, 1909.

1505. Tschörtner, H. D. Gerhart Hauptmanns Bibliographie.
Berlin: Deutsche Staatsbibliothek, 1971.

1506. Voight, Felix Alfred. Gerhart Hauptmann und die
Antike. Berlin: E. Schmidt, 1965.

1507. _____. Hauptmann und Shakespeare. Goslar: Verlag
Deutsche Volksbücherei, 1947.

1508. Woerner, U. C. Gerhart Hauptmann. Berlin: A. Duncker,
1901.

1509. Zabludowski, N. Die Bewältigung des Raumproblems in
den dramatischen Jugendwerken Gerhart Hauptmanns. Danzig:
1933.

In Other Languages:

1510. Lossis Cesare de. Gerhart Hauptmann e l'òpera sua
letterària. Florence: Successori Le Monnier, 1899.

1511. Proost, Karal Frederik. Gerhart Hauptmann, zijn leven
en werken. Zeist: J. Ploegsma, 1924.

                          Articles

1512. Allen, Genevieve M. "The Problem of Individualism in
Relation to Society in Ibsen, Maeterlinck and Hauptmann."
Poet Lore. Vol. 32 (Summer, 1921), pp. 262-6.

1513. Atkins, H. G. "Hauptmann's Influence in the History
of German Drama." 19th Century. Vol. 128 (November, 1940),
pp. 488-91.

1514. Bader, D. "Gerhart Hauptmanns Beurteilung in Ungarn
zwischen den beiden Weltkriegen." Annales (University of
Budapest Sectio Philologgica). Vol. 7 (1967), pp. 133-46.

1515. Behl, C. F. W. "Der Einzelne und die Masse im Werke
Gerhart Hauptmanns." Germanic Review. Vol. 33 (October,
1958), pp. 168-75.

1516. _____. "Gerhart Hauptmann und Ida Orloff."
Schlesien. Vol. 2 (1967), pp. 95-96.

1517. _____. "Neues von und über Gerhart Hauptmann."
Schlesien. Vol. 12 (1967), pp. 179-82.

1518. Bosdari, A. de. "Gerhart Hauptmann nel suo sessan-
tesimo anno." Nuova Antologia. Vol. 248 (July 1, 1924),
pp. 53-66.

1519. Coates, W. A. "Dostoyevski and Gerhart Hauptmann."
American Slavonic Review. Vol. 4 (December, 1945), pp. 107-27.

1520. Drews, Richard. "Der Dramatiker Gerhart Hauptmann.
Zum 90. Geburtstag des Dichters." Weltbühne. Number 47
(1952), n. pag.

1521. Dziallas, Paul. "Gerhart Hauptmann in Karikatur,
Satire und Parodie." Schlesien. Vol. 13 (1968), pp. 96-106.

1522. Eloesser, Arthur. "Gerhart Hauptmanns Buch der Lei-
denschaft." Neue Rundschau. Vol. 40, Part 2 (December, 1929),
pp. 815-18.

1523. Foster, F. M. "The Work of Gerhart Hauptmann." Colonnade. Vol. 7 (February, 1914), pp. 152-62.

1524. Garten, Hugo F. "Gerhart Hauptmann, a Revaluation."
German Life and Letters. Vol. 3 (October, 1949), p. 32.

1525. Grützmacher, R. H. "Die geistigen Schichten in Gerhart Hauptmanns Lebensanschauung." Preussische Jahrbücher.
Vol. 230 (November, 1932), pp. 106-19.

1526. Grummann, P. H. "Criticism of Gerhart Hauptmann."
Poet Lore. Vol. 22 (March-April, 1911), pp. 117-27.

1527. _____. "Criticism of Hauptmann's Dramas from
'The Sunken Bell' to 'Pippa.'" Poet Lore. Vol. 21 (July-
August, 1910), pp. 285-99.

1528. Guthrie, William Norton. "Gerhart Hauptmann."
Sewanee Review. Vol. 3 (May, 1895), pp. 278-89.

1529. Haskell, J. S. "Quellenstudien zu Gerhart Hauptmann."
German Society Quarterly. Vol. 2 (March, 1915), pp. 46-47,
and (January, 1915), pp. 81-9.

1530. Hell, Victor. "Die Ehe im Zeitalter des Naturalismus.
Ihre Soziologie und aesthetic Funktion im Werk von Zola,
Ibsen und G. Hauptmann." Recherches germaniques. Vol. 3
(1973), pp. 125-34.

1531. Hennecke, H. "Sprache, Gedanke und Lyrik im Lebens-
werke Gerhart Hauptmanns: aus Anlass des Erscheinens der
Ahrenlese." Neue Rundschau. Vol. 52 (April, 1941), pp.
201-14.

1532. Heuser, F. W. J. "Gerhart Hauptmann: zu seinem Leben
und Schaffen." Germanic Review. Vol. 37 (January, 1962),
pp. 79-80.

1533. _____. "Personal and Literary Relations of
Hauptmann and Wedekind." Modern Language Notes. Vol. 66
(November, 1921), pp. 395-402.

1534. Hülsen, H. von. "Der siebzigjährige Gerhart Hauptmann." Westermanns Monatshefte. Vol. 153 (November, 1932),
PP. 209-12.

1535. "Hauptmann and the Nietzschean Philosophy." Poet Lore.
Vol. 24 (September-October, 1913), pp. 34-7.

1536. Henderson, Archibald. "Gerhart Hauptmann, Social
Idealist." Arena. Vol. 33 (March, 1905), pp. 251-7.

1537. Ihering, Herbert. "Die Berliner Hauptmanntradition."
Sonntag. Number 46 (1952), pp. 5, 9.

1538. _____. "Produktive Theatergeschichte. Zum 5.
Todestag Gerhart Hauptmanns." Aufbau. Number 6 (1951),
pp. 560-2.

1539. Kayser, R. "Neue Hauptmann Literatur." Neue Rundschau. Vol. 43, Part 2 (November, 1932), pp. 714-16.

1540. Kaiser, Gerhard. "Die Tragikomödien Gerhart Hauptmanns," in Eckhard Catholy and Winifried Hellmanns, eds.
Festschrift für Klaus Ziegler. Tübingen: Niemeyer, 1968,
pp. 269-89.

1541. Koezy, Karol. "Plebiscyst fornoslaski i Gerhart
Hauptmann." Zaranie Slaskie. Vol. 29 (1966), n. pag.

1542. Leder, Lily. "Gerhart Hauptmann und sein dramatisches
Werk." Theater der Zeit. Number 3 (1953), pp. 9-15.

1543. Lederer, Max. "Gerhart Hauptmann." German Quarterly.
Vol. 20 (1947), pp. 46-48.

1544. McInnes, Edward. "The Domestic Dramas of Gerhart
Hauptmann: Tragedy or Sentimental Pathos?" German Life and
Letters. Vol. 20 (1966), pp. 53-60.

1545. Mayer, Hans. "Das dramatische Werk Gerhart Hauptmanns," in G. Hauptmann. Werke in acht Bänden. Vol. 4
Berlin: Aufbau-Verlag, 1962, n. pag.

1546. _____. "Die dramatischen Meisterwerke Gerhart
Hauptmanns." Heute und Morgen. Vol. 5 (1952), pp. 317-22.

1547. _____. "Einführung in das dramatische Werk
Gerhart Hauptmanns," in G. Hauptmann. Dramen in vier Bänden.
Vol. 1. Berlin: Aufbau-Verlag, 1956, n. pag.

1548. Mencken, Henry Lewis. "Hauptmann, His Works and His
Present Position." Smart Set. Vol. 39 (March, 1913), pp.
153-5.

1549. Muret, M. "M. Gerhart Hauptmann, se penche sur son
passé." Journal des Débats. Vol. 39, Part 2 (September 16,
1932), pp. 475-7.

1550. Osborne, John. "Hauptmann's Later Naturalistic Dramas: Suffering and Tragic Vision." Modern Language Review. Vol. 63 (1968), pp. 628-35.

1551. Pohl, G. "Gerhart Hauptmanns letzte Tage." Deutsche Rundschau. Vol. 75 (June, 1949), pp. 526-32.

1552. Reichart, Walter A. "Bibliographie der gedruckten und ungedruckten Dissertationen über Gerhart Hauptmann und sein Werk." Philobiblon. Vol. 11 (1967), pp. 121-34.

1553. _____. "Gerhart Hauptmann's Dramas on the American Stage." Masque & Kothurn. Vol. 7 (1962), pp. 223-32.

1554. _____. "Gerhart Hauptmann's Germanen und Römer." Modern Languages Association. Vol. 44 (September, 1929), pp. 901-10.

1555. _____. "Gerhart Hauptmann since 1933." Books Abroad. Vol. 20 (1946), pp. 125-29.

1556. _____. "Gerhart Hauptmann, War Propaganda, and George Bernard Shaw." Germanic Review. Vol. 33 (October, 1958), pp. 176-80.

1557. _____. "Grundbegriffe im dramatischen Schaffen Gerhart Hauptmanns." PMLA. Vol. 82, pp. 142-51.

1558. _____. "Hauptmann before Vor Sonnenaufgang." Journal of English and German Philosophy. Vol. 28 (October, 1929), pp. 518-31.

1559. _____. "The Totality of Hauptmann's Work." Germanic Review. Vol. 21 (1946), pp. 143-9.

1560. Scholz, K. "The Art of Translation with Special Reference to the Prose of Hauptmann and Sudermann." German-American Annals. Vol. 20 (January--April, 1918), pp. 1-70.

1561. Schrimpf, Hans J. "Das unerreichte Soziale: Die Komödien Gerhart Hauptmanns Der Biberpelz und Der rote Hahn," in Hans Steffan Das deutsche Lustspiel. Vol. II, Göttingen: Vandenhoeck und Ruprecht, 1966, pp. 25-60.

1562. Seidlin, Oscar. "Taking Leave of Gerhart Hauptmann." South Atlantic Quarterly. Vol. 46 (July, 1947), pp. 359-64.

1563. Studt, W. "Frühste Dichtungen Gerhart Hauptmanns: neue Funde aus den Jahren 1875-1881." Germanic Review. Vol. 33 (October, 1958), pp. 181-96.

1564. Wahr, F. B. "Theory and Composition of the Hauptmann Drama." Germanic Review. Vol. 17 (1942), pp. 167-73.

1565. Wegner, Peter-Christian. "Gerhart Hauptmann als Leser: Ein Beitrag zur Auswertung der Büchersammlung des Dichters." Germanischromanische Monatsschrift. Vol. 23 (1973), pp. 365-76.

1566. Wiehr, Josef. "The Naturalistic Plays of Gerhart Hauptmann." Journal of English and Germanic Philology. Vol. 6 (1906), pp. 1-71, 163-73.

1567. Zeydel, E. H. "Note of Georg Büchner and Gerhart Hauptmann." Journal of English and German Philosophy. Vol. 44 (January, 1945), pp. 87-8.

1568. Ziolkowski, T. "Gerhart Hauptmann and the Problem of Language." Germanic Review. Vol. 38 (November, 1963), pp. 245-306.

Theses and Dissertations

1569. Bachman, Charles R. "Hardy and Hauptmann: The Variations of Fatalism." Ph.D. Dissertation. University of Indiana, 1966.

1570. Brammer, Ursula Guenther. "Selbstbildnis in Gerhart Hauptmanns Dramen." Ph.D. Dissertation. University of Pittsburgh, 1972.

1571. Cappel, Edith. "The Reception of Gerhart Hauptmann in the United States." Ph.D. Dissertation. Columbia University, 1952.

1572. Clare, Hazel S. "Eros in the Works of Hauptmann." Ph.D. Dissertation. New York University, 1941.

1573. Clemens, Gurney W. "Environment in Gerhart Hauptmann's Works." Ph.D. Dissertation. Johns Hopkins University, 1934.

1574. Flygt, Sten G. "Conceptions of the Tragic in German Drama from Schiller to Hauptmann." Ph.D. Dissertation. Northwestern University, 1939.

1575. Gassner, Sigrid. "Gerhart Hauptmann und die dramatische Kurzform." Ph.D. Dissertation. Columbia University, 1973.

1576. Gohla, Kurt B. "Natur und Naturgefühl in Werken Gerhart Hauptmanns." Ph.D. Dissertation. New York University, 1952.

1577. Gunvaldsen, Kaare M. "Gerhart Hauptmann's Dramatic Conception of the Artist." Ph.D. Dissertation. University of Wisconsin, 1949.

1578. Hachigian, Margarete. "Teichoskopie im deutschen Drama von Klopstock bis Hauptmann." Ph.D. Dissertation. University of Massachusetts, 1970.

1579. Hill, Mary C. "The Problem of Religion in the Life and Works of Gerhart Hauptmann." Ph.D. Dissertation. Northwestern University, 1948.

1580.   Hortenbach, Jenny Christa.   "Freiheitsstreben und Destruktivität. Frauen in den Dramen August Strindbergs und Gerhart Hauptmanns." Ph.D. Dissertation, University of California, 1962.

1581.   Kipa, Albert Alexander.   "Gerhart Hauptmann in Russia: 1889-1917: Reception and Impact." Ph.D. Dissertation. University of Pennsylvania, 1972.

1582.   Klemm, F. A.   "The Death Problem in the Life and Works of Gerhart Hauptmann." Ph.D. Dissertation. University of Pennsylvania, 1939.

1583.   Muller, Siegfried Hermann.   "Gerhart Hauptmann and Goethe." Ph.D. Dissertation. Columbia University, 1950.

1584.   Owen, Carroll H.   "The Treatment of History in Gerhart Hauptmann's Dramas." Ph.D. Dissertation. Cornell University, 1938.

1585.   Quimby, Mary Agnes.   "The Nature Background in the Dramas of Gerhart Hauptmann." Ph.D. Dissertation. University of Pennsylvania, 1918.

1586.   Rahde, Heinz Friedrich.   "Der Eros bei Gerhart Hauptmann." Ph.D. Dissertation. University of Utah, 1965.

1587.   Reichert, Walter Albert.   "Hauptmann's Relation to the State." Ph.D. Dissertation. University of Michigan, 1930.

1588.   Rempel, Margareta.   "Leo Totstoy, Gerhart Hauptmann and Maxim Gorky--A Comparative Study." Ph.D. Dissertation. University of Iowa, 1960.

1589.   Scholtz, Karl William Henry.   "The Art of Translation, with Special References to English Renditions of the Prose Dramas of Gerhart Hauptmann and Herman Sudermann." Ph.D. Dissertation. University of Pennsylvania, 1918.

1590.   Schutze, Martin.   "Gerhart Hauptmann's Plays and their Literary Relations." Ph.D. Dissertation. University of Pennsylvania, 1899.

1591.   Shaw, Leroy R.   "The Concept of 'Kulturluge' in Hauptmann's Early Work." Ph.D. Dissertation. University of California, 1954.

1592.   Stoeckius, Alfred.   "Naturalism in the Recent German Drama with Special Reference to Gerhart Hauptmann." Ph.D. Dissertation. Columbia University, 1903.

1593.   Stoeklein, George A.   "Romanticism in the Character of Gerhart Hauptmann and in his Prose Dramas." Ph.D. Dissertation. University of Pennsylvania, 1934.

1594. Temoyan, A. Betty. "The Art of Characterization in Some of the Dramas of Gerhart Hauptmann." Ph.D. Dissertation. Bryn Mawr University, 1965.

1595. Trumbauer, Walter. "Gerhart Hauptmann and John Galsworthy: A Parallel." Ph.D. Dissertation. University of Pennsylvania, 1917.

1596. Van Duren, Arthur, Jr. "Ibsen and Hauptmann." Ph.D. Dissertation. University of Michigan, 1930.

1597. Walsh, Dwight Rolfe. "Diety in Drama. The Representation of the Absolute in Some Plays of Ibsen, Strindberg and Hauptmann." Ph.D. Dissertation. Harvard University, 1963.

1598. Weisert, John L. "The Dream in Gerhart Hauptmann." Ph.D. Dissertation. Columbia University, 1949.

HERMANN SUDERMANN

(1857-1928)

Selected Full-length Plays:

> Die Ehre (Honor, 1889)
> Sodoms Ende (The Destruction of Sodom, The Man and His Picture, 1891)
> Die Heimat (Home, Magda, 1893)
> Die Schmetterlingsschlacht (The Battle of Butterflies, 1894)
> Das Glück in Winkel (Happiness in a Corner, The Vale of Content, 1895)
> Morituri (1896)
> Die Drei Reiherfedern (The Three Heron-feathers, 1898)
> Johannis (John, John the Baptist, 1898)
> Johannisfeuer (St. John's Fire, The Fires of St. John, 1900)
> Es lebe das Leben (Here's to Life, 1902)
> Der Sturmgeselle Sokrates (The Storm Trooper Socrates, 1903)
> Stein unter Steinen (A Stone Among Stones, 1905)
> Das Blumenboot (The Flower Float, 1905)
> Rosen (Roses, 1907)
> Strandkinder (Beach Children, 1910)
> Der Bettler von Syrakus (The Beggar of Syracus, 1911)
> Der gute Ruf (The Good Reputation, 1913)
> Die Lobgesänge des Claudian (Claudius' Song of Praise, 1914)
> Die entgötterte Welt (World Without God, 1916)

Der Katzensteg (The Cat's Bridge, 1917)
Die Raschoffs (The Raschoffs, 1919)
Notruf (Emergency Call, 1920-21)

Books

1599. Busse, Kurt. Hermann Sudermann: Sein Werk und sein Wesen. Stuttgart und Berlin: Cotta, 1927.

1600. Cannon, Harry Sharp. Sudermann's Treatment of Verse. Tübingen: H. Laupp, Jr., 1922.

1601. Duglor, Thomas. Hermann Sudermann: ein Dichter an der Grenzscheide zweier Welten. Troisdorf: Wegweiserverlag, 1958.

1602. Kaweran, Waldemar. Hermann Sudermann. Magdeburg and Leipzig: Verlag von B. Elischer nach Folger, 1897.

1603. Kerr, Alfred. Herr Sudermann. Berlin: Verlag Helianthus, 1903.

1604. Knortz, K. Sudermann's Dramen. Halle: M. Grosse, 1908.

1605. Landsberg, Hans. Hermann Sudermann. Berlin: Gose und Tetzloff, 1906.

1606. Schoen, Henri. Hermann Sudermann, poète dramatique et romancier. Paris: H. Didier, 1904.

1607. Seibel, George. Hauptmann and Sudermann. Girand, Kansas: Julius Co., 1935.

1608. Sudermann, Hermann. Book of My Youth. New York: Harper, 1923.

Theses and Dissertations

1609. Bockstahler, Oscar Leo. "A Study of the Influence of Friedrich Nietzsche on the Thoughts and Works of Hermann Sudermann." Ph.D. Dissertation. University of Michigan, 1932.

1610. Mathers, R. H. "Sudermann and the Critics: An Analysis of the Criticism of Sudermann's Works and of His Revolt against Literary Criticism of His Time." Ph.D. Dissertation. University of Southern California, 1951.

1611. Scholtz, Karl William Henry. "The Art of Translation with Special Reference to English Renditions of the Prose Dramas of Gerhart Hauptmann and Hermann Sudermann." Ph.D. Dissertation. University of Pennsylvania, 1918.

1612. Whitaker, Paul Knowlton. "The Inferiority Complex in Hermann Sudermann's Life and Works." Ph.D. Dissertation. The Ohio State University, 1943.

1613. Drummer, E. Heyse. "Hermann Suderman, a Contributor to American Culture." American-German Review. Vol. 13, no. 3 (1947), pp. 26-9.

1614. Ende, Amelia von. "The Works of Hermann Sudermann." Theatre. Vol. 16 (July, 1912), pp. 5-8.

1615. Fechter, P. "Hermann Sudermann, zum achtzigsten Geburtstag." Deutsche Rundschau. Vol. 252 (September, 1937), pp. 211-14.

1616. Florer, Warren W. "Recent German Criticism: Hermann Sudermann." Poet Lore. Vol. 16 (September, 1905), pp. 116-23.

1617. Frentz-Sudermann, Hans. "Hermann Sudermann, an Appreciation." German-American Review. Vol. 16, no. 1 (1949-50), pp. 24-26.

1618. "Hermann Sudermann, 1857-1928; eine individualanalytische und schaffenspsychologische Studie." Journal für Psychologie und Neurologie. Vol. 42 (1931), pp. 231-413.

1619. Lavison, Richard H. "Hermann Sudermann and Edith Wharton." Revue de Littérature Comparée. Vol. 41 (1967), pp. 125-31.

1620. Meyer, Richard M. "Hermann Sudermann." International Monthly. Vol. 6 (1902), pp. 140-54.

1621. Scholz, K. "The Art of Translation, with Special Reference to the Prose Dramas of Hauptmann and Sudermann." German-American Annals. Vol. 20 (January-April, 1918), pp. 1-70.

1622. Shaw, C. G. "Critical Sketch." Colonnade. Vol. 8 (August, 1914), pp. 70-6.

1623. Spiero, H. "Hermann Sudermann." Western Monatshefte. Vol. 143 (October, 1927), pp. 217-21.

1624. Whitaker, Paul K. "The Inferiority Complex in Hermann Sudermann's Life and Works." Monatshefte. Vol. 40 (1948), pp. 68-81.

LUDWIG THOMA

(1867-1971)

Selected Full-length Plays:

Die Medaille (The Medal, 1901)
Die Lokalbahn (The Branch Line, 1902)
Die Schusternazi (1905)
Moral (Morality, Morals, 1908)
Erster Klasse (First Class, 1910)
Lottchens Geburtstag (Lottchen's
    Birthday, 1911)
Magdalena (1910)
Das Säuglingsheim (The Baby Farm, The
    Nursery, 1913)
Die Sippe (The Tribe, 1913)
Christnacht (Christ's Night, 1914)
Der Erste August (The First of August,
    1915)

Books

1625. Brehm, Friedl. Sehnsucht nach Unterdrückung: Zensur und Presserecht bei Ludwig Thoma. Feldafing: F. Brehm, 1957.

1626. _____. Zehn haben neun Meinungen: Kritik und Kritiker bei Ludwig Thoma. Feldafing: F. Brehm, 1958.

1627. Herzog, Wilhelm. Menschen, denen ich begegnete. Munich and Bern: Francke, 1959.

1628. Stemplinger, Eduard. Ludwig Thoma als Altbayer. Altotting: Bücher der Heimat, 1948.

1629. Thoma, Ludwig. Ein Leben in Briefen, 1875-1921. Munich: R. Piper, 1963.

1630. Thumser, Gerd. Anekdoten und Ludwig Thoma. Munich: Bechtle, 1968.

1631. _____. Ludwig Thoma und seine Welt. Munich: Desch, 1966.

1632. Ziersch, Roland. Ludwig Thoma. Mühlacker: Stieglitz-Verlag, 1964.

Articles

1633. Heilbronner, Walter L. "A Reappraisal of Ludwig Thoma." German Quarterly. Vol. 30, no. 4 (November, 1957), pp. 247-53.

Theses and Dissertations

1634. Heilbronner, Walter L. "Ludwig Thoma as a Social and Political Critic and Satirist." Ph.D. Dissertation. University of Michigan, 1955.

FRANK WEDEKIND

(1864-1918)

Selected Full-length Plays:

    Der Schnellmaler, oder Kunst und Mammon
        (The Wholesale Painter or Art for
        Profit, The Lightning Artist or Art
        and Mammon, 1886
    Elins Erweckung (Elin's Awakening, 1887)
    Die junge Welt (The Young World, 1889)
    Der Liebestrank (The Love Potion, also
        played as Fritz Schwigerling, 1892)
    Der Erdgeist (The Earth Spirit, 1893)
    Frühlings Erwachen (Spring's Awakening,
        Dame Nature, 1896)
    Der Kammersänger (The Tenor, The Heart
        of a Tenor, The Court Singer, 1899)
    Marquis von Keith (1901)
    Die Büchse der Pandora (Pandora's Box,
        1901)
    So ist das Leben (Such Is Life, 1902)
    Hidalla (1904)
    Tod und Teufel (Death and Damnation,
        1905)
    Totentanz (Dance of Death, 1905)
    Musik (Music, 1906)
    Oaha, die Satire der Satire (Oaha, the
        Satire on Satire, 1908)
    Die Zensur (Censorhip , 1909)
    Schloss Wetterstein (Castle Wetterstein,
        1910)
    Franziska (1912)
    Simson, oder Scham und Eifersucht (Simson,
        or Shame and Jealousy, 1913)
    Felix und Galathea (1914)
    Bismark (1915)
    Herakles (Hercules, 1917)

Books

1635. Blei, Franz. Über Wedekind, Steinheim und das Theater. Leipzig: K. Wolff, 1915.

1636. Dehnow, Fritz. Frank Wedekind. Leipzig: Reisland, 1922.

1637. Duwe, Willi. Die dramatische Form Wedekinds in ihrem Verhältnis zur Ausdruckskunst. Munich: Lebenslauf, 1936.

1638. Elster, Hanns Martin. Frank Wedekind und seine besten Bühnenwerke. Berlin: F. Schneider, 1922.

1639. Fechter, Paul. Frank Wedekind: der Mensch und das Werk. Berlin: Verlegt bei Erich Lichtenstein, 1920.

1640. Gittleman, Sol. Frank Wedekind. New York: Twayne, 1969.

1641. Kapp, Julius. Frank Wedekind, seine Eigenart und seine Werke. Berlin: H. Barsdorf, 1909.

1642. Kempner, Hans. Frank Wedekind als Mensch und Künstler. Leipzig: Verlag für Literatur, Kunst und Musik, 1908.

1643. Kutscher, Artur. Frank Wedekind, sein Leben und seine Werke. Munich: G. Müller, 1922.

1644. Lemp, Richard, ed. Ludwig Thoma zum 100. Geburtstag. Munich: Stadtbibliothek, 1967.

1645. Munich Stadtbibliothek. Frank Wedekind zum 100. Munich: Richard Lemp, 1964.

1646. Pissin, Raimund. Frank Wedekind. Berlin: Gose and Tetzlaff, 1906.

1647. Proost, Karel Frederik. Frank Wedekind, zijn leven en werken. Zeist: J. Ploegsma, 1928.

1648. Rothe, Friedrich. Frank Wedekinds Dramen: Jugendstil und Lebensphilosophie. Stuttgart: J. B. Metzler, 1968.

1649. Seehaus, Günler. Frank Wedekind und das Theater, 1898-1959. Munich: Laokoön Verlag, 1964.

1650. Shaw, Leroy. The Playwright and Historical Change: Dramatic Strategies in Brecht, Hauptmann, Kaiser, Wedekind. Madison: University of Wisconsin Press, 1970.

1651. Ude, Karl. Frank Wedekind. Mühlacher: Stieglitz-Verlag, Handle, 1966.

1652. Volker, Klaus. Frank Wedekind. Velber b. Hannover: Friedrich, 1965.

Theses and Dissertations

1653. Force, Edward. "The Development of Wedeking Critic-ism." Ph.D. Dissertation. Indiana University, 1964.

1654. McIntyre, James R. "Epic Elements in the Drama of Frank Wedekind." Ph.D. Dissertation. Michigan State Uni-versity, 1973.

1655. Neumann, Edith S. "Der Künstler und sein Verhältnis zur Welt in Frank Wedekinds Dramen." Ph.D. Dissertation. Tulane University, 1970.

1656. Pampel, Brigitte C. G. "The Relationship of the Sexes in the Works of Strindberg, Wedekind and O'Neill." Ph.D. Dissertation. Northwestern University, 1973.

1657. Westervelt, William Osborne. "Frank Wedekind and the Search for Morality." Ph.D. Dissertation. University of Southern California, 1967.

Articles

1658. Brecht, Bertholt. "An Expression of Faith in Wedekind." Drama Review. Vol. 6, no. 1 (Spring, 1961), pp. 26-7.

1659. Clark, Barrett H. "Appreciation." International. Vol. 8 (November, 1914), pp. 333-6.

1660. Ende, Amelia von. "The Works of Frank Wedekind." Theatre. Vol. 16 (July, 1912), pp. 5-8.

1661. Fay, F. "Criticism of Frank Wedekind's Work." Drama. No. 19 (August, 1915), pp. 478-94.

1662. Friedman, E. "Sketch." Colonnade. Vol. 7 (January, 1914), pp. 134-7.

1663. Hern, Nicholas. "Frank Wedekind: An Introduction." Theatre Quarterly. Vol. 1, no. 2 (April-June, 1971), pp. 8-15.

1664. Heuser, F. W. J. "Personal and Literary Relations of Hauptmann and Wedekind." Modern Language Notes. Vol. 66 (November, 1921), pp. 395-402.

1665. Hill, Claude. "Wedekind in Retrospect." Modern Drama. Vol. 3 (1960), pp. 82-92.

1667. Maclean, Mary. "Jean Giraudoux and Frank Wedekind." Australian Journal of French Studies. Vol. 4 (1967), pp. 97-105.

1668. Neumann, Editha S. "Musik in Frank Wedekinds Bühnenwerken." German Quarterly. Vol. 44 (1971), pp. 185-90.

1669. Rasch, Wolfdietrich. "Sozialkritische Aspekte in Wedekinds dramatischer Dichtung: Sexualität, Kunst und Gesellschaft," in Helmet Kreuzer and Kate Hamburger, eds. Gestalttungsgeschichte und Gesellschaftsgeschichte. Stuttgart: Metzler, 1969, pp. 409-26.

1670. Theis, Otto Frederick. "Frank Wedekind." Poet Lore. Vol. 24 (July-August, 1913), pp. 237-47.

1671. Ude, Karl. "Eine Ehe wie im Drama: Frank Wedekind--
wie seine Frau Tilly ihn sah." Welt und Wort. Vol. 25
(1970), pp. 205-7.

1672. Weales, Gerald. "The Slippery Business of Frank Wedekind." American-German Review. Vol. 34, no. 1, pp. 41-44.

VII IRELAND

General Commentaries

Books

1673. Bell, Sam H. The Theatre in Ulster: A Survey of the Dramatic Movement in Ulster from 1902 to the Present Day. Dublin: Gill and Macmillan, 1972.

1674. Boyd, Ernest A. Ireland's Literary Renaissance. New York: John Lane Co., 1916.

1675. _____. Contemporary Drama of Ireland. Boston: Little, Brown & Co., 1917.

1676. Byrne, Dawson. The Story of Ireland's National Theatre: The Abbey Theatre. Dublin and Cork: The Talbot Press, Ltd., 1929.

1677. Coxhead, Elizabeth. J. M. Synge and Lady Gregory. London: Longmans, Green, 1962.

1678. Duggan, George Chester. Stage Irishman: A History of the Irish Play and Stage Characters from the Earliest Times. London and New York: Longmans, 1937.

1679. Ellis-Fermor, Una M. The Irish Dramatic Movement. London: Methuen and Co., Ltd., 1939.

1680. Gregory, Isabella Augusta Persse. Our Irish Theatre. New York: G. Putnam's Sons, 1913.

1681. Howarth, Herbert. Irish Writers, 1880-1940. London: Rockliff, 1958.

1682. Malone, Andrew E. Irish Drama. London: Constable & Co., 1929.

1683. Mikhail, E. H. A Bibliography of Modern Irish Drama, 1899-1970. Seattle: University of Washington Press, 1972.

1684. Monahan, Michael. Nova Hibernia: Irish Poets and Dramatists of Today and Yesterday. New York: M. Kennerly, 1914.

1685. O'Donovan, Michael. A Short History of Irish Literature. New York: Putnam, 1967.

1686. O'Driscoll, Robert, ed. Theatre and Nationalism in Twentieth Century Ireland. Toronto: University of Toronto Press, 1971.

1687. Payne, Ben Iden. A Life in a Wooden O: Memoirs of the Theatre. New Haven: Yale University Press, 1976.

1688. Robinson, Lennox. The Irish Theatre. London: Macmillan & Co., 1939.

1689. Sahal, N. Sixty Years of Realistic Irish Drama. Bombay: Macmillan, 1971.

1690. Salerno, Henry I. English Drama in Transition, 1880-1920. New York: Pegasus Press, 1968.

1691. Setterquist, Jan. Ibsen and the Beginnings of Anglo-Irish Drama. Cambridge: Harvard University Press, 1951.

1692. Skelton, Robin. Irish Renaissance: A Gathering of Essays, Memoirs, Letters and Dramatic Poetry. Dublin: Dolman, 1965.

1693. Weygandt, C. Irish Plays and Playwrights. Boston and New York: Houghton Mifflin Co., 1913.

1694. Wieczorek, Hubert. Irische Lebenshaltung im neuen irischen Drama. Breslau: Priebatsch, 1937.

1695. Williams, Harold. Modern English Writers, 1890-1914. London: Sidgwich and Jackson, 1919.

Theses and Dissertations

1696. Byars, John Arthur. "The Heroic Type in the Irish Legendary Dramas of W. B. Yeats, Lady Gregory, and J. M. Synge 1903-1910." Ph.D. Dissertation. University of North Carolina, 1964.

1697. McGuire, James Brady. "Realism in Irish Drama." Ph.D. Dissertation. Trinity College, Dublin, 1954.

Articles

1698. Ervine, St. John Greer. "The Irish Dramatist and the Irish People." Forum. Vol. 51 (June, 1914), pp. 940-8.

1699. Tennyson, Charles. "Irish Plays and Playwrights." Quarterly Review. Vol. 215 (July, 1911), pp. 219-43.

1700. _____ . "The Rise of the Irish Theatre." Contemporary Review. Vol. 100 (August, 1911), pp. 240-2.

1701. Walbrook, H. M. "Irish Dramatists and their Countrywomen." Fortune. Vol. 99 (November, 1913), pp. 957-62; and Living Age. Vol. 279 (December 27, 1913), pp. 789-93.

ST. JOHN [GREER] ERVINE

(1883-1971)

Selected Full-length Plays:

> Mixed Marriage (1911)
> The Magnanimous Lover (1912)
> Jane Clegg (1913)
> The Critics (1913)
> The Orangemen (1914)
> John Fergusson (1915)

Books

1702. Ervine, St. John. The Theatre in My Time. London: Rich and Cowan, 1933.

1703. Hogan, Robert Goode. After the Irish Renaissance. Minneapolis: University of Minnesota Press, 1967.

Theses and Dissertations

1704. Haile, Virginia A. "The Dramas and Dramatic Criticism of St. John Greer Ervine." Ph.D. Dissertation. University of Indiana, 1949.

1705. Scofield, J. M. "The Dramatic Works of Mr. St. John Ervine." Master's Thesis. University of Wales, 1952.

Articles

1706. Ervine, St. John Greer. "Concerning Heroes." The New Republic. Vol. 23 (June 9, 1920), pp. 47-9.

1707. _____ . "On Learning to Write Plays." Living Age. Vol. 308 (January 1, 1921), pp. 36-9.

1708. Ervine, St. John Greer. "Some Impressions of My
Elders." The North American. Vol. 240 (February-August,
1920), pp. 225-37, 402-10, 669.

1709. _____. "Women and Theatre." Living Age. Vol.
309 (May 7, 1921), pp. 367-9.

1710. "An Irish Dramatist and the Irish People." Forum.
Vol. 51 (June, 1914), pp. 940-8.

1711. McQuilland, L. J. "Appreciation and Criticism of St.
John Ervine." Bookman (London). Vol. 57 (January, 1920),
pp. 145-8.

1712. Morris, L. R. "Ulster Realist." Outlook. Vol. 125
(June 23, 1920), pp. 388-9.

1713. "St. John Ervine and His Work." Living Age. Vol.
305 (April 3, 1920), pp. 45-50.

1714. Sutton, G. "The Critic as Dramatist." Bookman (London). Vol. 65 (February, 1924), pp. 279-81.

1715. "The Versatile Genius of St. John Ervine." Current
Opinion. Vol. 58 (June, 1915), pp. 426-7.

1716. Woodbridge, H. E. "Realism and St. John Greer Ervine."
Sewanee Review. Vol. 33 (April, 1925), pp. 199-209.

1717. "Writer of the Hour in Ireland." Touchstone. Vol. 6
(October, 1919), pp. 42-6.

LADY [ISABELLA] AUGUSTA GREGORY

(1852-1932)

Selected Full-length Plays:

>   A Losing Game (1902)
>   The Twisting of the Rope (1904)
>   Spreading the News (1904)
>   The White Cockade (1905)
>   Kincora (1905)
>   Hyacinth Halvey (1906)
>   The Canavans (1906)
>   Dervorgilla (1907)
>   The Travelling Man (1910)
>   The Dragon (1919)
>   Aristotle's Bellows (1921)

Books

1718. Adams, Hazard. Lady Gregory. Lewisburg, Pennsylvania: Bucknell University Press, 1973.

1719. Chislett, William, Jr. Moderns and Near Moderns. London: Grafton Press, 1928.

1720. Coxhead, Elizabeth. Lady Gregory: A Literary Portrait. London: Macmillan, 1961.

1721. Dedio, Anne. Das dramatische Werk von Lady Gregory. Cooper Monograph No. 13. Bern: Francke, 1967.

1722. Gregory, Isabella Augusta. Lady Gregory's Journals, 1916-1930. London: Putnam and Co., 1946.

1723. _____. Seventy Years: Being the Autobiography of Lady Gregory. Gerrards Cross: Smythe, 1974.

1724. Saddlemeyer, Ann. In Defense of Lady Gregory, Playwright. Dublin: Dolman Press, 1966.

Theses and Dissertations

1725. Merriman, Daise C. "Lady Gregory, A Social Historian." M.A. Thesis. The Ohio State University, 1922.

1726. Murphy, Daniel. "The Letters of Lady Gregory to John Quinn." Ph.D. Dissertation. Columbia University, 1962.

1727. Regan, M. J. "Lady Gregory: The Dramatic Artist." Master's Thesis. National University of Ireland, 1952.

1728. Young, L. D. "The Plays of Lady Gregory." Ph.D. Dissertation. Trinity College, Dublin, 1957.

Articles

1729. Ayling, Ronald. "Charwoman of the Abbey." Shaw Review. Vol. 4, no. 3 (1961), pp. 7-15.

1730. Bowen, Anne. "Lady Gregory's Use of Proverbs in Her Plays." Southern Folklore. Vol. 3, no. 4 (December, 1939), pp. 231-243.

1731. Bregy, K. "Lady Gregory and the Lore of Ireland." Forum. Vol. 48 (October, 1912), pp. 465-72.

1732. Edwards, A. C. "The Lady Gregory Letters to Sean O'Casey." Modern Drama. Vol. 8, no. 1 (May, 1965), pp. 95-111.

1733. Jeffares, A. N. "New Faces: A New Explanation." Review of English Studies. Vol. 23 (October, 1947), pp. 349-53.

1734. "Lady Gregory's Irish Plays." Contemporary Review. Vol. 102 (October, 1912), pp. 602-4.

1735. McHugh, Roger. "Sean O'Casey and Lady Gregory." James Joyce Quarterly. No. 8 (1970), pp. 119-23.

1736. Malone, A. E. "The Plays of Lady Gregory." Yale Review. Vol. 14 (April, 1925), pp. 540-51.

1737. Marcus, Hans. "Unveröffentliche Briefe der Lady Isabella A. Gregory." Archiv. Vol. 167, pp. 216-22.

1738. Mikhail, E. H. "The Theatre of Lady Gregory." Bulletin of Bibliography. Vol. 27 (January-March, 1970), pp. 9-10.

1739. Moore, George. "Sketch." English Review. Vol. 16 (January, 1914), pp. 167-80.

1740. _____. "Yeats, Lady Gregory and Synge." English Review. Vol. 16 (1913-14), pp. 167-180, 350-364.

1741. Murphy, Daniel J. "The Lady Gregory Letters to G. B. Shaw." Modern Drama. Vol. 10, no. 4 (February, 1968), pp. 331-345.

1742. Saddlemeyer, Ann. "Image Maker for Ireland: Lady Augusta Gregory," in Robin Skelton and Ann Saddlemeyer, eds. The World of W. B. Yeats: Essays in Perspective. Dublin: Dolman Press, 1965, pp. 195-202.

1743. Storer, E. "Dramatists of Today." Living Age. Vol. 281 (May 9, 1914), pp. 332-6.

1744. Toksvig, Signe. "A Visit to Lady Gregory." North American Review. Vol. 214 (1921), pp. 190-200.

EDWARD MARTYN

(1859-1923)

Selected Full-length Plays:

> The Heather Field (1895)
> The Bending of the Bough (written
>   with George Moore, 1900)
> Grangecolman (1912)
> The Dream Physician (1914)

Books

1745. Courtney, Marie. Edward Martyn and the Irish Theatre. New York: Vantage Press, 1956.

1746. Ellis-Fermor, Una. The Irish Dramatic Movement. London: Methuen, 1939.

1747. Gwynn, Denis Rolleston. Edward Martyn and the Irish Revival. London: J. Cape, 1930.

1748. Setterquist, Jan. Ibsen and the Beginnings of Anglo-Irish Drama. Cambridge: Harvard University Press, 1951.

Articles

1749. MacDonagh, John. "Edward Martyn." Dublin Magazine. Vol. N.S. 1, no. 6 (January, 1924), pp. 465-7.

1750. McFate, Patricia. "The Bending of the Bough and The Heather Field: Two Portraits of the Artists." Éire-Ireland. Vol. 8, no. 1 (1973), pp. 52-61.

1751. O'Conor, Norreys Jephson. "A Dramatist of Changing Ireland." Sewanee Review. Vol. 30, no. 3 (July, 1922), pp. 277-85.

1752. Saddlemeyer, Ann and Robin Skelton. "All Art Is a Collaboration? George Moore and Edward Martyn," in The World of W. B. Yeats. Seattle: University of Washington Press, 1967, pp. 169-88.

1753. Setterquist, Jan. "Ibsen and Edward Martyn." Edda. Vol. 61 (1961), pp. 97-104.

[ESME STUART] LENNOX ROBINSON

(1886-1958)

Selected Full-length Plays:

>   The Clancy Name (1908)
>   The Cross Roads (1909)
>   Harvest (1910)
>   Patriots (1912)
>   The Dreamers (1915)
>   The White-Headed Boy (1916)
>   The Lost Leader (1918)

Books

1754. O'Neill, Michael J. Lennox Robinson. New York: Twayne Publishers, 1964.

1755. Robinson, Lennox. Curtain Up, an Autobiography. London: M. Joseph, 1942.

1756. _____ . Ireland's Abbey Theatre, a History, 1899-1951. London: Sidgwick and Jackson, 1951.

1757. Robinson, Thomas J. and Nora Robinson Dorman. Three Homes. London: M. Joseph, 1938.

Theses

1758. Peake, Donald James. "Selected Plays of Lennox Robinson: A Mirror of the Anglo-Irish Ascendancy." Ph.D. Dissertation. Southern Illinois University, 1972.

JOHN MILLINGTON [EDMUND] SYNGE

(1871-1909)

Selected Full-length Plays:

In the Shadow of the Glen (1903)
The Tinker's Wedding (1903)
The Well of the Saints (1905)
The Playboy of the Western World (1907)
Deirdre of the Sorrows (1910)

Books

1759. Bickley, Francis Lawrence. J. M. Synge and the Irish Dramatic Movement. Boston and New York: Houghton, 1912.

1760. Bourgeois, Maurice. John Millington Synge and the Irish Theatre. London: Constable and Co., 1913.

1761. Bushrui, Suheil B., ed. Sunshine and the Moon's Delight: A Centenary Tribute to John Millington Synge, 1871-1909. London: Colin Smythe Ltd., 1972.

1762. Chislett, William, Jr. Moderns and Near Moderns. London: Grafton Press, 1928.

1763. Corkery, Daniel. Synge, and Anglo-Irish Literature: A Study. Dublin and Cork: Cork University Press, Educational Co. of Ireland, 1931.

1764. _____. Synge and Anglo-Irish Literature. New York: Longmans, Green and Co., 1931.

1765. Gerstenberger, Donna Loraine. John Millington Synge. New York: Twayne Publishers, 1964.

1766. Grene, Nicholas. Synge: A Critical Study of the Plays. London: Macmillan, 1975.

1767. Howe, Percival Presland. J. M. Synge, a Critical Study. London: Secker, 1912.

1768. Johnston, Denis. John Millington Synge. New York: Columbia University Press, 1965.

1769. Krieger, Hans. J. M. Synge, ein Dichter der keltischen Renaissance. Marburg: N. G. Elwert, 1916.

1770. Levitt, Paul M. J. M. Synge: A Bibliography of Published Criticism. New York: Barnes and Noble, 1974.

1771. Masefield, John. John M. Synge, A Few Personal Recollections with Biographical Notes. New York and London: Macmillan, 1915.

1772. Price, Alan. Synge and Anglo-Irish Drama. London:
Methuen, 1961.

1773. Saddlemyer, Ann. J. M. Synge and Modern Comedy. Dublin: Dolmen Press, 1968.

1774. Strong, L. A. J. John Millington Synge. London:
Allen & Unwin, 1941.

1775. Synge, John Millington. The Autobiography of J. M.
Synge. Dublin: Dolmen Press, 1945.

1776. Tilgher, Adriano. Studi su teàtro contemporàneo.
Rome: Libreria di scienze e lettere, 1928.

1777. Yeats, W. B. Synge and the Ireland of His Time.
Churchtown: The Cuala Press, 1911.

Articles

1778. Allen, B. S. "Synge: A Problem of His Genius." Colonnade. Vol. 2. (January, 1916), pp. 5-15.

1779. Barnett, Pat. "The Nature of Synge's Dialogue." in
Henry Salerno. English Drama in Transition, 1880-1920. New
York: Pegasus Press, 1968, n. pag.

1780. Bennett, C. A. "The Plays of John Millington Synge."
Yale Review. (January, 1912), pp. 192-205.

1781. Blake, Warren Barton. "A Great Irish Playwright: John
M. Synge." Theatre Magazine. Vol. 13 (June, 1911), n. pag.

1782. _____ . "John Synge and His Plays." Dial. Vol.
50 (January 16, 1911), pp. 37-41.

1783. Bourgeois, Maurice. "Synge and Loti." Westminster
Review. Vol. 179 (May, 1913), pp. 532-6.

1784. Casey, Helen. "Synge's Use of the Anglo-Irish Idiom."
English Journal. Vol. 27, no. 9 (November, 1938), pp. 773-6.

1785. Dubois, Paul L. "Le théâtre irlandais: Synge." Revue
des Deux Mondes. Vol. 27 (June 1, 1935), pp. 637-44.

1786. Faulk, C. S. "John Millington Synge and the Rebirth
of Comedy." Southern Humanities Review. Vol. 8 (1974),
pp. 431-48.

1787. Fausset, Hugh I'A. "Synge and Tragedy." Fortnightly.
Vol. 115 (January-June, 1924), pp. 258-73.

1788. Figgis, Darrell. "The Art of J. M. Synge." Fortnightly Review. Vol. 96 (December, 1911), pp. 1056-68.

1789. Gaskell, Ronald. "The Realism of J. M. Synge." Critical Quarterly. Vol. 5 (August, 1963), pp. 242-8.

1790. Greene, David H. "J. M. Synge: A Centenary Appraisal."
Eire. Vol. 6, no. 4 (1971), pp. 71-86.

1791. _____. "An Adequate Text of J. M. Synge." Modern Language Notes. Vol. 61 (November, 1946), pp. 466-7.

1792. Gregory, Augusta I. "Synge." English Review. Vol.
13 (March, 1913), pp. 556-66.

1793. Grigson, G. "Synge." New Statesman. Vol. 64 (October 19, 1962), p. 528.

1794. Hart, William. "Synge and the Christian Ethos."
Studies. Vol. 61 (1972), pp. 85-96.

1795. Helmholtz, Bastien von. "John Synge and the Habits
of Criticism." Egoist. Vol. 1, no. 3 (February 2, 1914),
pp. 53-4.

1796. Henn, T. R. "John Millington Synge: A Reconsideration." Hermathena: A Dublin University Review. Vol. 112
(1971), pp. 5-21.

1797. Leech, Clifford. "John Synge and the Drama of His
Time." Modern Drama. Vol. 16 (December, 1973), pp. 223-37.

1798. Masefield, John. "John M. Synge." Contemporary Review. Vol. 99 (April, 1911), pp. 470-8.

1799. Mercier, Vivian. "Irish Comedy: The Probable and the
Wonderful." University Review (Dublin). Vol. 1, no. 8
(Spring, 1956), pp. 45-53.

1800. Michie, Donald M. "Synge and His Critics." Modern
Drama. Vol. 15 (March, 1973), pp. 427-31.

1801. Mikhail, E. H. "French Influences on Synge." Revue
de Littérature Comparée. Vol. 42 (1968), pp. 429-31.

1802. Moore, George. "Sketch." English Review. Vol. 16
(January, 1914), pp. 167-80.

1803. _____. "Yeats, Lady Gregory and Synge." The
English Review. Vol. 16 (1913-1914), pp. 167-80, 350-64.

1804. Orr, Robert H. "The Surprise Ending: One Aspect of
the Dramatic Technique of J. M. Synge." English Literature
in Translation. Vol. 15 (1972), pp. 105-15.

1805. Pritchell, V. S. "Synge and Joyce." New Statesman
and Nation. Vol. 21 (April 19, 1941), p. 143.

1806. Rajan, Balachandra. "Yeats, Synge and the Tragic
Understanding." Yeats Studies. Vol. 2 (1972), pp. 66-79.

1807. Reynolds, Lorna. "Collective Intellectual: Yeats, Synge and Nietzsche." Essays and Studies by Members of the English Association. Vol. 26 (1973), pp. 83-98.

1808. _____. "The Rhythms of Synge's Dramatic Prose." Yeats Studies. Vol. 2 (1972), n. pag.

1809. Scudder, Vida D. "The Irish Literary Drama." Poet-Lore. Vol. 16 (Spring, 1905), pp. 40-53.

1810. Sherman, Stuart P. "John Synge." Nation. Vol. 95 (December 26, 1912), pp. 608-11.

1811. Storer, E. "Work of Millington Synge." British Review. Vol. 5 (January, 1914), pp. 73-80.

1812. Strong, Lawrence A. "John Millington Synge." Bookman (USA). Vol. 73 (April, 1973), n. pag.

1813. Strong, Leonard A. G. "John Millington Synge." Dublin Magazine. Vol. N. S. 7, no. 2 (April-June, 1932), pp. 12-32.

1814. Sultan, Stanley. "The Gospel According to Synge." Papers on Language and Literature. Vol. 4 (1968), pp. 428-41.

1815. Sutton, G. "J. M. Synge: Critical Sketch." Bookman (London). Vol. 69 (March, 1926), pp. 299-301.

1816. Tupper, J. W. "J. W. Synge and His Work." Dial. Vol. 54 (March 16, 1913), pp. 233-5.

1817. Warner, Alan. "Astringent Joy: The Sanity of Synge." Wascana Review. Vol. 6 (1971), pp. 5-13.

1818. Woods, Anthony S. "Synge Stayed at Home by the Fireside." New Catholic World. Vol. 141 (1935), pp. 46-52.

1819. Yeats, Jack Butler. "Synge and the Irish." Harper's Weekly. Vol. 55 (November 25, 1911), p. 17.

1820. Yeats, William Butler. "The Death of Synge, and Other Pages From an Old Diary." Dial. Vol. 84 (April, 1928), pp. 271-88.

1821. Zydler, Tomasz. "John Millington Synge and the Irish Theatre." Kwartalnik Neofilologiczny. Vol. 18 (1971), pp. 383-96.

Theses and Dissertations

1822. Bigley, B. M. "Perspectivism in Ibsen, Synge and Hofmannstahl." Ph.D. Dissertation. Yale University, 1973.

1823. Clement, K. E. "John Millington Synge." M.A. Thesis. University of Colorado, 1927.

1824. Estill, Adelaide D. "The Sources of Synge." Ph.D. Dissertation. University of Pennsylvania, 1937.

1825. Flood, Jeanne A. "John Millington Synge: A Study of His Aesthetic Development." Ph.D. Dissertation. University of Michigan, 1968.

1826. Greene, David Herbert. "The Drama of J. M. Synge. A Critical Study." Ph.D. Dissertation. Harvard University, 1944.

1827. Howland, Kathleen. "Synge--A Tragic Life Imposes A Tragic Drama." M.A. Thesis. University of Kansas, 1950.

1828. Kilroy, James Francis. "Dominant Themes and Ironic Techniques in the Works of J. M. Synge." Ph.D. Dissertation. University of Wisconsin, 1965.

1829. McKinley, C. F. "John Millington Synge." Ph.D. Dissertation. Trinity College, Dublin, 1950-1951.

1830. Medine, Patricia A. "The Art of John Millington Synge." Ph.D. Dissertation. University of Wisconsin, 1972.

1831. Newlin, Nicholas. "The Language of Synge's Plays: The Irish Element." Ph.D. Dissertation. University of Pennsylvania, 1950.

1832. Price, A. F. "The Art of John Synge." M.A. Thesis. University of London, 1951-1952.

1833. Sponberg, Arvid F. "J. M. Synge: Man of the Theatre." Ph.D. Dissertation. University of Michigan, 1974.

1834. Sullivan, James T. "A Gay Goodnight: A Study of Irish Tragedy." Ph.D. Dissertation. Brandeis University, 1974.

1835. Takacs, Dalma S. "J. M. Synge as a Dramatist." Ph.D. Dissertation. Columbia University, 1972.

VIII ITALY

General Commentaries

Books

In English:

1836. Kennard, Joseph Spencer. The Italian Theatre. Vol. 2
New York: W. E. Rudge, 1922.

1837. MacClintock, Lander. Contemporary Drama of Italy.
Boston: Little, 1920.

1838. McLeod, Addison. Plays and Players in Modern Italy.
Chicago: C. H. Sergel, 1912.

In Italian:

1839. Ancheschi, Luciano. L'Idèa del Teàtro e la Crisi del
Naturalismo. Bologna: Calderini, 1971.

1840. Appollonio, Mario. Stòria del teàtro italiano. Two
Volumes. Florence: G. C. Sansoni, 1943-1951.

1841. Barbiera, Raffaello. Vite ardenti del teàtro, 1700-
1900. Milano: Fratelli Treves, 1931.

1842. Barbina, Alfredo. Teàtro verista siciliano. Bologna:
Cappelli, 1970.

1843. Borghese, Guiseooe Antonio. Tèmpo di edificàre.
Milan: Fratelli Treves, 1923.

1844. _____. La vita e il lìbro. Turin: Bocca, 1910.

1845. Croce, Alda. Il teàtro italiano della secónda metà
dell'Ottocènto. Bari: G. Laterz, 1940.

1846. Croce, Benedetto. La Letteratúra della Nuova Itàlia.
Bari: G. Laterza & figli, 1940.

1847. D'Amico, Sandro and Silvia d'Amico. Il Teàtro Italiano. Milano-Roma: Treves-Trezzani-Tumminelli, 1932.

1848. D'Amico, Sylvia and E. Possenti, eds. Teàtro italiano.
Five Volumes. Milan: Nuova accadèmia editrice, 1955-6.

1849. Gobetti, Piero. Opera critica. Turin: Baretti, 1927.

1850. Levi, Cesare. Autori drammatici italiani. Bologna:
N. Zanichelli, 1922.

1851. Levi, Eugenio. Il còmico di caràttere da Teofrasto a
Pirandello. Turin: G. Einaudi, 1959.

1852. Manganella, Renato. Le opere e gli uomini. Rome:
Roux-Varengo, 1904.

1853. Marzot, Giulio. Battàglia veristiche dell'Ottocènto.
Milan: Principato, 1941.

1854. Petronio, Giuseppe. Dall' illuminismo al Verismo:
Saggi e proposte. Padova: Manfredi, 1962.

1855. Pomilio, Mario. Dal naturalismo al verismo. Naples:
Liberia Liguori, 1963.

1856. Praga, Marco. Oronache teatrali. Milan: Treves,
1919-1929.

1857. Pullini, Giorgio. Teàtro italiano fra due secoli,
1850-1950. Florence: Parenti, 1958.

1858. Simoni, Renato. Trent'anni di cronace drammàtica.
Turin: Società editrice torinses, 1952.

1859. Tonelli, Luigi. L'evoluzione del teàtro contemporàneo
in Itàlia. Palermo, 1913.

1860. _____ . Il teàtro contemporàneo italiano. Milan:
Edizioni Corbaccio, 1936.

1861. _____ . Il teàtro italiano dalle origini ai
giórni nostri. Milan: Modernissima, 1924.

1862. Vergani, Orio. Teàtro milanese. Bologna: Guanda,
1958.

Articles

1863. Ayer, Charles C. "Foreign Drama on the English and
American Stage." Colorado Studies. Vol. 10, no. 3 (1913),
pp. 149-161.

1864. Giacomo, Salvatore. "Una difésa del realism," in
Il Teàtro e le cronache. Catania, 1936, n. pag.

1865. Gregersen, Halfden. "Visiting Italian Interpreters
of Ibsen in Barcelona and Madrid." Hispanic Review. Vol. 3,
no. 2 (1935), pp. 166-9.

1866. Rod, Édouard. "Les veristes italiens," in Études sur
le XIX siècle. Paris: Perrin et cie, 1888, n. pag.

1867. Tonelli, Luigi. "Italian Drama of Today." Drama.
Vol. 17 (March, 1927),p. 81.

CARLO BERTOLAZZI

(1870-1916)

Selected Full-length Plays:

Ave Maria (Hail Mary, 1887)
Mamma Teresa (1888)
I Coniugi Barbaccini (The Barbaccini
    Marriage, 1888)
Trilogia di Gilda (The Trilogy of Gilda,
    1889)
La Lezióne per domani (The Lesson for
    Tomorrow, 1890)
Ona Scèna de la vita (The Theatre of
    Life, 1890)
Preludio (Prelude, 1892)
El Sogn de Milan (The Dream of Milan,
    1894)
Strozzin (Extortion, 1895)
La maschera (The Mask, 1896)
Il Successore (1896)
La Gibigianna (The Reflection, 1898)
L'Egoista (The Egoist, 1900)
L'Amis de tutti (The Friend to All, 1899)
La Casa del sono (The House of Sleep,
    1901)
Lulu (1903)
Il Diàvolo e l'acqua santa (The Devil and
    ·Holy Water, 1904)
Lorenzo e il suo avvocàto (Lorenzo and
    His Lawyer, 1905)
La Sfrontata (The Idle Woman, 1907)
Ombra del cuore (The Shade of the Heart,
    1908)
I Giorni di fèsta (The Feast Days, 1908)
La Principessina (The Young Princess,
    1908)
Il Matrimònio della Lena (Lenna's
    Marriage, 1909)
La Zitrella (The Main, 1915)
I Fratèlli Bandiera (The Bandiera
    Brothers, 1916)

Articles

1868. Ghilardi, Ferdinando. "Carlo Bertolazzi: Il teàtro di Milano," in Studi sulla cultura lombardia. Milan: Publications della Università Cattòlica del Sacro Cuore, 1972, n. pag.

1869. Portinari, Folco. "Realismo e realtà (Per messe per uno studio sul teàtro di Bertolazzi)." L'Appròdo Letteràrio. Vol. 51 (1970), pp. 73-90.

ROBERTO BRACCO

(1861-1943)

Selected Full-length Plays:

> Non fare a altri (Don't Do Unto Others,
>   1886)
> Fracássa (1887)
> Lui, lei, lui (Him, Her, Him, 1887)
> Un'avventúra di viàggio (An Adventurous
>   Voyage, 1888)
> Le Disilluse (The Disenchanted, 1888)
> Una Donna (A Woman, 1892)
> Infedèle (The Unfaithful One, Comtesse
>   Coquette, 1894)
> Il triónfo (The Triumph, 1895)
> Don Pietro Caruso (1895)
> Tragedie dell'animo (The Tragedy of the
>   Soul, 1899)
> Il Dirítto di vivere (The Law of Life,
>   1901)
> Sperduti nel buio (Lost in the Dark, 1901)
> Maternita (Motherhood, 1906)
> La Píccola Fonte (The Little Fountain, 1906)
> Nòtte di Néve (A Snowy Night, Night of
>   Snow, 1906)
> Fantàsmi (Phantasms, 1906)
> Nelina (1908)
> Il Perfètto amore (The Perfect Love, 1910)
> Il Píccolo Santo (The Little Saint, 1912)
> Nemméno un bacio (Not Even a Kiss, 1912)
> L'Amánte Lontàno (The Distant Lover, 1916)
> I Pazzi (The Insane Ones, 1922)

Books

1870. Altomare, Leonida. Il Teàtro di Roberto Bracco nella dramàtica contemporànea: studio critico. Molfetta: Premiato Stabilim grafico, 1913.

1871. Altrocchi, Rudolph and Martha Bloch, eds. Il Píccolo Santo, 1929. New York and London: Century, 1929.

1872. Cristaldi, Raimondo. E fórse verra un giórno, Con-
fidènza di Roberto Bracco. Milan: Airoldi, 1949.

1873. Flora, Francesco. Saggi di poètica moderna. Messina-
Florence: G. d'Anna, 1948.

1874. Galeota, Umberto. Roberto Bracco. Naples: Arti
grafiche Ardenza, 1967.

1875. Parisi, Pasquale. Roberto Bracco: La sua vita, La
sua arte, I suoi critici. Palermo: R. Sandron, 1923.

Theses and Dissertations

1876. Aiello, Gaetano Rudolph. "The Tristezza of Roberto
Bracco." Ph.D. Dissertation. Harvard University, 1932.

Articles

1877. Altrocchi, Rudolph. "Bracco and the Drama of the Subconscious." North American Review. Vol. 224 (March, 1927),
pp. 151-62.

1878. DeCadeval, Rudy. "Roberto Bracco." Alla Bottega.
Vol. 6, no. 2 (1969), pp. 35-40.

1879. Quargnolo, Mario. "La lunga contesa fra bracco e il
fascismo." Osservatore Politico Letterario. Vol. 13, no. 3
(1967), pp. 41-47.

1880. Stauble, Antonio. "Profilo di Roberto Bracco." Nuova
Antologia. Vol. 504 (1968), pp. 98-104.

LUIGI CAPUANA

(1839-1915)

Selected Full-length Plays:

> Giacinta (1888)
> Spèra di sole (The Sphere of the Sun,
>   1893)
> Malía (Enchantment, 1895)
> I Ribelli (The Rebels, 1908)
> Lu Cavalieri Pidagna (Cavaliere Pidagna's
>   Family, 1909)
> Cumpanatico (1911)
> Un Vampiro (A Vampire, 1912)
> Un paranintu (A Matchmaker, 1914)
> La tríste lusínga (The Dull Seduction,
>   1914)
> Don Rammunnu Limoli (1915)
> Quaquarà (The Quaker Woman, 1916)

Books

1881. Capuana, Luigi. Gli ismi contemporànei: Verismo, sim-
bolismo, idealismo, cosmopolitismo ad altri saggi de critica
letterària ed artística. Milan: Fratelli Fabbri, 1973.

1882. DiBlasi, Conrado. Luigi Capuana: Vita, Amicizie,
Relazioni Letterarie. Minea: Bibliotèca Capuana, 1954.

1883. Frattarolo, Renzo. Conclusióni su Leopardi ed altri
studi. Ravenna: Longo, 1968.

1884. Madrignani, Carlo A. Capuana e il naturalismo. Bari:
Laterza, 1970.

1885. Mauro, Walter, ed. Capuana, antología degli scritti
critici. Bologna: Calderini, 1971.

1886. Petrini, Enzo. Luigi Capuana. Florence: Industria
tipografica florentina, 1954.

1887. _____. Bibliografia di Luigi Capuana (1839-
1968). Rome: Ciranna, 1969.

1888. _____. Luigi Capuana: ad usodie Concorsi Magis-
trali. Rome: Ciranna, 1966.

1889. Scalia, Samuel Eugene. Luigi Capuana and His Times.
New York: S. F. Vanni, 1952.

1890. Torraca, Francesco. Saggi e Rassegne. Livorno: Tipi
di F. Vigo, 1885.

1891. Traversa, Vincenzo Paolo. Luigi Capuana, Critic and
Novelist. Paris and the Hague: Mouton, 1968.

1892. Vetro, Pietro. Luigi Capuana: la vita e le òpere.
Catania: Stúdio editoriale Moderno, 1922.

Articles

1893. Caccia, E. "Luigi Capuana." I Minori IV, 1962, n. pag.

1894. Centorbi, Giovanni. "Luigi Capuana spiritista fotò-
grafo e acquafortista." Osservatóre Politico Letterària.
Vol. 13 (November, 1967), pp. 75-83.

1895. Luti, G. Capuana Moderno." Inventàrio VI. Vol. 4.

1896. Norman, H. L. "The Scientific and the Pseudo-Scientific
in the Works of Luigi Capuana." PMLA. Vol. 53 (September,
1938), pp. 869-85.

1897. Tonelli, L. "Il caràttere e l'òpera di Luigi Capuana."
Nuova Antologia. Vol. 259 (May 1, 1928), pp. 5-18.

1898. Trombatore, G. "Capuana e il verísmo." <u>Arena</u>. January-March, 1954), n. pag.

PAOLO FERRARI

(1822-1889)

<u>Selected Full-length Plays</u>:

Goldoni e le sue sedici commedie nuove
    (Goldoni and His Sixteen New Comedies,
    1852)
La Satira e Parini (Satire and Parini,
    1856)
Il Duèllo (The Duel, 1858)
Amore senza stíma (Love Without Value,
    1868
Cause ed effetti (Cause and Effect, 1871)
Ridícolo (Ridicule, 1872)
Amici e rivaldi (Friends and Rivals,
    1874)
Il Suicidio (The Suicide, 1875)
Le Due Dame (Two Ladies, 1877)
Per vendétta (For Vengeance, 1879)
Maria e Mario (1880)
Alberta Pregalli (1880)
Giogetta cieca (Georgette, the Blind
    Woman, 1881)
Giovanni Pico della Mirandola (1882)
Fàlse Famiglie (False Families (1885)
Il Signor Lorenzo (1886)
La Separazióne (The Separation, 1886)
Fulvio Testi (1888)

Books

1899. Bellis, Niccolo de. <u>Il teàtro di Paolo Ferrari</u>.
Rome: Maglione e Strini, 1922.

1900. Castrucci, Clotilde. <u>Il teàtro di Paolo Ferrari</u>.
Città di Castello: S. Lapi, 1898.

1901. D'Amico, Silvia. <u>Dramma: sàcro e profàno</u>. Rome:
Tumminelli, 1942.

1902. Ferrigni, Pietro F. L. Coccoluto. <u>Il teàtro di Paolo
Ferrari</u>. Milan: Carlo Aliprandi, 1922.

1903. Ferrari, Vittorio. <u>Paolo Ferrari, la vita, il teàtro</u>.
Milan: Baldini, Castoldi e Co., 1899.

1904. Fortis, Leone. <u>Paolo Ferrari, Ricòrdi e note</u>. Milan:
Fratelli Treves, 1889.

1905. Lodi, L. Paolo Ferrari, ricerche. Bologna, 1877.

Articles

1906. Apollonio, Carla. "Paolo Ferrari." Letteratúra italiana, I minóri. Vol. 4 (1962), n. pag.

1907. Levi, C. "Paolo Ferrari nel prímo centenàrio della nàscita." Il Marzocco. Vol. 2, no. 4 (1922), n. pag.

1908. _____. "Paolo Ferrari nelle sui pubblicazióni." Nuova Antologia. Vol. 240 (April 1, 1925), pp. 293-7.

1909. Pariset, C. "Da un cartéggio inèdito di Paolo Ferrari." Nuova Antologia. Vol. 263 (February 1, 1929), pp. 318-29.

1910. Valeri, D. "L'efficàcia del teàtro francese nel teàtro di Paolo Ferrari." Revista d'Italia. (February, 1909), p. 81.

PAOLO GIACOMETTI

(1816-1882)

Selected Full-length Plays:

> Il Poèta e la ballerína (The Poet and the
>   Ballerina, 1841)
> Le Metamorfòsi politiche (The Political
>   Metamorphosis, 1849)
> La Mòrte civile (The Civil Death, The
>   Outlaw, 1861)

Books

1911. Costetti, G. La Compagnia reale Sarda e il teàtro Italiàno dal 1821 al 1893. Milan: M. Kantorowicz, 1893.

1912. Soavi, Georgio. Il mio Giacometti. Milan: All'insegna del pesce d'oro, 1966.

Theses and Dissertations

1913. Wilkinson, Gerald Thomas. "The Dramatic Works of Paolo Giacometti." Ph.D. Dissertation. Harvard University, 1928.

Articles

1914. Valori, G. "Paolo Giacometti bersaglière del teàtro Italiàno." Convivio. Vol. 7 (1937), n. pag.

1915. Veo, E. "L'amnistía di Pio e Paolo Giacometti." Nuova Antologia. Vol. 258 (March 1, 1928), pp. 130-2.

GIUSEPPE GIACOSA

(1847-1906)

Selected Full-length Plays:

> Tristi amori (Unhappy Love, 1887)
> I Dirítti dell'ànima (The Rights of the
>   Soul, 1894)
> Come le fòglie (Like Falling Leaves,
>   As the Leaves (1900)
> Il più forte (The Stronger), 1904)

Books

1916. Donelli, P. Giuseppe Giacosa. Milan: Mondadori,
1948.

1917. Momigliano, A. Ultimi studi. Florence: Nuova Italia,
1954.

1918. Nardi, Piero. Vita e tèmpo di Giuseppe Giacosa.
Milan: A Mondadori, 1949.

1919. Rumor, Mariano. Giuseppe Giacosa, saggio. Padova:
Casa editrice dott. A Milani, 1940.

Articles

1920. Pandolfi, Vito. "Il móndo di Giuseppe Giacosa." Il
Dramma. (1956), pp. 239-40.

1921. Smith, S. "Critical Sketch." Drama. No. 10 (May,
1913), pp. 5-31.

1922. Vannucci, Pasquale. "Giuseppe Giacosa con Fogazzaro
e con Pascoli." Brigata. Vol. 14, no. 10 (1970), pp. 1-5.

MARCO PRAGA

(1862-1929)

Selected Full-length Plays:

> Le vérgini (The Virgins, 1889)
> La móglie ideale (The Ideal Wife, 1890)
> L'amico (The Friend, 1893)
> Il Bell'Apollo (Handsome Apollo, 1894)
> L'ondina (The Water Sprite, 1904)
> La Porta chiúsa (The Closed Door, 1913)
> Il divòrzio (The Divorce, 1915)

Books

1923. Praga, Marco. Cronache teatrali. Milan: Treves,
1919-1929.

Articles

1924. D'Ambra, L. "Marco Praga." Nuova Antologia. Vol.
263 (February 16, 1929), pp. 533.

1925. D'Amico, Silva. "Appunti su Marco Praga." Pegaso.
(March, 1929), p. 63-5.

1926. Munaro, G. "Praga e le sue cronache teatràle."
Cremona. January-February, 1960, n. pag.

1927. Rigotti, D. "Si torna a Marco Praga." Fièra Letterària. October 14, 1962), p. 5.

GIOVANNI VERGA

(1840-1922)

Selected Full-length Plays:

> In portinería (In the Porter's Lodge,
>   1884)
> La lúpa (The She-wolf, 1896)
> Dal tuo al mio (From Yours to Mine,
>   1930)
> Rose cadúce (Ephemeral Roses, post-
>   humously published, 1928)

Books

1928. Abete, Giovanna. Indivíduo e società in Giovanni Verga.
Rome: A.B.E.T.E., 1964.

1929. Alexander, Alfred. Giovanni Verga: A Great Writer and
His World. London: Grant and Cutler, 1972.

1930. Asor Rosa, Alberto. Il càso Verga. Pulmermo: Palumbo,
1972.

1931. Barsotti, Anna. Verga drammatúrgo: Fra commèdia
borghése e teàtro verista siciliano. Florence: Nuova Itàlia,
1974.

1932. Bergin, Thomas G. Giovanni Verga. Westport, Connecticut: Greenwood, 1969.

1933. Bohm, Dorothee. Zeitlosigkeit und entgleitende Zeit
als Konstitutive Dialektik im Werke von Giovanni Verga. Münster: Aschendorffsche Verlagsbuchhandlung, 1967.

1934. Capuana, Luigi. Verga e D'Annunzio. A cúra di Mario
Pomilio. Bologna: Cappelli, 1972.

1935. Cecchetti, Giovanni. Il Verga maggiore. Florence:
Nuova Itàlia, 1968.

1936. Debenedetti, Giacomo. Verga e il naturalismo. Milan:
Garzant, 1976.

1937. Di Zenzo, Floro. Verismo e non di Giovanni Verga.
Naples: Glaux, 1967.

1938. Esposito, Vittoriano. Saggi polèmici. Aveggzno:
Eirene, 1971.

1939. Ferrante, Luigi. Verga: La vita, il pensièro, i tèsti
esemplàri. Milan: Accademia, 1972.

1940. Ferrone, Siro. Il teàtro del Verga. Rome: Bulzoni,
1972.

1941. Giachery, Emerico. Verga e D'Annuncio. Milan: Silva,
1967.

1942. Mazzone, Alfredo. Polèmiche verghiane. Catania:
Edigraf, 1971.

1943. Niccolai, Giovanni. Giovanni Verga: I romànzi a stàmpa
del período catanese. Florence: Edizióni della comunità di
laboro, 1970.

1944. Principato, Marco. Malavòglia di Giovanni Verga.
Palermo: Palumbo, 1971.

1945. Raya, Gino. La Lingua del Verga. Florence: Le Monnier,
1969.

1946. _____. Bibliografia Verghiana, 1840-1971. Roma:
Ciranna, 1972.

1947. Reppucci, Gabriele. Questionàrio su Verga e Pirandello e pàgine di crítica. Florence: Sandron, 1970.

1948. Russo, Luigi. Giovanni Verga. Naples: Ricciardi,
1920.

1949. Viti, Gorizio. Verga Verista. Florence: Le Monnier,
1961.

1950. Vono, Fausto. Giovanni Verga. Milan: Le Stelle,
1969.

Theses and Dissertations

1951. Iannace, Gaetano Antonio. "Sofferènza e Progrèsso nel personaggi di Giovanni Verga." Ph.D. Dissertation. New York University, 1964.

Articles

1952. Cambon, G. "Verga's Mature Style." Comparative Literature. Vol. 14 (Spring, 1962), pp. 143-52.

1953. Cecchitti, G. "Verga and D. H. Lawrence's Translations." Comparative Literature. Vol. 9 (Fall, 1957), pp. 333-44.

1954. Chandler, S. Bernard. "The Primitive World of Giovanni Verga." Mosaic. Vol. 5 (1972), pp. 117-28.

1955. Hartley, K. H. "Giovanni Verga and Zola." Journal of the Australian Universities Language and Literature Association. May, 1962, pp. 7-76.

1956. Klein, J. W. "Pietro Mascagni and Giovanni Verga." Music and Letters. Vol. 44 (October, 1963), pp. 350-7.

1957. Madrignani, Carlo A. "La nuòva crítica marxísta su Verga." Belfagor. Vol. 25 (1970), pp. 80-87.

1958. Masiello, Vitilio. "La lingua del Verga tra mimesi dialettàle e realismo crítico." Dimensióni. Vol. 15 (1970). pp. 51-68.

1959. Trombatore, Gaetano. "Arte sociàle in Giovanni Verga." Rinàscita. Vol. IV, no. 3 (1947), n. pag.

IX NORWAY AND SWEDEN

General Commentaries

Books

1960. Beyer, Harald. A History of Norwegian Literature.
New York: New York University Press for the American-Scandinavian Foundation, 1956.

1961. Blankner, Frederika, ed. A History of Scandinavian Literature. New York: Dial Press, 1938.

1962. Boyesen, H. H. Essays on Scandinavian Literature.
New York: C. Scribners Sons, 1895.

1963. Brandes, Georg M. Henrik Ibsen, Bjørnstjerne Bjørnson. London: W. Heinemann, 1899.

1964. Elster, Kristian. Fra Tid til Anden. Oslo: H. Aschehoug, 1920.

1965. Gabrieli, Mario. Storia delle letterature Scandinavia.
Milan: Nuova accademia, 1958.

1966. Heiberg, Gunnar E. R. Franske visitter. Kristiania:
H. Aschehoug, 1919.

1967. _____. Ibsen og Bjørnson paa scenen. Kristiania:
H. Aschehoug & Co., 1918.

1968. _____. Norsk Teater. Kristiania: Aschehoug,
1920.

1969. Jorgenson, Jorgen T. History of Norwegian Literature.
New York: Macmillan, 1933.

1970. Lanquist, John. Essayer: ny samling. Stockholm: A. Bonnier, 1913.

1971. Lucas, Frank Laurence. The Drama of Ibsen and Strindberg. New York: Macmillan, 1962.

1972. McFarlane, James W. Ibsen and the Temper of Norwegian Literature. London and New York: Oxford University Press, 1960.

1973. Rønneberg, Anton J. Nationaltheatret gjennom femti år. Oslo: Gydendal, 1949.

Articles

1974. Kielland, E. "New Aspects of Norwegian Literature." American Scandinavian Review. Vol. 45 (June, 1957), p. 150.

1975. Marker, Lise-Lone and Frederick J. "William Bloch and Naturalism in the Scandinavian Theatre." Theatre Survey. Vol. 15, no. 2 (1974), pp. 85-104.

BJØRNSTJERNE [MARTINIUS] BJØRNSON

(1832-1910)

Selected Full-length Plays:

       De Nygifte (The Newly-Married, 1865)
       Redaktoren (The Editor, 1874)
       Ein Fallit (The Bankrupt, 1875)
       Kongen (The King, 1877)
       Det Ny System (The New System, 1879)
       Leonarda (1879)
       En Handske (The Gauntlet, 1883)
       Over Aevne I (Beyond Human Power, Beyond
          Our Power I, 1883)
       Geografi og Koerlighed (Love and Geog-
          raphy, 1885)
       Over Aevne II (Beyond Human Power II,
          1895)
       Paul Lange og Tora Parsberg (1898)
       Laboremus (1901)
       Paa Storhove (At Storhove, 1902)
       Daglannet (Dag's Farm, 1905)
       Naar den ny Vin blomstrer (When the New
          Wine Blooms, When the Young Vine
          Blooms, 1909)

Books

1976. Brandes, George. Ibsen. Bjørnson. The Macmillan Co., New York and London: 1899.

1977. Bull, Francis. Bjørnstjerne Bjørnson. Oslo: H.
Aschehoug, 1923.

1978. Gran, Gerhard von der Lippe. Bjørnstjerne Bjørnson.
Copenhagen: Schonbergske forlag, 1916.

1979. Heiberg, Gunnar E. R. Ibsen og Bjørnson paa scenen.
Kristiania: H. Aschehoug, 1918.

1980. Larson, Harold. Bjørnstjerne Bjørnson: A Study in
Norwegian Nationalism. New York: King's Crown Press, 1944.

1981. Michl, Jozef B. Bjornstjerne Bjornson. Bratislava:
Ob zor, 1970.

1982. Møller, Herluf. Fem År: Studier i Bjørnsons Ungdoms-
digtning. Copenhagen: Gyldendal, 1968.

1983. Noreng, Harald. Bjørnsons skuespill på svensk scene.
Oslo: Gyldendal, 1967.

1984. Payne, William Morton. Bjornstjerne Bjornson, 1832-
1910. Chicago: McClurg, 1910.

Theses and Dissertations

1985. Paulson, Arthur C. "The Norwegian-American Reaction
to Ibsen and Bjørnson." Ph.D. Dissertation. University of
Iowa, 1933.

Articles

1986. Aas, "1832: Bjørnstjerne Bjørnson." Bookman, Vol. 83
(December, 1932), pp. 165-9.

1987. Anker, Ella "Bjornson and His Christianity." Contemporary Review. Vol. 98 (November, 1910), pp. 621-8.

1988. Archer, William. "Bjørnson: Novelist, Dramatist,
Lyrist and Politician." Athenaeum. Vol. 1 (April 3, 1910),
pp. 522-3, and Living Age. Vol. 265 (May 28, 1910), pp.
550-4.

1989. Boyesen, H. H. "Conversations with Bjørnson." Cosmopolitan. Vol. 15 (1893), pp. 413.

1990. _____. "The Dramas of Bjørnson." North American
Review. Vol. 116 (1873), p. 109.

1991. Buchanan, R. "Bjørnstjerne Bjørnson." Contemporary
Review. Vol. 21 (1873), p. 45.

1992. Bull, F. "Le Premier Séjour à Rome d'Ibsen et de
Bjørnson." Revue de Littéraire Comparée. Vol. 9 (January,
1929), pp. 105-16.

1993. Collin, C. "B. Bjørnson." Review of Reviews. New
York: Vol. 6 (1893), pp. 411.

1994. Downs, Brian W.. "Bjornson and Tragedy." Scandinavia.
Vol. 1 (1962), pp. 17-28.

1995. Drougard, E. "Villiers de l'Isle-Adam et Bjørnstjerne
Bjørnson." Revue Littérature Comparée. Vol. 17 (October,
1937), pp. 750-4.

1996. Forster, G. B. "The Message of Bjørnson." Open
Court. Vol. 38 (June, 1924), pp. 321-31.

1997. Koht, H. "Bjørnstjerne Bjornson." American Scandinavian Review. Vol. 20 (December, 1932), pp. 551-64.

1998. Larsen, H. A. "Norway's Beating Heart: Bjørnson, the
Guardian of his Country." Craftsman. Vol. 9 (January, 1911),
pp. 362-71.

1999. Leach, H. G. "Bjørnson the Prophet." American Scandinavian Review. Vol. 21 (January, 1933), pp. 26-8.

2000. Lescoffier, J. "Bjørnson à la Recherche de la France."
Revue de Littérature Comparée. Vol. 12 (October, 1932), pp.
801-20.

2001. _____. "Pour lire Bjørnson." Mercure de France.
Vol. 240 (December 1, 1932), pp. 355-68.

2002. Livingston, S. "B. Bjørnson." Canadian Magazine.
Vol. 1 (1893), p. 93.

2003. Lunde, Johannes. "Økonomisk krise og moralsk drama:
'En Fallit' i lys av Bjørnson inntrykk fra den okonomiske
krisen i Bergen, 1857-59." Edda. Vol. 54 (1967), p. 90.

2004. Machray, R. "Sketch of Bjørstjerne Bjørnson." Fortnightly Review. Vol. 95 (March, 1911), pp. 519-33.

2005. _____. "The Literary Work of Bjornson." Fortnightly Review. Vol. 95 (March, 1911), pp. 519-33.

2006. Maury, L. "Bjornson: à propos d'une thèse récente."
Revue Politique et Littéraire. Vol. 71 (March 4, 1933).
pp. 149-52.

2007. Nansen, P. "Last Meeting with Bjørnson." Fortnightly
Vol. 93 (June, 1910), pp. 1161-4.

2008. Nordav, M. "Bjornson's Paris Days." Bookman (N.Y.).
Vol. 32 (September, 1910), pp. 63-7.

2009. Noreng, Harald. "Bjørnstjerne Bjørnson på svenske
scener." Lund: Vetenskaps-societeten, 1966, pp. 97-103.

2010. Ofstad, Erna. "Gjensyn med Bjørnson-myten." Samtiden. Vol. 77 (1968), pp. 67-78.

2011. Orbeck, A. "Bjørn Bjørnson and the Norwegian Stage." American Scandinavian Review. Vol. 12 (June, 1924), pp. 340-5.

2012. Payne, W. M. "Bjørnstjerne Bjørnson as Dramatist." Drama. No. 3 (August, 1911), pp. 3-15.

2013. Pineau, L. "Bjørnstjerne Bjørnson." Journal des Débats. Vol. 40, Part 2 (September 8, 1933), pp. 391-3.

2014. _____. "Bjørnstjerne-Bjørnson d'après la correspondance d'Ibsen." Journal des Débats. Vol. 32, Part 2 (October 9, 1925), pp. 597-9.

2015. Schofield, William Henry. "Personal Impressions of Bjørnson and Ibsen." Atlantic Monthly. Vol. 81 (April, 1898), pp. 567-75.

2016. Stahl, Bernard. "Bjørnson and His Plays." Theatre Magazine. Vol. 11 (April, 1910), p. 112.

2017. _____. "Bjornson and His Women Types." Independent. Vol. 68 (May 5, 1910), pp. 967-71.

2018. Stampenbourg, Baron de. "Bjørnson in Norwegian Politics." Independent. Vol. 53 (January 31, 1901), pp. 255-7.

2019. Stanton, T. "Souvenirs of Bjørnson." Independent. Vol. 56 (January 14, 1904), pp. 73-5.

2020. Sturtevant, Albert M. "Possible Traces of Ibsen's Influence on Bjørnson." Scandinavian Studies. Vol. 20 (1948), pp. 92-5.

2021. Tweedie, Mrs. Alec. "Bjørnson and Ibsen." Temple Bar. Vol. 98 (1893), pp. 536.

2022. Wilcox, L. C. "Bjørnstjerne Bjørnson." North American Review. Vol. 192 (July, 1910), pp. 44-55.

KNUT HAMSUN

(1859-1952)

Selected Full-length Plays:

> Vet rigets port (At the Gates of the
>   Kingdom, 1895)
> Livets spil (Game of Life, 1896)
> Aftenrøde (Red of Evening, 1898)
> Munken Vendt (Vendt the Monk, 1902)
> Droning Tamara (Tamara the Queen,
>   1903)
> Livet i vold (In the Grip of Life,
>   1910)

Books

2023. Beyer, Edvard. Hamsun og vi. Oslo: Aschehoug, 1959.

2024. Bull, Francis, ed. Knut Hamsun: festskrift til 70 aarsdagen. Oslo: Gyldendal, 1929.

2025. _____ . Knut Hamsun paa ny. Oslo: Norske studentersamfund, 1953.

2026. Hamsun, Marie A. Under grullregen. Oslo: Aschehoug, 1959.

2027. Hamsun, Tore. Knut Hamsun, min far. Oslo: Gyldendal, 1952.

2028. _____ . Knut Hamsun, mein Vater. Leipzig: P. List, 1940.

2029. Kristensen, Sven, ed. Fremmede digtere i det 20 århundrede. Copenhagen: Gad, 1967.

2030. Landquist, John. Knut Hamsun. Copenhagen: Gyldendal, 1917.

2031. _____ . Knut Hamsun, sein Leben und sein Werk. Tübingen: A. Fischer, 1927.

2032. Nag, Harald S. Hamsun i russisk åndsliv. Oslo: Gyldendal, 1969.

2033. Nybø, Gregory. Knut Hamsuns Mysterier. Oslo: Gyldendal, 1969.

2034. Ostby, Arvid. Knut Hamsun: En bibliografi. Oslo: Gyldendal, 1972.

2035. Schepens, Piet. Knut Hamsun. Bruges: Desclée DeBrouwer, 1965.

Articles

2036. Anderson, Arlow W. "Knut Hamsun's America." Nor-wegian-American Studies. Vol. 23 (1967), pp. 175-203.

2037. Beyer, Edvard. "Knut Hamsun," in Sven M. Kristensen, ed. Fremmede digtere i det 20 århundrede. Vol. 1. Copenhagen: G. F. C. Gad, 1967, pp. 29-49.

2038. Beyer, Harald. "Ein Dichter un sein Volk--Knut Hamsun und Norwegen," in Heinrich Jessen, ed. Zur Kultur des Nordens. Lubeck: Deutsche Auslandsgesellschaft, 1969, p. 235.

2039. Dale, Johannes A. and Hallvard Lie. "Olof Øyslebø: Hamsun gjennom stilen." Edda. Vol. 54 (1965), pp. 145-93.

2040. Fechter, P. "Knut Hamsun." Deutsche Rundschau. Vol. 220 (August, 1929), pp. 150-4.

2041. _____. "Knut Hamsun, zum 80. Geburtstag." Deutsche Rundschau. Vol. 260 (August, 1939), pp. 113-17.

2042. Friese, Wilhelm. "Hamsun und der Jugendstil," in Vaxelverkan mellan skønlitteraturen och andra konstarter: Sixth International Study Conference on Scandinavian Literature. Vol. 12. Uppsala: Student Service, 1966, pp. 91-100.

2043. Gustafson, A. "Hamsun's Growth of the Soil." American-Scandinavian Review. Vol. 27 (September, 1939), pp. 198-214.

2044. Haakonsen, Daniel. "Fins det en moral i Ibsens skuespill?" in Gustav Albeck, ed. Festskrift til Jens Kruuse den 6 April 1968. Aarhus: Universitets-forlaget, p. 179.

2045. Lesser, J. "Knut Hamsun." Life and Letters Today. Vol. 22 (August, 1939), pp. 160-6.

2046. Marken, Amy van. "Hamsun och sekelskiftets Kvinnog-estaltning," in Vaxelverkan mellan skønlitteraturen och andra konstarter: Sixth International Study Conference on Scandinavian Literature. Vol. 12. Uppsala: Student Service, 1966, pp. 75-90.

2047. Markey, T. L. "Själfstaett Folk, Hamsun, and Rousseau." Edda. Vol. 54 (1967), pp. 346-55.

2048. Naess, Harald. "Knut Hamsun and America." Scandinavian Studies. Vol. 39 (1967), pp. 305-28.

2049. Nag, Martin. "Hamsun i Finnegans Wake." Edda. Vol. 54 (1967), pp. 356-60.

2050. Shurkamp, P. "Knut Hamsun: Geschichte eines Mannes und eines Dichters." Neue Rundschau. Vol. 45, Part 2 (September, 1934), pp. 329-36.

2051. Waal, Carla. "The Plays of Knut Hamsun." <u>Quarterly</u>
<u>Journal of Speech</u>. Vol. 57 (1971), pp. 75-82.

2052. Worster, W. W. "The Works of Knut Hamsun." <u>Fort-</u>
<u>nightly Review</u>. Vol. 108 (December, 1920), pp. 1003-13.

HENRIK [JOHAN] IBSEN

(1828-1906)

<u>Selected Full-length Plays</u>:

> De Unges Forbund (The League of Youth,
>   1869)
> Kjoerlighedens Komedie (Love's Comedy,
>   1873)
> Keyser og Galilaeer (The Emperor and
>   the Galilean, 1873)
> Peer Gynt (1876)
> Samfundets Støtter (The Pillars of
>   Society, 1877)
> Et Dukkehjem (A Doll's House, Nora,
>   1879)
> Gjengangere (Ghosts, 1881)
> Ein Folkefiende (An Enemy of the People,
>   1882)
> Vidanden (The Wild Duck, 1884)
> Brand (1885)
> Rosmersholm (1886)
> Fruen fra Havet (The Lady from the
>   Sea, 1888)
> Hedda Gabler (1890)
> Bygmester Solness (The Master Builder,
>   1893)
> Lille Eyoff (Little Eyoff, 1895)
> John Gabriel Borkman (1897)
> Naar vi Doede vaagner (When We Dead
>   Awaken, 1899)

Books

<u>In English</u>:

2053. Anstensen, Ansten. <u>The Proberb in Ibsen: Proverbial</u>
<u>Sayings and Citations as Elements in his Style</u>. New York:
Columbia University Press, 1936.

2054. Bentley, Eric. <u>The Theatre of Commitment</u>. New York:
Columbia University Press, 1936.

2055. Bradbrook, Muriel Clara. <u>Ibsen, the Norwegian: A</u>
<u>Revaluation</u>. London: Chatto and Windus, 1946.

2056. Brandes, Georg. <u>Henrick Ibsen: A Critical Study</u>.
London: Macmillan, 1899.

2057. Bull, Francis. Ibsen, The Man and the Dramatist.
Oxford: Clarendon Press, 1954.

2058. Colby, Frank Moore. Constrained Attitudes. New York:
Dodd, Mead, 1910.

2059. Downs, Brian Westerdale. Ibsen: The Critical Back-
grounds. Cambridge: Cambridge University Press, 1946.

2060. _____. Ibsen: The Intellectual Background. London: Cambridge University Press, 1946.

2061. _____. A Study of Six Plays by Ibsen. Cambridge:
Cambridge University Press, 1950.

2062. Egan, Michael. Ibsen: The Critical Heritage. London:
Routledge and K. Paul, 1972.

2063. Eikland, Peter J. Ibsen Studies. Northfield, Minnesota: St. Olaf College Press, 1934.

2064. Eller, William Henri. Ibsen in German, 1870-1900.
Boston: R. G. Badger, 1918.

2065. Ellis, Henry Havelock. New Spirit. Washington, D.C.:
National Home Library Foundation, 1935.

2066. Firkins, Ina Ten Ayck. Henrik Ibsen: A Bibliography
of Criticism and Biography. New York: W. H. Wilson Company,
1921.

2067. Fjelde, Rolf, ed. Ibsen: A Collection of Critical
Essays. Englewood Cliffs, New Jersey: Prentice Hall, 1965.

2068. Flores, Angel. Henrik Ibsen: A Marxist Analysis.
New York: Critics Group, 1937.

2069. Franc, Miriam Alice. Ibsen in England. Folcroft,
Pa.: Folcroft Press, 1970.

2070. Gosse, Edmund. Henrik Ibsen. New York: C. Scribner's
Sons, 1910.

2071. _____. Northern Studies. New York: A Lovell,
1890.

2072. Gregersen, Halfdan A. I. Ibsen and Spain, a Study in
Comparative Drama. Cambridge: Harvard University Press,
1936.

2073. Grumman, Paul Henry. Henrik Ibsen: An Introduction
to His Life and Works. New York: University Publishers,
1928.

2074. Heiberg, Hans. Ibsen. London: George Allen and
Unwin, 1969.

2075. Heiberg, Hans. Ibsen: A Portrait of the Artist.
Coral Gables: University of Miami Press, 1969.

2076. Heller, Otto. Henrick Ibsen: Plays and Problems. New
York: Houghton Mifflin, 1912.

2077. Henderson, Archibald. Interpreters of Life and the
Modern Spirit. New York and London: M. Kennerley, 1911.

2078. Holtan, Orley I. Mythic Patterns in Ibsen's Last
Plays. Minneapolis: University of Minnesota, University
Press, 1970-1971.

2079. Ibsen, Henrik. The Correspondence of Henrik Ibsen.
New York: Hasdell House, 1970.

2080. _____. Letters and Speeches. New York: Hill and
Wang, 1964.

2081. _____. Speeches and New Letters. Boston: Badger, 1910.

2082. Jaeger, Henrik Bernhard. Henrik Ibsen, A Critical
Biography. Chicago: McClurg, 1901.

2083. Johnston, Brian. The Ibsen Cycle. New York: Twayne
Publishers, 1974.

2084. Jorgenson, Jorgen Theodore. Henrik Ibsen: A Study in
Art and Personality. Northfield, Minnesota: St. Olaf College, 1945.

2085. Key, Ellen Karolina Sofia. The Torpedo under the Ark:
Ibsen and Women. Chicago: Ralph Fletcher Seymour Co., 1912.

2086. Kildal, Arne. Speeches and New Letters by Henrik
Ibsen. Boston: R. G. Badger, 1910.

2087. Koht, Halvdan. Life of Ibsen. New York: Norton,
1931.

2088. Knight, G. Wilson. Henrik Ibsen. New York: Grove
Press, 1962.

2089. Lavrin, Janko. Ibsen: An Approach. New York: Russell
& Russell, 1968.

2090. Lockwood, Edith. Ibsen: Poet, Philosopher, and
Psychologist. A Revaluation of His Life Work. Bristol: West-
bury-on-Trym, 1948.

2091. Lucas, Frank Laurence. The Drama of Ibsen and Strindberg. New York: Macmillan, 1962.

2092. Lyons, Charles R. Henrik Ibsen: The Divided Consciousness. Carbondale: University of Southern Illinois Press,
1971.

2093. Macfall, Chambers Haldane Cooke. Ibsen, the Man, His Art and His Significance. New York: M. Shepard Co., 1907.

2094. McFarlane, James W. Discussions of Henrik Ibsen. Boston: Heuty, 1962.

2095. _____, ed. Henrik Ibsen: A Critical Anthology. New York: Penguin, 1970.

2096. _____, ed. The Oxford Ibsen. Oxford University Press, 1966.

2097. _____. Ibsen and the Temper of Norwegian Literature. London: Oxford University Press, 1960.

2098. Meyer, Hans Georg. Henrik Ibsen. New York: Ungar, 1972.

2099. Meyer, Michael L. Henrik Ibsen. Oslo: Gyldendal, 1970-1971.

2100. _____. Ibsen: A Biography. Garden City, New York: Doubleday, 1970-1961.

2101. _____. Henrik Ibsen: The Making of a Dramatist, 1828-1964. London: Hart-Davis, 1967.

2102. Moses, Montrose. Henrik Ibsen: The Man and His Plays. Boston: Little Brown, 1920.

2103. Muir, Kenneth. Last Periods of Shakespeare, Racine, Ibsen. Detroit: Wayne State University Press, 1961.

2104. Northam, John R. Ibsen: A Critical Study. London: Cambridge University Press, 1973.

2105. _____. Ibsen's Dramatic Method: A Study of the Prose Dramas. London: Faber & Faber, 1953.

2106. Roberts, Richard Ellis. Henrik Ibsen: A Critical Study. London: Secker, 1912.

2107. Rose, Henry. Henrik Ibsen: Poet, Mystic and Moralist. New York: Baskell House, 1973.

2108. Russell, Edward R. and Percy Cross Standing. Ibsen on His Merits. New York: Haskell House, 1971.

2109. Shaw, George Bernard. The Quintessence of Ibsenism. London: Constable, 1913.

2110. Sprinchorn, Evert, ed. Ibsen: Letters and Speeches. New York: Hill and Wang, 1964.

2111. Tedford, Ingrid. Ibsen Bibliography, 1928-1957. Oslo: Oslo University Press, 1961.

2112. Tennant, Peter F. Ibsen's Dramatic Technique. Cambridge: Cambridge University Press, 1948.

2113. Tysdahl, Bjøorn J. Joyce and Ibsen: A Study in Literary Influence. New York: Humanities Press, 1968.

2114. Watson, William. Excursions in Criticisms. London:
Mathews and Lane, 1893.

2115. Weigand, Hermann. The Modern Ibsen: A Reconsideration. New York: Henry Holt, 1925.

2116. West, Edward Joseph. Shaw's Criticism of Ibsen: A
Reconsideration. Colorado: Colorado University Series in
Language and Literature, 1953.

2117. Zucker, Adolph E. Ibsen, the Master Builder. New
York: Octagon Books, 1973.

In German:

2118. Bahr, Hermann. Zur Überwindung des Naturalismus.
Stuttgart: Kohlhammer, 1968.

2119. Bien, Horst. Henrik Ibsens Realismus: Zur Genesis
und Methode des klassichen kritisch-realistischen Dramas.
Berlin: Rutten and Loening, 1970.

2120. George, David E. Henrik Ibsen in Deutschland: Rezept
und Revision. Göttingen: Vandenhoeck Ruprecht, 1968.

2121. Gran, Gerhard von des Lippe. Henrik Ibsen, der Mann
und sein Werk. Leipzig: F. A. Brockhaus, 1928.

2122. Jacobs, Montague. Ibsens Bühnentecknik. Dresden:
Sibullenverlag, 1920.

2123. Landsberg, Hans. Ibsen. Berlin: Gose und Tetzlaff,
1904.

2124. Lothar, Rudolph. Henrik Ibsen. Berlin: Verlag von
E. A. Seemann, 1902.

2125. Woener, Roman. Henrik Ibsen. Munich: C. H. Beck'sche
Verlagsbuchhandlung, 1900.

In Norwegian:

2126. Blanc, Tharald H. Henrick Ibsen og Kristiania Theater,
1850-1899. Oslo: J. Dybwad, 1906.

2127. Bull, Francis, Halvdan Koht and Didrik Arup Seip.
Ibsens drama: Innledning til Hundreårsutgaven av Henrik Ibsens Samlede verker. Oslo: Gyldendal, 1972.

2128. Dahl, Willy. Ibsen. Oslo: Aschehoug, 1974.

2129. Duve, Arne. Ibsen-bak Kulissene. Oslo: Gyldendal,
1970-1971.

2130. Ebbell, Clara T. I ungdomsbyen med Henrik Ibsen.
Grimstad: Ibsenhuset og Grimstad Bymusuem, 1966.

2131. Gran, Gerhard von der Lippe. Henrik Ibsen: festskrift
i anledning af 70de fødselsdag. Bergen: J. Grieg, 1898.

2132. _____ . Henrik Ibsen. Liv og Vaerker. Kristiania:
H. Aschehoug, 1918.

2133. _____ . Ibsen og Bjørnson. Kristiania: Malling,
1915.

2134. Heiberg, Gunnar E. R. Ibsen og Bjørnson paa scenen.
Kristiania: H. Aschehoug, 1918.

2135. Lindvig, Anne-Marie. Ibsen-årbok: Bibliografi, 1952-
1971. Porsgrunn bibliotek, 1972.

2136. Nag, Martin. Ibsen i russisk åndsliv. Oslo: Gyldendal, 1967.

2137. Noreng, Harald, ed. Ibsen pa Festpillscenen. Bergen:
Eide, 1968.

2138. Ostvedt, Einar. Henrik Ibsen, barndom og ungdom.
Skien: Rasmussen, 1973.

2139. _____ . Henrik Ibsen: Miljø og mennesker. Oslo:
Gyldendal, 1968.

2140. _____ . Henrik Ibsen og haus barndomsmiljø.
Skien: Ibsenforbundet, 1966.

2141. _____ . Henrik Ibsen som student og blant studen-
ter. Skien: Ibsenforbundet, 1971.

2142. _____ . Med Henrik Ibsen i fjellheimen. Henrik
Ibsens egne tegninger og malerier. Skien: Rasmussen, 1967.

2143. Tedford, Ingrid. Ibsen bibliography, 1928-1957.
Oslo: Norsk Bibliografisk bibliotek, 1961.

All Other Languages:

2144. Bull, Francis. Henrik Ibsen et Georg Brandes. Copenhagen: Gyldendal, 1939.

2145. Como, Julio Alfredo. Cuatro puntales del teatro
moderno. Buenos Aires: Tinglado, 1948.

2146. Croce, Benedetto. Poesía e non poesía. Bari: G.
Laterza, 1923.

2147. D'Amico, Silvio. Ibsen. Milan: Treves, 1928.

2148. Doumic, Rene. De Scribe à Ibsen: causeries sur le théâtre contemporain. Paris: Perrin et Cie, 1913.

2149. Farinelli, Arturo. La tragèdia di Ibsen. Bologna: N. Zanichelli, 1923.

2150. Hansen, Joseph. Henrik Ibsen. La satire sociale dans son théâtre. Luxemburg: Th. Schroell, 1904.

2151. Jacobbi, Ruggero. Ibsen: La vita, il pensièro, i testi esemplàri. Milan: Accadèmia, 1972.

2152. Michalik, Jan. Twórszość Ibsena w sadach krytyki polskiej, 1875-1906. Wroclaw: Ossolineum, 1971.

2153. Proost, Karel Frederik. Ibsen Essays. Zeist: J. Ploegsma, 1919.

2154. Sajko, Rosanda. Henrik Ibsen in Proe Drame Livan Cankarja. Ljobljana: Mestno gledalisce, 1966.

2155. Suarès, André. Trois Hommes: Pascal, Ibsen, Dostoievsky. Paris: Gallimard, 1935.

2156. Torslow, Stig, ed. Ibsens brevvaxling med Dramatiska teatern. Stockholm: Dramatiska teatern, 1973.

Theses and Dissertations

2157. Amble, Kjell. "The Spirit of Ibsen, Problems of English Translation in Three of His Plays." Ph.D. Dissertation. Northwestern University, 1964.

2158. Anderson, Annette. "Ibsen in America." Ph.D. Dissertation. University of Iowa, 1931.

2159. Anstensen, Ansten. "The Proverb in Ibsen: Proverbial Sayings and Citations as Elements in His Style." Ph.D. Dissertation. Columbia University, 1936.

2160. Bigley, B. M. "Perspectivism in Ibsen, Synge and Hofmannsthal." Ph.D. Dissertation. Yale University, 1973.

2161. Bolz, Klaus-Dieter. "Die Bühnengestalten Henrik Ibsens im Licht der Psychiatrie." Ph.D. Dissertation. University of Würzburg, 1970.

2162. Clay, James Herbert. "The Problem of What is Real in the Drama. An Analysis of Ibsen's Realism and Maeterlinck's Symbolism." Ph.D. Dissertation. University of Illinois, 1957.

2163. Deer, Irving. "Ibsen's Search for Dramatic Form." Ph.D. Dissertation. University of Minnesota, 1956.

2164. Eller, William Henri. "Ibsen in Germany." Ph.D. Dissertation. University of Wisconsin, 1916.

2165. Ellett, Melvin K. "Organic Unity in the Social-Problem Plays of Henrik Ibsen." Ph.D. Dissertation. Stanford University, 1970.

2166. Franc, Miriam Alice. "Ibsen in England." Ph.D. Dissertation. University of Pennsylvania, 1918.

2167. Gregersen, Halfdan I. "Ibsen and Spain. A Study in Comparative Drama." Ph.D. Dissertation. Columbia University, 1936.

2168. Gregory, William Alfred, Jr. "A Rite-Role Analysis of Thirteen Ibsen Plays." Ph.D. Dissertation. University of Minnesota, 1957.

2169. Hattstaedt, Edwin William. "Der Nationalethische Gedanke in Drama Ibsens." Ph.D. Dissertation. Marquette University, 1940.

2170. Hawes, James William. "The Importance of the Major Discovery and Reversal in the Dramas of Henrik Ibsen." Ph.D. Dissertation. University of Kansas, 1966.

2171. Hehir, Diana F. O. "Ibsen and Joyce: A Study of Three Theses." Ph.D. Dissertation. Johns Hopkins University, 1972.

2172. Huber, Robert. "Ibsens Bedeutung für das englishe Drama." Ph.D. Dissertation. University of Marburg, 1914.

2173. Paulson, Arthur C. "The Norwegian-American Reaction to Ibsen and Bjørnson, 1850-1900." Ph.D. Dissertation. University of Iowa, 1933.

2174. Paulus, Gretchen. "Ibsen and the English Stage, 1889-1903." Ph.D. Dissertation. Radcliffe College, 1959.

2175. Pearce, John Calvin. "Bourgeois Tragedy, the Ibsen Synthesis." Ph.D. Dissertation. University of Southern California, 1961.

2176. Sheldon, James Gail. "The Orientation of Nicholas Berdyaev: His Relation to Jacob Boehme, Fyodor Dostoyevsky, Friedrich Nietzsche and Henrik Ibsen." Ph.D. Dissertation. University of Indiana, 1954.

2177. Swanson, Carl Alvin. "Ibsen and the French Drama." Ph.D. Dissertation. University of Chicago, 1930.

2178. Thune, Ensaf. "Main Currents of Ibsen Interpretation in England and America." Ph.D. Dissertation. University of Washington, 1963.

2179. Twetley, A. Corine. "Ibsen the Playwright: A Study of His Theatrical Apprenticeship and Its Influence on the Construction of His Plays." Ph.D. Dissertation. Yale University, 1945.

2180. Van Duren, Arthur, Jr. "Ibsen and Hauptmann." Ph.D. Dissertation. University of Michigan, 1930.

2181. Weisberg, Lynne B. W. "Ibsen and English Criticism: Early Critical Reactions to Ibsen and Their Aftermath in Modern Ibsenism." Ph.D. Dissertation. University of Michigan, 1973.

2182. Wiehr, Josef. "Hebbel und Ibsen." Ph.D. Dissertation. University of Pennsylvania, 1907.

Articles

2183. Adams, R. M. "Henrick Ibsen: The Fifty-First Anniversary." Hudson Review. Vol. 10 (Fall, 1957), pp. 415-23.

2184. Adler, J. H. "Ibsen, Shaw and Candida." Journal of English and Germanic Philology. Vol. 58 (January, 1962), pp. 50-58.

2185. Allen, Genevieve M. "The Problem of Individualism in Relation to Society in Ibsen, Maeterlinck and Hauptmann." Poet Lore. Vol. 32 (Summer, 1921), pp. 262-6.

2186. Allen, M. O. "The Clergy in Ibsen's Plays." Religion in Life. Vol. 39 (Spring, 1962), pp. 279-93.

2187. Anderson, S. "Genius of Ibsen." New Statesman and Nation. Vol. 37 (April 2, 1949), pp. 326.

2188. Archer, C. "Ibseniana: Letters from William Archer to Charles Archer." London Mercury. Vol. 36 (October, 1927), pp. 525-37.

2189. Archer, William. "From Ibsen's Workshop: The Genesis of His Dramas." Fortnightly Review. Vol. 86 (December, 1909), pp. 976-92.

2190. Arestad, Sverre. "Ibsen's Concept of Tragedy." PMLA. Vol. 74 (June, 1959), pp. 285-97.

2191. _____. "Ibsen, Strindberg and Naturalist Tragedy." Theatre Annual. Vol. 24 (1969), pp. 6-13.

2192. Barnes, J. T. "Ibsen's Tragic Themes." Lock Haven Review. Series 1, no. 5 (1963), pp. 11-26.

2193. Barranger, M. S. "Ibsen Bibliography, 1957-67." Scandinavian Studies. Vol. 4 (1969), pp. 243-58.

2194. Behrens, C. "Ibsen and Denmark." American Scandinavian Review. Vol. 16 (April, 1928), pp. 224-31.

2195. Bennett, L. "Ibsen as a Pioneer of the Woman's Movement." Westminster Review. Vol. 173 (March, 1910), pp. 278-85.

2196. Bentley, Eric. "Ibsen: Pro and Con." Theatre Arts. Vol. 34 (1950), pp. 39-44.

2197. _____. "The Theatres of Wagner and Ibsen." Kenyon Review. Vol. 6, no. 4 (Autumn, 1944), pp. 542-69.

2198. Bjorkman, E. "The Ibsen Myth." Forum. Vol. 45 (May, 1911), pp. 565-83.

2199. _____. "The Optimism of Ibsen." Living Age. Vol. 277 (June 21, 1913), pp. 716-23, and Contemporary Review. Vol. 103 (April, 1913), pp. 544-54.

2200. Blindheim, Joan T. "Bringing Ibsen to Life." The Norseman. (1966), pp. 155-59.

2201. Bradbrook, Muriel C. "Ibsen and the Past Imperfect." Ibsenforbondet: Arbox. Vol. II (1970-1971), pp. 7-25.

2202. Brochur, Georg. "My Memories of Henrik Ibsen." The Mask. Vol. 14, no. 1 (January-March, 1928), p. 7010.

2203. Brustein, Robert. "Ibsen and Revolt." Tulane Drama Review. Vol. 7, no. 1 (Fall, 1962), pp. 113-51.

2204. Burchart, C. B. "Ibsen and England." Norseman. Vol. 5 (1947), pp. 149-56.

2205. Butler, A. Maynard. "View of Ibsen." Contemporary Review. Vol. 81 (May, 1902), pp. 709-19.

2206. Carlson, M. "Henrik Ibsen and Finnegan's Wake." Comparative Literature. Vol. 12 (Spring, 1960), pp. 133-41.

2207. Clive, G. "Teleological Suspension of the Ethical in Nineteenth Century Literature." Journal of Religion. Vol. 34 (April, 1954), pp. 75-87.

2208. Cocco, Maria Rosaria. "Malodorous Ibsen." Annali Instituto Universitàrio Orientàle, Seziόne Germànica. Vol. 11 (1968), pp. 171-93.

2209. Decker, C. R. "Ibsen's Literary Reputation and Victorian Taste." Studies in Philology. Vol. 32 (October, 1935), pp. 362-45.

2210. Dimond, S. G. "The Philosophy of H. Ibsen." London Quarterly Review. Vol. 194 (1928), pp. 175-86.

2211. Edwards, H. "Henry James and Ibsen." American Literary Review. Vol. 24 (May, 1952), pp. 208-23.

2212. Ellis-Fermor, Una. "Ibsen and Shakespeare as Dramatic Artists." Edda. Vol. 56 (1956), pp. 364-80.

2213. _____. "Ibsen and the Artist." Queen's Quarterly. Vol. 53, no. 2 (1946), pp. 200-8.

2214. Engleslad, L. F. "Henrik Ibsen and the Modern Theatre." World Theatre. Vol. 6, Part 1 (1957), pp. 5-26.

2215. Evans, Edward Payson. "Henrik Ibsen: His Early Career as Poet and Playwright." Atlantic Monthly. Vol. 65 (May, 1890), pp. 577-88.

2216. Ewbank, Inga-Stinta. "Ibsen and the Far More Difficult Art of Prose." Ibsenforbundet: Årbox. Vol. II (1970-1971), pp. 60-83.

2217. Farquhar, E. F. "Recruiting Ibsen for the Allies." Drama. Vol. 8 (August, 1918), pp. 317-28.

2218. Fergusson, Francis. "Exiles and Ibsen's Work." Hound and Horn. Vol. 5, no. 3 (April-June, 1932), pp. 345-53.

2219. Fife, R. H. and A. Anstensen. "Henrik Ibsen on the American Stage." American Scandinavian Review. Vol. 16 (April, 1928), pp. 218-28.

2220. Findlaler, R. "Two Brands of Ibsen." 20th Century. Vol. 168 (October, 1960), pp. 337-42.

2221. Fjelde, Rolf. "The Dimensions of Ibsen's Dramatic World." Ibsenforbundet: Arbox. Vol. 2 (1970-1971), pp. 60-83.

2222. Flom, G. T. "Henrik Ibsen: Some Aspects of His Life and Work." Scandinavian Studies. Vol. 10 (1928), pp. 67-78.

2223. Garman, Douglas. "Ibsen's Early Development." Left Review. Vol. 3, no. 4 (May, 1937), pp. 215-23.

2224. Gerould, D. C. "George Bernard Shaw's Criticism of Ibsen." Comparative Literature. Vol. 15 (Spring, 1963), pp. 130-45.

2225. Gilman, Robert. "The Drawing Room and Beyond," in Common and Uncommon Masks. New York: Random House, 1971, p. 53

2226. Goodman, Randolph. "Playwatching with a Third Eye." Columbia University Forum. Vol. 10 (1967), pp. 18-22.

2227. Gosse, E. "A Visit to the Friends of Ibsen. Modern Languages Review. Vol. 13 (July, 1918), pp. 282-91.

2228. Granville-Barker, Harley. "The Coming of Ibsen," in Walter de la Mare, ed., In the Eighteen Eighties. Cambridge: Cambridge University Press, 1930, pp. 159-96.

2229. Grummann, P. H. "Ibsen in His Maturity." Poet Lore.
Vol. 29 (March–April, 1918), pp. 229-40.

2230. Haakonsen, Daniel. "The Play-Within-the Play in Ibsen's Realistic Drama." Ibsenforbundet: Arbox. Vol. II
(1970-1971), pp. 101-17.

2231. Hamilton, C. "Ibsen Once Again." Bookman. Vol. 47
(January, 1918), pp. 426-31.

2232. Hatch, Robert. "The Persistence of Ibsenism." Hori-
zon. Vol. 4, no. 3 (January, 1962), pp. 106-8.

2233. Haugen, Einar. "Ibsen in the Mill Race." Scandinavian Studies. Vol. 17, no. 8 (1943), pp. 313-7.

2234. _____. "Ibsen's Mill Race Once Again." Scandinavian Studies. Vol. 26 (1954), pp. 115-7.

2235. _____. "The Living Ibsen." Quarterly Journal
of Speech. Vol. 41 (1955), pp. 19-26.

2236. Haun, Myrtle L. "Social Problems as Ibsen Found Them
and As They Are Today." Scandinavian Studies. Vol. 6
(1929), pp. 176-9.

2237. Henderson, Archibald. "Henrik Ibsen and Social Progress." Arena. Vol. 33 (January, 1905), pp. 23-30.

2238. Irvine, W. "Shaw's Quintessence of Ibsenism." South
Atlantic Quarterly. Vol. 46 (April, 1947), pp. 252-62.

2239. Jacobs, E. "Henrik Ibsen and the Doctrine of Self-
Realization." Journal of English and German Philology. Vol.
38 (July, 1939), pp. 416-30.

2240. Jennings, R. "Ibsen Without Ibsenism, 1828-1928."
Spectator. Vol. 140 (March, 1928), pp. 422-3.

2241. Johnston, Brian. "The Boyg and the Sphinx in Ibsen's
Theatre." Yale Review. Vol. 60, pp. 366-82.

2242. _____. "The Corpse and the Cargo: The Hegelian
Past in Ibsen's Naturalistic Cycle." Drama Review. Vol. 13,
no. 2 (1968), pp. 47-66.

2243. Kaasa, Harris. "Ibsen and the Theologians." Scandinavian Studies. Vol. 43, pp. 356-84.

2244. Kaufmann, F. W. "Ibsen's Conception of Truth."
Germanic Review. Vol. 32 (April, 1957), pp. 83-93.

2245. Kenner, Hugh. "Joyce and Ibsen's Naturalism."
Sewanee Review. Vol. 59 (January, 1951), pp. 75-99.

2246. Kildahl, E. "Ibsen's Contrasting Clergy." Educational Theatre Journal. Vol. 15 (December, 1963), pp. 348-357.

2247. Knorr, Helena. "Ibsen and the Ethical Drama of the Nineteenth Century." Poet Lore. Vol. 10 (January-March, 1898), pp. 49-65.

2248. Knudsen, Trygve. "Phases of Style and Language in the Works of Henrik Ibsen." Scandinavia. Vol. 2 (1963), pp. 1-20.

2249. Koht, H. "Shakespeare and Ibsen." Journal of English and German Philology. Vol. 44 (January, 1945), pp. 79-86.

2250. Kruuse, Jens. "The Function of Humor in the Later Plays of Ibsen." Ibsenforbundet: Arbox. Vol. 2. (1971), p. 42.

2251. Lawson, R. "Ibsen the Individualist." Fortune. Vol. 99 (August, 1913), pp. 314-27.

2252. Lerner, Michael G. "Edouard Rod and the Introduction of Ibsen into France." Revue de Littérature Comparée. Vol. 43 (1969), pp. 69-82.

2253. Lundeberg, O. K. "Ibsen in France: A Study of the Ibsen Drama, Its Introduction, Vogue and Influence on the French Stage." Scandinavian Studies. Vol. 8 (1924), p. 93.

2254. McCarthy, M. "Will and Testament of Ibsen." Partisan Review. Vol. 23 (Winter, 1956), pp. 74-80.

2255. Magoun, Francis P., Jr. "Ibsen: Women's Votes and Women's Lib." Neuphilologische Mitteilungen. Vol. 74, pp. 727-29.

2256. Meyer, Annie N. "The Bare Bones of Ibsen." Drama. Vol. 8 (August, 1918), pp. 369-75.

2257. Meyer, Michael. "Ibsen: The Years of Failure." Listener. Vol. 77 (1967), pp. 225-27.

2258. Mori, Mitsuya. "Ibsen's Dramatic Irony." Ibsen-forbundet: Arbox. Vol. 2(1970-1971), pp. 118-39.

2259. Mortizen, J. "Henrik Ibsen: His Aim and Influence." 20th Century. Vol. 3 (March, 1911), pp. 503-7.

2260. Neserius, P. G. "Ibsen's Social and Political Ideas." American Political Science Review. Vol. 19 (February, 1925), pp. 25-37.

2261. Nixon, Barbara. "Has Ibsen Dated?" Left Review. Vol. 2, no. 7 (April, 1936), pp. 326-9.

2262. Northam, John. "Ibsen in England." Ibsenforbundet: Arbox. (1973), pp. 139-44.

2263. Orton, W. A. "The Ethics of Henrik Ibsen." Westminster Review. Vol. 174 (August, 1910), pp. 163-70.

2264. Osborne, John. "Zola, Ibsen and the Development of the Naturalist Movement in Germany." Arcadia. Vol. 2 (1967), pp. 196-203.

2265. Otten, Terry. "Ibsen and Albee's Spurious Children." Comparative Drama. Vol. 2 (1968), pp. 83-93.

2266. Quinn, Arthur Hobson. "Ibsen and Herne--Theory and Facts." American Literature.. Vol. 19, no. 2 (1947), pp. 171-7.

2267. Raphael, Robert. "From Hedda Gabler to When We Dead Awaken: The Quest for Self-Realization." Scandinavian Studies. Vol. 36 (1964), pp. 34-47.

2268. Rienert, Otto. "Archetypes of Ambiguity." Edda. Vol. 54 (1967), pp. 288-94.

2269. Rodenbeck, John. "The Irrational Knot: Shaw and the Uses of Ibsen." Shaw Review. Vol. 12 (1969), pp. 66-76.

2270. Roe, Frederick W. "Ibsen as a Dramatist." Sewanee Review. Vol. 13 (1905), pp. 305-18.

2271. Schechner, Richard. "Unexpected Visitor in Ibsen's Late Plays." Educational Theatre Journal. Vol. 14 (May, 1962), pp. 120-7.

2272. Scholfield, William Henry. "Personal Impressions of Bjørnson and Ibsen." Atlantic Monthly. Vol. 81 (April, 1898), n. pag.

2273. Setterquist, Jan. "Ibsen and Synge." Studia Neophilogica. Vol. 24 (1952), pp. 69-154.

2274. Shatsky, Joel. "Heredity as a Metaphor in Ibsen's Plays." Edda. Vol. 74 (1974), pp. 227-34.

2275. Silverman, Dan P. "Ibsen's Quest for Moral Regeneration." Illinois Quarterly. Vol. 34 (L972), pp. 5-13.

2276. Simons, L. "Ibsen as an Artist." Westminster Review. Vol. 140 (November, 1893), pp. 506-13.

2277. Smith, L. W. "Ibsen, Emerson and Nietzsche, the Individualists." Popular Science. Vol. 78 (February, 1911), pp. 147-57.

2278. Sontum, B. "Personal Recollections of Henrik Ibsen." Bookman. Vol. 37 (May, 1913), pp. 247-56.

2279. Speer, Joan H. "The Rhetoric of Ibsenism: A Study of the Poet-as-Persuader." Southern Speech Communications Journal. Vol. 37 (1972), pp. 13-26.

2280. Sprinchorn, Evert. "Ibsen and the Immoralists." Comparative Literature Studies. Vol. 9 (1972), pp. 58-79.

2281. Stampenbourg, Baron D. "The Passing of Ibsen." Independent. Vol. 53 (November 7, 1901), pp. 2630-3.

2282. Steeves, H. R. "Note on Ibsen's Stock of Ideas." German Review. Vol. 6 (1931), pp. 193-4.

2283. Steinhauer, H. "The Metaphysics of Ibsenism." University of Toronto Quarterly. Vol. 2 (1932), pp. 74-91.

2284. Stillwell, C. L. "Ibsen: the Master Builder of Drama." Methodist Quarterly Review. Vol. 77 (October, 1928), pp. 587-600.

2285. Sturtevant, Albert M. "Possible Traces of Ibsen's Influence on Bjørnson." Scandinavian Studies. Vol. 20 (1948), pp. 92-5.

2286. Teall, Gardner C. "Portrait of Ibsen." Chapbook. Vol. 4, no. 3 (December 15, 1895), p. 158.

2287. Tennant, P. F. D. "Ibsen as a Stage Craftsman." Modern Language Review. Vol. 34 (October, 1939), pp. 557-68.

2288. Thompson, Alan R. "Ibsen the Detestable." Theatre Arts. Vol. 36, no. 8 (1952), pp. 22-3.

2289. _____. "Ibsen as a Psychoanatomist." Educational Theatre Journal. Vol. 3 (1951), pp. 34-9.

2290. Tornquist, F. "Ibsen and O'Neill: A Study in Influence." Scandinavian Studies. Vol. 37, pp. 211-35.

2291. Turco, Alfred, Jr. "Ibsen, Wagner and Shaw's Changing View of 'Idealism.'" Shaw Review. Vol. 17 (1974), pp. 78-85.

2292. Wade, A. "Ibsen in Translation." Drama. No. 39 (Winter, 1955), pp. 26-9.

2293. Weightman, John. "Ibsen and the Absurd." Encounter. Vol. 45, no. 4 (October, 1975), pp. 48-52.

2294. White, Robert. "Ibsen in France: Romain Rolland and Norwegian Drama." Journal of the Australasian Universities Language and Literature Association. Vol. 40, pp. 260-70.

2295. Williams, R. "Ibsen Restored." New Statesman. Vol. 60 (July 2, 1960), pp. 23-4.

In Norwegian:

2296. Bukdahl, Jørgen. "Ariccia: Omkring Henrik Ibsen problemet." Dansk Udsyn. Vol. 49, pp. 244-60.

2297. Chirkov, N. M. "Henrik Ibsen i August Strindberg." Skandinavskii Sbornik. Vol. 2 (1966), pp. 197-228.

2298. Haakonsen, Daniel. "Et marxistisk syn på Ibsen."
Ibsenforbundet: Årbok. Vol. 3 (1972), pp. 71-8.

2299. Håtun, Grete. "Ibsen-bibliografi--1969-1970." Ibsenforbundet: Årbok. Vol. 2 (1970-1971), pp. 181-95.

2300. Henricksen, Aage. "Henrick Ibsen som moralist."
Kritik. Vol. 2, pp. 69-84.

2301. Lysander, Per. "Henrik Ibsen och politiken: En åmbets-
man på teatern." Ord och Bild. Vol. 82, pp. 3-17.

2302. Nag, Martin. "Tolstoj og Ibsen." Ibsen forbundet:
Årbok. (1972), pp. 78-82.

2303. Nyholm, Kela. "Ibsen og Frankrig." Ord och Bild.
Vol. 66, no. 9 (1957), pp. 482-6.

2304. Persson, Ola. "Henrik Ibsen hoc det norska Språket."
Studiekamraten. Vol. 53 (1971), pp. 52-3.

2305. Vessby, Hadar. "Ibsen och scandinavismen." Nordisk
Tidskrift. Vol. 48, pp. 152-56.

All Other Languages:

2306. Bull, F. "Le Premier Séjour à Rome d'Ibsen et de
Bjørnson." Revue de Littéraire Comparée. Vol. 9 (January,
1929), pp. 105-16.

2307. Coussange, J. de. "L'Influence française dans l'oeuvre
d'Ibsen." Revue Littérature Compárée. Vol. 5 (April, 1925),
pp. 298-305.

2308. Guilbourg, Edmundo. "Benavente e Ibsen, Puntos de
contacto." Cuadernos Hispanoamericanos. Vol. 68 (1966),
pp. 527-36.

2309. Hell, Victor. "Die Ehe im Zeitalter des Naturalismus, Ihre Soziologie und aesthetic Funktion im Werk von Zola,
Ibsen und G. Hauptmann." Recherches germaniques. No. 3
(1973), pp. 125-34.

2310. Henrici, Waltruab B. "Anspielungen auf Ibsens Dramen
in Finnegan's Wake." Orbis Litterarum. Vol. 23 (1968),
pp. 127-60.

2311. Magnino, B. "Enrico Ibsen e Søren Kierkegaard."
Nuova Antologia. Vol. 258 (April 1, 1928), pp. 298-311.

2312. Manacorda, G. "Il pensièro religióso di Enrico Ibsen." Nuova Antologia. Vol. 268 (November 1, 1929), pp.
58-77.

2313. Maynial, E. "Ibsen et Fogazzaro." Revue de Littérature Comparée. Vol. 4 (January, 1924), pp. 92-108.

2314. Nicod, L. "Une nouvelle interprétation du Canard sauvage d'Ibsen par Wyller." Revue Politique et Littéraire.
Vol. 76 (September, 1938), p. 356.

2315. Noreng, Harald. "Die soziale Struktur in Ibsens
Gegenwartsdramen." Skandinavistik. Vol. 1, pp. 17-39.

2316. Rouveyre, A. "Un amour du viel Ibsen." Mercure de
France. Vol. 203 (April 1, 1928), pp. 29-52.

2317. Vladesco, T. "Entre Ibsen et Tolstoi: réflexions sur
l'anarchisme." Mercure de France. Vol. 206 (September,
1928), pp. 569-87.

[JOHAN] AUGUST STRINDBERG

(1849-1912)

Selected Full-length Plays:

> Fritänkaren (The Freethinker, 1869)
> Lycko-Pers Resa (Lucky Pehr, 1883)
> Fadren (The Father, 1887)
> Kamraterna (Comrades, 1887)
> Fröken Julie (Miss Julie, Countess
>   Julia, Lady Julie, 1888)
> Den Starkare (The Stronger, 1890)
> Fordringsagare (Creditors, 1890)
> Himmelstrickets Nycklar (Keys to the
>   Kingdom of Heaven, 1892)
> Bandet (The Link, The Bond, 1893)
> Debit och Kredit (Debit and Credit,
>   1893)
> Infor Doden (Facing Death, 1893)
> Brott och Brott (There Are Crimes and
>   Crimes, Crime and Crime, 1899)
> Forsta Varningen (First Warning, 1901)
> Kronbruden (The Crown Bride, The Bridal
>   Crown, 1901)
> Pask (Easter, 1901)
> Svanehvit (Swanwhite, 1901)
> Dödsansen (The Dance of Death, The Last
>   Dance, 1901)
> Ett Drömspel (The Dream Play, 1902)
> Oväder (Thunderstorm, Stormweather
>   1907)
> Brända Tomten (After the Fire, The
>   Burned House, 1907)
> Spöksonaten (The Spook Sonata, The
>   Ghost Sonata, 1908)
> Stora landsvägen (The Great Highway,
>   The Highway, 1910)

Books

2318. Berendsohn, Walter A. August Strindberg. Amsterdam: Rodopi, 1974.

2319. Bergman, Gösta M. Den moderna teaterns genombrott, 1890-1925. Stockholm: Bonnier, 1966.

2320. Bergman, Bo. Predikare. Stockholm: Bonnier, 1967.

2321. Boethius, Uif. Strindberg och kvinnofrågan: Till och med Giftas I. Stockholm: Prisma, 1969.

2322. Borland, Harold H. Nietzsche's Influence on Swedish Literature with Special Reference to Strindberg, Ola Hansson, Heidenstam and Fröding. Goteberg: Wettergren and Kerber, 1957.

2323. Bulman, Joan. Strindberg and Shakespeare. Shakespeare's Influence on Strindberg's Historical Drama. London: J. Cape, 1933.

2324. Campbell, George Archibald. Strindberg. New York: The Macmillan Company, 1933.

2325. Dahlström, Carl Enoch William Leonard. Strindberg's Dramatic Expressionism. Ann Arbor: University of Michigan Press, 1930.

2326. Gabrieli, Mario. August Strindberg: uno studio. Göteborg: Elander, 1945.

2327. Gierow, Carl-Olof. Documentation-évocation: Le Climat littéraire et théâtral en France des années 1886 et Mademoiselle Julie de Strindberg. Stockholm: Almqvist and Widsell, 1967.

2328. Grant, Vernon W. Great Abnormals: The Pathological Genius of Kafka, van Gogh, Strindberg and Poe. New York: Hawthorn, 1968.

2329. Järv, Harry, ed. Strindbergsfejden. Stockholm: Bo Cavefors Bokförlag, 1967.

2330. Jaspers, Karl. Strindberg und vanGogh. Berlin: P. Stringer, 1926.

2331. Klaf, Franklin S. Strindberg: The Origins of Psychology in Modern Drama. New York: Citadel Press, 1963.

2332. Lamm, Martin. August Strindberg. New York: Blom, 1970-1971.

2333. Lind-af-Hageby, Emile Augusta. August Strindberg: The Spirit of Revolt. New York: D. Appleton and Co., 1913.

2334. Lind-af-Hageby, Emile Augusta. August Strindberg: A
Study. London: A. K. Press, 1928.

2335. Lucas, Frank Laurence. The Drama of Ibsen and Strindberg. New York: Macmillan, 1962.

2336. Lundberg, Sten and Erland Norin. Studiehandledning
till August Strindberg, Roda rummet. Stockholm: Tiden, 1970-
1971.

2337. Madsen, Børge Gedsø. Strindberg's Naturalistic Theatre; Its Relation to French Naturalism. New York: Russell
and Russell, 1973.

2338. McGill, Vivian J. August Strindberg, the Bedeviled
Viking. New York: Coward-McCann, 1930.

2339. Mortensesn, Brita M. and Brian W. Downs. Strindberg:
An Introduction to His Life and Work. Cambridge: Cambridge
University Press, 1969.

2340. Olejelund, Lars Ivan. Svenska genier. Stockholm:
L. Ts. Forlag, 1967.

2341. Ollen, Gunnar. Strindbergs dramatik. Stockholm:
Prisma, 1967.

2342. Proost, Karel Frederik. August Strindberg, zign leven
en werken. Zeist: J. Ploegma, 1922.

2343. Reinhart, Ono. Strindberg: A Collection of Critical
Essays. Englewood Cliffs: Prentice-Hall, Inc., 1971.

2344. Soderstrom, Goran. Strindberg och bildkonsten. Stockholm: Forum, 1972.

2345. Sprigge, Elizabeth. The Strange Life of August Strindberg. New York: Macmillan, 1949.

2346. Steene, Brigitta. The Greatest Fire: A Study of August Strindberg. London: Feffer and Simons, 1973.

2347. Swerling, Anthony, ed. In Quest of Strindberg: Letters to a Seeker. Cambridge: Trinity Lane Press, 1972.

2348. _____. Strindberg's Impact in France, 1920-1960.
Cambridge: Trinity Lane Press, 1971.

2349. Uppvall, Axel. August Strindberg, a Psychoanalytic
Study. Boston: R. G. Badger, 1920.

2350. Werein, Algot. Vandring kring en sjö: Studier, minnen,
betraktelser. Lund: Gleerup, 1967.

2351. Willers, Uno. Strindberg om sig själv. Stockholm:
Bonnier, 1968.

2 352. Wilson, Colin. <u>Strindberg: A Play in Two Scenes</u>.
New York: Random House, 1972.

Theses and Dissertations

2353. Axel, John Uppvall. "August Strindberg. A Psycho-
analytic Study." Ph.D. Dissertation. Clark University, 1919.

2354. Bjarnason, Loftur L. "Categories of Søren Kierkegaard's Thought in the Life and Writings of August Strindberg." Ph.D. Dissertation. Stanford University, 1951.

2355. Dahlström, Carl Enoch William Leonard. "Strindberg's
Dramatic Expressionism." Ph.D. Dissertation. University of
Michigan, 1928.

2356. Dawson, William Meredith. "The Female Characters of
August Strindberg, Eugene O'Neill and Tennessee Williams."
Ph.D. Dissertation. University of Wisconsin, 1964.

2357. Hartman, Murray. "Strindberg and O'Neill: A Study in
Influence." Ph.D. Dissertation. New York University, 1972.

2358. Hortenbach, Jenny Christa. "Freiheitsstreben und
Destruktivität. Frauen in den Dramen August Strindbergs und
Gerhart Hauptmanns." Ph.D. Dissertation. University of
California, 1962.

2359. Jacobs, Elizabeth R. "Strindberg and the Problem of
Suffering." Ph.D. Dissertation. University of Wisconsin,
1964.

2360. Madsen, Børge Gedsø. "The Impact of French Naturalists and Psychologists on August Strindberg's Plays of the
1880's and Early 1890's." Ph.D. Dissertation. University
of Minnesota, 1958.

2361. Pampel, Brigette C. G. "The Relationship of the Sexes
in the Works of Strindberg, Wedekind and O'Neill." Ph.D.
Dissertation. Northwestern University, 1972.

2362. Passerini, Edward M. "Strindberg's Absurdist Plays:
An Examination of the Expressionistic, Surrealistic and
Absurd Elements in Strindberg's Drama." Ph.D. Dissertation.
University of Virginia, 1972.

2363. Rapp, Esther J. "Strindberg's Reception in England
and America." Ph.D. Dissertation. University of Colorado,
1940.

2364. Scanlan, David E. "Traditional Comic Form in Strindberg's Naturalistic Plays." Ph.D. Dissertation. University
of Minnesota, 1970-71.

2365. Sprinchorn, Evert Manfred. "The Modern Scandinavian
Drama, 1900-1959." Ph.D. Dissertation. Columbia University,
1960.

2366. Uppvall, Axel Johan. "August Strindberg, A Psycho-analytic Study with Special Reference to the Oedipus Complex." Ph.D. Dissertation. Clark University, 1920.

2367. Walsh, Dwight Rolfe. "Deity in Drama. The Representation of the Absolute in Some Plays of Ibsen, Strindberg and Hauptmann." Ph.D. Dissertation. Harvard, 1963.

Articles

2368. Abdank, C. d'. "Strindberg and Bjørnson." Theatre. Vol. 20 (July, 1914), pp. 27.

2369. Åkerhjelm, H. "August Strindberg." American Scandinavian Review. Vol. 26 (December, 1938), pp. 312-17.

2370. Alin, Hans. "Några Strindbergsminnen." Meddelanden från Strindbergssällskapet. Vol. 40-41 (1968), pp. 12-15.

2371. Baumgartner, Walter. "Drömtekniken i Strindbergs och Kafkas verk." Svensk Litteraturtidskrift. Vol. 31, no. 3 (1968), pp. 18-26.

2372. Benekikt, Ernst. "Grillparzer und Strindberg: Eine vergleichende Charakterstudie." Jahrbuch der Grillparzer-Gesellscaft. Vol. 6 (1967), pp. 139-59.

2373. Benston, A. N. "From Naturalism to the Dream Play: a Study of the Evolution of Strindberg's Unique Theatrical Form." Modern Drama. Vol. 7 (February, 1965), pp. 382-98.

2374. Berg, Curt. "Alltjämt lika spánnande." Bokvännen. Vol. 22 (1967), pp. 219-22.

2375. Bergman, G. M. "Strindberg and the Intema Teatern." Theater Research. Vol. 9 (1967), pp. 14-47.

2376. Berendsohn, Walter A. "August Strindberg og Kvinderne." Vor riden. (1965-1966), pp. 498-512.

2377. Berman, H. "Dual Personality of August Strindberg." Out West. Vol. 4 (November, 1912), pp. 329-31.

2378. _____. "The Essence of August Strindberg." Colonnade. Vol. II (February, 1916), pp. 58-63.

2379. Beyer, William. "The State of the Theatre: The Strindberg Heritage." School and Society. Vol. 71 (1950), pp. 23-8.

2380. Bjørkman, E. "Poor Translations of Strindberg's Work for American Productions." Drama. No. 3 (August, 1911), pp. 175-9.

2381. Brett, A. "Psychological Abnormalities in August Strindberg." Journal of English and Germanic Philology. Vol. 20 (1921), pp. 47-98.

2382. Brustein, Robert. "Male and Female in August Strindberg." Drama Review. Vol. 7, no. 2 (Winter, 1962), pp. 130-
74.

2383. Burkhard, Arthur. "August Strindberg and Modern German Drama." German Quarterly. Vol. 6 (1933), pp. 163-74.

2384. Chirkov, N. M. "Henrik Ibsen i August Strindberg."
Skandinavskii Sbornik. Vol. II (1966), pp. 197-223.

2385. Clark, Barrett H. "Strindberg, Reinhardt, and Berlin."
Drama. No. 14 (May, 1914), pp. 270-9.

2386. Clarke, J. "Work of August Strindberg." Colonnade.
Vol. 7 (May, 1914), pp. 262-8.

2387. Dahlström, Carl E. W. L. "August Strindberg--1849-
1912: Between Two Eras." Scandinavian Studies. Vol. 21
(1949), pp. 1-18.

2388. _____. "Strindberg and Naturalistic Tragedy."
Scandinavian Studies. Vol. 30 (1958), pp. 1-8.

2389. _____. "Strindberg and the Problems of Naturalism." Scandinavian Studies. Vol. 16 (1941), pp. 213-9.

2390. _____. "Theomachy: Zola, Strindberg, Andreyev."
Scandinavian Studies. Vol. 17 (November, 1942), pp. 121-32.

2391. _____. "The Parisian Reception of Strindberg's
Plays." Scandinavian Studies. Vol. 19 (1949), pp. 195-207.

2392. Ekenvall, Asta. "Strindberg's och Kvinnans fysiol-
ogi." Bonniers L. Herar Magasin. Vol. 38 (1969), pp. 457-64.

2393. Farinelli, A. "Strindberg." Nuova Antologia. Vol.
402 (March 1, 1969), pp. 49-66.

2394. Gassner, John. "The Influence of Strindberg in the
U.S.A." World Theatre. Vol. II (Spring, 1962), pp. 21-30.

2395. _____. "Strindberg in America." Theatre Arts.
Vol. 33 (May, 1949), pp. 49-52.

2396. Goodman, Randolph. "Playwatching with a Third Eye."
Columbia University Forum. Vol. 10, no. 1 (1967), pp. 18-22.

2397. Gravier, Maurice. "Strindberg and the French Drama."
World Theatre. Vol. 2 (Spring, 1962), pp. 45-60.

2398. _____. "Strindberg auf der Bühne unserer Zeit."
Maske und Kothurn. Vol. 14 (1968), pp. 29-43.

2399. Gustafson, A. "Recent Development and Future Pros-
pects in Strindberg Studies." Modern Philology. Vol. 46
(August, 1948), pp. 49-62.

2400. Gustafson, A. "Six Recent Doctoral Dissertations on Strindberg." Modern Philology. Vol. 52 (August, 1954), pp. 52-6.

2401. Harrison, A. "The Life of August Strindberg." English Review. Vol. 12 (November, 1912), pp. 604-20.

2402. Hartman, J. W. "An Appreciation of August Strindberg's Work." International. Vol. 7 (January, 1913), pp. 5-6.

2403. Haugen, E. I. "Strindberg the Regenerated: A Study of the Moral Personality in a Group of his Later Plays." Journal of English and German Philology. Vol. 29 (April, 1930), pp. 237-70.

2404. Hauptmann, Ira. "Strindberg's Realistic Plays." Yale/Theatre. Vol. 5, no. 3 (1974), pp. 87-94.

2405. Heden, E. von. "Strindberg: Leben and Dichtung." Nation. (May 4, 1927), pp. 508-9.

2406. Henderson, A. "August Strindberg: Universalist." South Atlantic Quarterly. Vol. 13 (January, 1914), pp. 29-42.

2407. Jolivet, A. "Strindberg et Nietzsche." Revue de Littérature Comparée. Vol. 19 (July, 1939), pp. 390-406.

2408. _____. "Le théâtre de Strindberg." Modern Languages Notes. Vol. 48 (February, 1933), pp. 122-3.

2409. Josephson, A. G. S. "Strindberg in English." Dial. Vol. 56 (April 1, 1914), pp. 300-3.

2410. Kaufmann, R. J. "Strindberg: The Absence of Irony." Drama Survey. Vol. 3 (L964), pp. 463-76.

2411. Kejzlar, Radko. "Strindberg och den moderna teatern: Nagra anmärkningar med anledning av Mr. Lucas' bok." Meddelanden från Strindbergssällskapet. Vol. 40-41 (1968), pp. 16-23.

2412. Lamm, M. "Strindberg and the Theatre." Tulane Drama Review. Vol. 6 (1961), pp. 132-9.

2413. Lanem, A. M. "Strindbergs Dramen." Modern Language Review. Vol. 22 (July, 1927), pp. 354-6.

2414. Madsen, Børge Gedsø. "Strindberg as a Naturalistic Theorist: The Essay 'Om modernt drama och modern teater.'" Scandinavian Studies. Vol. 20 (1958), pp. 85-98.

2415. Marchand, J. "America's Acquaintance with August Strindberg." Bookman. Vol. 38 (December, 1913), pp. 435-6.

2416. Maury, L. "Les Confessions de Strindberg." Revue Politiques et Litteraires. Vol. 65 (March 5, 1927), pp.149-52.

2417. Melchinger, Siegfried. "German Theatre People Face to Face with Strindberg." World Theatre. Vol. 2 (Spring), 1962), pp. 31-44.

2418. Morgan, M. "Strindberg and the English Theatre." Modern Drama. Vol. 7 (1964), pp. 161-73.

2419. Moricera, M. D. "A Strindberg o L've Tolstrom." Scandinavskij Sbornik. Vol. 14 (1969), pp. 302-11.

2420. Moronek, James E. "Anthropomorphic Scenery." Theatre Crafts. Vol. 1 (1967), pp. 34-39.

2421. Mudford, P. G. "The Theatre of France: A View of the Consistency of Strindberg's Dramatic Craft." Theatre Research. Vol. 11, pp. 133-40.

2422. Obehauer, K. J. "Strindbergs Entwicklung." Preussische Jahrbücher. Vol. 205 (July, 1926), pp. 37-57.

2423. Ollen, Gunnar. "Strindberg, 1962." World Theatre. Vol. 2 (Spring, 1962), pp. 4-20.

2424. _____. "Svensk dramatik på dansk scen." Studiekamraten. Vol. 50 (1968), pp. 25-8.

2425. Olsson, Nils L. "Strindberg, Nils Anderson och 'Syndabocken.'" Svensk Litteraturtidskrift. Vol. 30, pp. 70-8.

2426. Oster, Rose-Marie G. "Hamm and Hummel--Beckett and Strindberg on the Human Condition." Scandinavian Studies. Vol. 41 (1969), pp. 330-45.

2427. Parsons, Mabel H. "Strindberg, Reality and the Dream Play." Poet Lore. Vol. 26 (November-December, 1915), pp. 763-73.

2428. Plasberg, Elaine. "Strindberg and the New Poetics." Modern Drama. Vol. 15 (1972), pp. 1-14.

2429. Rothenberg, Albert. "Autobiographical Drama: Strindberg and O'Neill." Literature and Psychology. Vol. 17 (1967), pp. 95-114.

2430. Samuel, H. B. "Strindberg and His Plays." Fortnightly. Vol. 97 (June 1, 1912), pp. 1116-31.

2431. Senelick, Laurence. "Strindberg, Antoine and Lugné-Poë: a Study in Cross-Purposes." Modern Drama. Vol. 15 (1973), pp. 391-401.

2432. Sitwell, O. "The Man Who Drove Strindberg Mad." Life and Letters Today. Vol. 28 (February, 1941), pp. 141-8.

2433. Sprigge, Elizabeth. "Strindberg--Towards an Interpretation." Life and Letters. Vol. 53 (June, 1947), pp. 182-91.

2434. Sprinchorn, Evert. "Strindberg and the Greater Naturalism." Vol. 13, no. 2 (1968), pp. 119-29.

2435. _____. "The Zola of the Occult: Strindberg's
Experimental Method." Modern Drama. Vol. 17 (1974), pp.
351-66.

2436. "Strindberg and American Cities." New York Dramatic
Mirror. Vol. 33 (March 3, 1915), p. 5.

2437. Stubbs, P. C. "The Work of August Strindberg." Green
Book. Vol. 8 (September, 1912), pp. 518-26.

2438. Svanberg, Victor. "Strindberg i skjortärmarna."
Bonniers Litterära Magasin. Vol. 38 (1969), pp. 442-46.

2439. Svedfelt, Torsten. "Strindberg, Munch och Quickborn."
Bokvännen. Vol. 24 (1969), pp. 51-56.

2440. Svenaeus, Gösta. "Uttrycksmedlens dialog: Tecknaven
Victor Hugo--målaren August Strindberg." Studiekamraten.
Vol. 49 (1967), pp. 51-54.

2441. Thompson, V. "Strindberg and His Plays." Bookman.
Vol. 47 (January, 1918), pp. 361-9.

2442. Trotskii, I. "Reminiscences of August Strindberg."
Living Age. Vol. 58 (February 22, 1913), pp. 495-9.

2443. Uppvall, Axel J. "Life and Work of August Strindberg." Poet Lore. Vol. 31 (Spring, 1920), pp. 69-156.

2444. _____. "Strindberg in Light of Psychoanalysis."
Scandinavian Studies. Vol. 21 (August, 1949), pp. 133-50.

2445. Walter, Jürgen. "Wolfgang Borchert und August Strindberg." Moderna Språk. Vol. 61 (1967), pp. 263-74.

2446. Winstock, John. "Strindberg and Women's Lib." Germanic Notes. Vol. 2, pp. 58-62.

2447. Williams, Raymond. "Strindberg and the New Drama in
Britain." World Theatre. Vol. 2 (Spring, 1962), pp. 61-66.

X RUSSIA

General Commentaries

Books

2448. Bakshy, Alexander. The Path of the Russian Stage. London: C. Palmer and Hayward, 1918.

2449. Baring, Maurice. Outline of Russian Literature. London: Williams and Norgate, 1915.

2450. Carter, Huntley. New Spirit in the Russian Theatre, 1917-1928. New York: Brentano, 1929.

2451. Davies, Ruth O. The Great Books of Russia. Norman, Okla.: University of Oklahoma Press, 1968.

2452. Derzhavin, Konstantin Nikolaievich. A Century of the State Dramatic Theatre, 1832-1932. Leningrad: State Publishing House, 1932.

2453. Ettinger, Amrei and Joan M. Gladstone. Russian Literature, Theatre and Art: A Bibliography of Works in English, Published 1900-1945. London: Hutchinson, 1947.

2454. Fennell, John, ed. Nineteenth-Century Russian Literature: Studies of Ten Russian Writers, London: Faber & Faber, 1973.

2455. Fülöp-Miller, René and Joseph Gregor. The Russian Theatre: Its Character and History. Philadelphia: J. B. Lippincott, 1929.

2456. Gorkii, Maksim. Reminiscences of Tolstoy, Checkhov, and Andreev. London: Hogarth Press, 1934.

2457. Gourfinkel, Nina. Théâtre russe contemporain. Paris: La Renaissance du livre, 1931.

2458. Hingley, Ronald. Russian Writers and Society, 1825-1904. New York: McGraw-Hill, 1967.

2459. Lo Gatto, Ettore. Il teàtro russo. Milan: Fratèlli Treves, 1937.

2460. Lukács, György. Der russische Realismus in der Welt-literatur. Berlin: Aufbau-Verlag, 1948.

2461. Macleod, J. T. G. Actors Across the Volga: A Study of the 19th Century Russian Theatre and of Soviet Theatres in War. London: G. Allen & Unwin Ltd., 1946.

2462. Mirshii, Dmitrii. Contemporary Russian Literature, 1881-1925. New York: Knopf, 1933.

2463. _____. History of Russian Literature. New York, 1934.

2464. Nemirovich-Danchenko, Vasilli. My Life in the Rus-sian Theatre. Boston: Little Brown, 1936.

2465. Saylor, Oliver. The Russian Theatre. New York: Brentano's 1922.

2466. Simmons, Ernest J. Introduction to Russian Realism. Bloomington, Indiana: Indiana University Press, 1965.

2467. Slonim, Mark. Russian Theatre. New York: Collier Books, 1962.

2468. Spector, Ivar. Golden Age of Russian Literature. Caldwell, Indiana: Caxton Printers, 1943.

2469. Strakhov, Nikolai N. Kriticheskie stat'io Turgeneve i Tolstrom. The Hague: Mouton, 1968.

2470. Struve, Gleb. Soviet Russian Literature. London: Routledge, 1935.

2471. Varneke, Boris V. History of the Russian Theatre. New York: Macmillan, 1951.

2472. Wiener, Leo. Contemporary Drama of Russia. Boston: Little, Brown, 1924.

Theses and Dissertations

2473. Shoemaker, Robert W. Russian Drama on the New York Stage, From the Beginning to 1920: Mainly as Seen by the Critics." Ph.D. Dissertation. University of Pennsylvania, 1951.

Articles

2474. Bjalik, B. "Niesčerpaemye volmožnosti realizma."
Voprosy Literatury. Vol. 12, no. 3 (1968), pp. 36-49.

2475. Guzieva, H. V. "Russkaja realističeskaja dramaturgija
1910-x godov." Russian Literature. Vol. 12, no. 3 (1969),
pp. 36-54.

2476. Houghton, Norris. "Russian Theatre in the 20th Century." Tulane Drama Review. Vol. 17, pp. 5-13.

2477. Kasper, K. "Tomantik und Realismus in der Sowjet-
literatur." Zeitschrift für Slawistik. Vol. 17 (1972), p. 488.

2478. Nabokoff, C. "Russian Drama in the XIXth and XXth
Centuries." Contemporary. Vol. 124 (May, 1922), pp. 637-44.

LEONID [NIKOLAIVICH] ANDREYEV

(also transliterated as Andreyeff, Andreiev,
Andreieff and Andreev, 1871-1919)

Selected Full-length Plays:

K'zvezdam (To the Stars, 1905)
Zhizn' Cheloveka (The Life of Man, 1906)
Savva (Ignis sanat) Savva, or Fire
    Cures, 1906)
Tsar Golod (King Hunger, 1907)
Chyornye Maski (The Black Maskers, 1908)
Dni nashey zhizni (Days of Our Life,
    1908)
Razskuz o semi poveshennykh (The Seven Who
    Were Hanged, 1908)
Anatema: Tragediia (Anathema: A Tragedy,
    1909)
Anfisa (1909)
Gaudeamus (1909)
Prekrasnyia Sabinianki (The Lovely Sabine
    Women, 1911)
Okean (The Ocean, 1911)
Professor Storitsyn (1912)
Yekaterina Ivanovna (1912)
Tot, kto poluchayet poshchechiny (He Who
    Gets Slapped, 1914)
Mysl (Thought, 1914)
Karol', Zakon i Svoboda (A Tragedy of
    Belgium, The Sorrows of Belgium, 1914)
Samson v okovakh (Samson in Chains, 1916)
Milye prizraki (The Dear Ghosts, Cherished
    Ghosts, The Dear Departing, 1916)
Sobachy vals (The Waltz of the Dogs, also
    played as Poema odinochestva, A Poem
    of Loneliness, 1916)

Books

2479. Gorky, Maxim. Reminiscences of Tolstoy, Chekhov and Andreyev. London: Hogarth Press, 1934.

2480. Kaun, Alexander S. Leonid Andreyev: A Critical Study. New York: B. H. Huebsch, 1924.

2481. Newcombe, Josephine M. Leonid Andreyev. New York: Ungar, 1973.

2482. Woodward, James B. Leonid Andreyev: A Study. Oxford: Clarendon Press, 1969.

2483. Yershov, Peter. Letters of Gorki and Andreev, 1899-1912. New York: Columbia University Press, 1958.

Theses and Dissertations

2484. King, Henry H. "Dostoyevsky and Andreyev: Gazers Upon the Abyss." Ph.D. Dissertation. Columbia University, 1936.

Articles

2485. Bevernis, M. "Zur Aufnahme Leonid Andreevs in Deutschland." Zeitschrift für Slawistik. Vol. 11, pp. 75-92.

2486. Block, A. "Reminiscences of Andreyev." Living Age. Vol. 317 (June 16, 1923), pp. 662-5.

2487. Dahlström, Carl E. W. L. "Theomachy: Zola, Strindberg, Andreyev." Scandinavian Studies. Vol. 17, no. 4 (November, 1942), pp. 121-32.

2488. Guzieva, N. "Dramaturgia Leonida Andreeva 1910-x godov." Russian Literature. Vol. 8, no. 4, pp. 64-79.

2489. Kayden, E. M. "Work of Andreev." Dial. Vol. 67 (November 15, 1919), pp. 425-8.

2490. "La tragédie russe." Revue de Paris. Vol. 29, Part 2 (April 1, 1922), pp. 499-519.

2491. Orton, W. "Leonid Andreyev." American Review. Vol. 3 (May, 1925), pp. 317-22.

2492. Pachmuss, Temira. "Leonid Andreev as Seen by Zinaida Gippius." Slavic and East European Journal. Vol. 9, pp. 141-154.

2493. Peltier-Zamoyska, H. "Leonid Andreev et le mal du siècle." Cahiers du Monde Russe et Soviétique. Vol. 4 (1963), pp. 205-29.

2494. Seltzer, T. "Life and Work of Leonid Andreieff." Drama. No. 13 (February, 1914), pp. 5-33.

2495. Sokoloff, A. "Leonid Andreieff." New Statesman. Vol. 14 (November 15, 1919), pp. 190-1.

2496. Turkevich, Ludmilla B. "Andreev and the Mask." Russian Literature Triquarterly. Vol. 7 (1973), pp. 267-84.

2497. Woodward, James B. "Leonid Andreyev and 'Conventionalism' in the Russian Theatre." Modern Language Review. Vol. 66 (1971), pp. 365-78.

2498. _____. "Leonid Andreev and Russkaia Volia." Études Slaves et Est-Européenes. Vol. 10 (1965-66), pp. 26-35.

ANTON [PAVLOVICH] CHEKHOV

(1860-1904)

Selected Full-length Plays:

> Ivanov (1887)
> Lebedinaya Pyesnya (The Swan Song, 1889)
> Chaika (The Seagull, 1896)
> Dyadya Vanya (Uncle Vanya, 1899)
> Tri Sestri (Three Sisters, 1901)
> Vishnevy Sad (The Cherry Orchard, The
>   Cherry Garden, 1904)

Books

In English:

2499. Brahms, Caryl. Reflections in a Lake: A Study of Chekhov's Four Greatest Plays. London: Weidenfeld and Nicholson, 1976.

2500. Bruford, Walter H. Anton Chekhov. New Haven: Yale University, 1957.

2501. _____. Chekhov and His Russia: A Sociological Study. London: Routledge and K. Paul, 1948.

2502. Chekhov, Anton. Anton Chekhov: Literary and Theatrical Reminiscences. New York: Blom, 1968.

2503. _____. Letters of Anton Pavlovitch Chekhov to Olga Leonardovna Knipper. New York: G. H. Doran (Doubleday), 1925.

2504. _____. Life and Letters of Anton Chekhov. New York, London and Toronto: Cassell, 1925.

2505. _____. The Selected Letters of Anton Chekhov. London and New York: Farrar, Straus, 1955.

2506. Brahms, Caryl. Reflections in a Lake: A Study of Chekhov's Four Greatest Plays. London: Weidenfeld and Nicholson, 1976.

2507. Chukovskii, Korniei Ivanovich. Chekhov the Man. New York: Hutchinson, 1945.

2508. Elton, Oliver. Chekhov, the Taylorian Lecture, 1929. London, Oxford: The Clarendon Press, 1929.

2509. Ermilov, Vladimir V. Anton Pavlovich Chekhov, 1860-1904. Moscow: Foreign Languages Publishing House, 1957.

2510. Friedland, Louis S., ed. Anton Chekhov's Letters on the Short Story, the Drama, and Other Literary Topics. New York: Blom, 1968.

2511. Gerhardie, William A. Anton Chehov, a Critical Study. London: R. Cobden-Sanderson, 1923.

2512. Gillès, Daniel. Chekhov: Observer Without Illusion. New York: Funk & Wagnalls, 1968.

2513. Gorky, Maxim. Reminiscences of Anton Chekhov. New York: Huebsch, 1921.

2514. Hingley, Ronald. A New Life of Anton Chekhov. New York: Knopf, 1976.

2515. _____. Chekhov: A Biographical and Critical Study. London: Allen and Unwin, 1950.

2516. Jackson, Robert L., ed. Chekhov: A Collection of Critical Essays. Englewood Cliffs, New Jersey: Prentice-Hall, 1967.

2517. Kotelianski, Samuel Solomonovitch, tr. and ed. Anton Chekhov: Literary and Theatrical Reminiscences. London: Routledge, 1927.

2518. _____, ed. The Life and Letters of Anton Chekhov. New York: George H. Doran, 1925.

2519. _____, and Leonard Woolf. The Notebooks of Anton Chekhov. New York: B. W. Hueback, 1921.

2520. Lucas, Frank Laurence. The Drama of Chekhov, Synge, Yeats and Pirandello. London: Cassell, 1936.

2521. Magarshack, David. Chekhov the Dramatist. New York: Auvergne Publishers, 1952.

2522. _____. The Real Chekhov: An Introduction to Chekhov's Last Plays. London: Allen and Unwin, 1972.

2523. Murray, John Middleton. Aspects of Literature. London: W. Collins Sons, 1921.

2524. Nemirovsky, Irene. _A Life of Chekhov_. London: Grey Walls Press, 1950.

2525. Oates, Joyce Carol. _The Edge of Impossibility: Tragic Forms in Literature_. New York: Vanguard, 1972.

2526. Rayfield, Donald. _Chekhov: The Evolution of His Art_. New York: Harper, Row, 1975.

2527. Saunders, Beatrice. _Tchekhov the Man_. Philadelphia: Dufour, 1961.

2528. Shestov, Lev. _Chekhov and Other Essays_. Ann Arbor: University of Michigan Press, 1966.

2529. Simmons, Ernest J. _Chekhov: A Biography_. Boston: Little, Brown, 1962.

2530. Speirs, Logan. _Tolstoy and Chekhov_. Cambridge: Cambridge University Press, 1975.

2531. Toumanvoa, N. A. _Anton Chekhov, the Voice of Twilight Russia_. New York: Columbia University Press, 1937.

2532. Valency, Maurice. _The Breaking String_. London and New York: Oxford University Press, 1966.

2533. Winner, Thomas G. _Chekhov and His Prose_. New York: Holt, Rinehart, Winston, 1966.

2534. Yachnin, Rissa. _Chekhov in English_. New York: New York Public Library, 1960.

In Russian:

2535. Balukhatyi, Sergei D. _Chekhov dramaturg_. Leningrad, 1936.

2536. _____. _Problemy dramaturgicheskogo analiza Chekhov_. Munich: Fink, 1969.

2537. Berdnikov, Georgii P. _Anton Pavlovich Chekhov_. Moscow: 1950.

2538. Derman, Abram Borisovich. _O masterstve Chekhova_. Moscow-Leningrad, 1959.

2539. Ermilov, Vladimir V. _Dramaturgiya Chekhova_. Moscow, 1948.

2540. Kotov, Anatolii. _Chekhov v vospominaniyakh sovremennikov_. Moscow, 1952.

2541. Paperni, Zinovii S. _A. P. Chekhov_. Moscow, 1960.

2542.   Polotskaya, Emma Artem'evna.   Anton Pavlovich Chekhov-Rekomendatelnyi ukazatel literatury.   Moscow: Publichnaia biblioteka, 1955.

2543.   Sakharova, Eugeniia Mikhailovna.   Anton Pavlovich Chekhov, 1860-1904--Pamyatka chitatelya i materialy y pom-shch bibliotekaryu.   Moscow: Publichnaia biblioteka, 1954.

In Other Languages:

2544.   Levander, Hans.   Anton Tjechov.   Stockholm: Natur og kulter, 1969.

2545.   Scheibitz, Christina.   Mensch und Mitmensch im Drama Anton Chehovs.   Goppingen: A. Kummerle, 1972.

2546.   Teodorescu, Leonida.   Dramaturgia lui Chekhov.   Bucharest: University of Bucharest, 1970.

Articles

2547.   Aldanov, M.   "Reflections on Chekhov."   Russian Review. Vol. 14 (April, 1955), pp. 83-92.

2548.   Bentley, Eric.   "Chekhov as Playwright."   Kenyon Review.   Vol. 2, no. 2 (1949), pp. 226-50.

2549.   Carr, E. H.   "Chekhov: Twenty-five Years After." Spectator.   Vol. 143 (July 20, 1929), pp. 72-3.

2550.   Collins, H. P.   "Chekhov: The Last Phase."   Contemporary Review.   Vol. 185 (July, 1954), pp. 37-41.

2551.   Corrigan, Robert.   "The Drama of Anton Chekhov," in Travis Bogard and William Oliver.   Modern Drama: Essays in Criticism.   New York: Oxford University Press, pp. 73-98.

2552.   _____.   "Some Aspects of Chekhov's Dramaturgy." Educational Theatre Journal.   Vol. 7 (May, 1955), pp. 107-14.

2553.   Cross, A. G.   "The Breaking String of Chekhov and Turgenev."   Slavonic and East European Review.   Vol. 47 (1970), pp. 510-3.

2554.   Croyden, Margaret.   "'People Just Eat Their Dinner': The Absurdity of Chekhov's Doctors."   Texas Quarterly.   Vol. 2, no. 3 (1968), pp. 130-37.

2555.   Davie, Donald, ed.   "Chekhov and the English," in Russian Literature and Modern English Fiction.   Chicago: University of Chicago Press, 1965, pp. 203-13.

2556.   Doyle, P. A.   "Chekhov in Erin."   Dublin Review.   Vol. 241 (1967), pp. 263-67.

2557. Fagin, N.B. "The Work of Anton Chekhov." Poet Lore. Vol. 32 (Autumn, 1921), pp. 416-24.

2558. Fludas, John. "Chekhovian Comedy: A Review Essay." Genre. Vol. 6, pp. 333-46.

2559. Freedman, Morris. "Chekhov's Morality of Work." Modern Drama. Vol. 5 (1962), pp. 83-93.

2560. Garnett, E. "Tchekov and His Art." Quarterly Review. Vol. 236 (October, 1921), pp. 257-69.

2561. Gordon C. "Notes on Chekhov and Maugham." Sewanee Review. (July, 1949), pp. 401-10.

2562. Halward, L. "Introduction to Literature." London Mercury. Vol. 37 (March, 1938), pp. 515-18.

2563. Hellman, Lillian. "Letters about Writers and Writing." Partisan Review. Vol. 21 (July, 1954), pp. 371-86.

2564. Jones, W. Gareth. "Chekhov's Undercurrent of Time." Modern Language Review. Vol. 64 (1969), pp. 111-121.

2565. Karlinsky, Simon. "Chekhov, Beloved and Betrayed." Delos. Vol. 3 (1969), pp. 192-7.

2566. Koteliansky, S. S. "Reminiscences of Chekhov by Actors of the Moscow Art Theatre." Spectator. Vol. 135 (October-November-December, 1925), pp. 701-2.

2567. Kramer, Karl D. "Chekhov at the End of the Eighties: A Question of Identity." Études Slaves et Est-Européennes. 1966, pp. 3-18.

2568. Krutch, Joseph Wood. "The Tragic-comedy of Chekhov." Nation. Vol. 128 (May 22, 1929), pp. 626-7.

2569. Laffilte, Sophie. "La Personnalité de Tchékhov." Canadian Slavonic Papers. Vol. 2 (1969), pp. 250-61.

2570. Lahr, John. "Pinter and Chekhov: The Bond of Naturalism." Tulane Drama Review. Vol. 13, no. 2 (1968), pp. 137-45.

2571. Lewis, F. R. "Anton Chekhov." London Quarterly Review. Vol. 160 (October, 1935), pp. 484-7.

2572. MacCarthy, D. "Tchekov." New Statesman. Vol. 26 (March, 6, 1926), pp. 645-6.

2573. McConkey, James. "In Praise of Chekhov." Hudson Review. Vol. 20 (1967), pp. 417-28.

2574. Meister, C. W. "Chekhov's Reception in England and America." American Slavic Review. Vol. 12 (February, 1953), pp. 109-21.

2575. Moravcevich, Nicholas. "The Dark Side of the Chekhovian Smile." Drama Survey. Vol. 5 (1967), pp. 237-51.

2576. Morgan, Victor. "Chekhov's Social Plays and Their Historical Background." Manchester Literary Club (England) English Papers. Vol. 64 (1939), pp. 96-114.

2577. Nabokoff, C. "Chekhov on the English Stage." Contemporary Review. Vol. 129 (1926), pp. 756-62.

2578. _____. "Chekhov and His Plays." Contemporary Review. Vol. 125 (1924), pp. 338-46.

2579. Pattrick, G. Z. "Chekhov's Attitude towards Life." Slavonic Review. Vol. 10 (April, 1932), pp. 658-68.

2580. Paul, Barbara. "Chekhov's 'Five Sisters.'" Modern Drama. Vol. 14 (1971), pp. 45-67.

2581. Pritchett, V. J. "Chekhov and the Soviet Writers." New Statesman and Nation. Vol. 25 (March 27, 1943), pp. 209.

2582. Senanu, K. E. "Anton Chekhov and Henry James." Ibadan Studies in English. Vol. 2 (1970), pp. 182-92.

2583. States, Bert O. "Chekhov's Dramatic Strategy." Yale Review. Vol. 56 (1967), pp. 212-24.

2584. Struve, Gleb. "On Chekhov's Craftsmanship." Slavic Review. Vol. 20 (1961), pp. 365-76.

2585. Styan, J. L. "The Delicate Balance: Audience Ambivalence in the Comedy of Shakespeare and Chekhov." Costerus. Vol. 2 (1972), pp. 159-84.

2586. _____. "The Idea of a Definitive Production of Chekhov In and Out of Period." Comparative Drama. Vol. 4 (1970), pp. 177-96.

2587. Wadsworth, P. B. "Tchekhov at Yalta." Bookman London). Vol. 84 (April, 1933), pp. 17, 18.

2588. Weightman, John. "Chekhov & Chekhovian." Encounter. Vol. 41 (August, 1973), pp. 51-53.

2589. Willcocks, M. P. "The Writings of Anton Chekhov." English Review. Vol. 34 (March, 1972), pp. 207-16.

2590. Winner, T. G. "Chekhov, literaturnaja biografija." American Slavic and East European Review. Vol. 14 (December, 1955), pp. 570-1.

Theses and Dissertations

2591. Gottlieb, Lois J. "Chekhov and Some Chekhovians in the English-Speaking Theatre, 1910-1935." Ph.D. Dissertation. University of Michigan, 1970.

2592. Kobler, Mary Turner Spencer. "Chekhov as Moralist: The Man with a Hammer." Ph.D. Dissertation. University of Texas, 1968.

2593. Meister, Charles W. "English and American Criticism of Chekhov." Ph.D. Dissertation. University of Chicago, 1949.

2594. Moravcevich, Nicholas. "Chekhovian Dramatic Innovations." Ph.D. Dissertation. University of Wisconsin, 1964.

2595. Raviv, Zeev. "The Productions of Chekhov's Plays on the American Professional Stage." Ph.D. Dissertation. Yale University, 1964.

2596. Toumanova, Nina A. "Anton Chekhov, the Voice of Twilight Russia." Ph.D. Dissertation. Columbia University, 1937.

2597. Tracy, Robert Edward. "The Flight of the Seagull. Chekhov's Plays on the English Stage." Ph.D. Dissertation. Harvard University, 1960.

2598. Urbanski, Henry. "Chekhov as Viewed by His Russian Literary Contemporaries." Ph.D. Dissertation. New York University, 1974.

MAXIM GORKY

(Pseudonym of Alexei Maximovich Pieskov, 1868-1936. Also transliterated as Gorki and Gorkii.)

Selected Full-length Plays:

> Meshchane (The Smug Citizen, Petty
>   Bourgeois, Philistines, 1901)
> Na dne (The Lower Depths, A Night's
>   Lodging, Night's Refuge, Submerged,
>   Underworld, 1902)
> Dachnik (Summerfolk, The Vacationists,
>   1904)
> Deti solntsa (The Children of the Sun,
>   1905)
> Vragi (Enemies, 1906)
> Varvary (The Barbarians, 1906)
> Chudaki (The Eccentricities, 1910)
> Vassa Zheleznova (1910)
> Deti Vstrecho (The Meeting, 1910)

Zykovy (The Zykovs, 1913)
Falshivaya (False Money, 1913)
Starik (The Old Man, The Judge, 1919)

Books

2599. Boras, Frank Marshall. Maxim Gorky, the Writer: An
Interpretation. Oxford: Clarendon Press, 1967.

2600. Dillon, Emile J. Maxim Gorky, His Life and Writings.
London: Isbister, 1902.

2601. Gorky, Maxim. Reminiscences. New York: Diver, 1946.

2602. Hare, Richard. Maxim Gorky, Romantic Realists and
Conservative Revolutionary. London: Oxford University Press,
1962.

2603. Holtzman, Filia. Young Maxim Gorky, 1868-1902. New
York: Columbia University Press, 1948.

2604. Kaun, Alexander Samuel. Maxim Gorky and His Russia.
New York: Ballou, 1931.

2605. Levin, Dan. Stormy Petrel: The Life and Works of
Maxim Gorky. New York: Appleton-Century, 1965.

2606. Metcenko, A. Zavescano Gor'kim: Rol' A. M. Gor'kogo
v razvitii socialisticeskogo realizma. Moscow: Xudozestven-
naga literatura, 1969.

2607. Olgin, Moissaye J. Maxim Gorky, Writer and Revolu-
tionist. London: Lawrence, 1933.

2608. Rempel, Margareta. Leo Tolstoy, Gerhart Hauptmann
and Maxim Gorky: A Comparative Study. Ames, Iowa: University of Iowa Press, 1959.

2609. Roskin, Alexander Iosifovich. From the Banks of the
Volga: the Life of Maxim Gorky. New York: Philosophical
Library, 1946.

2610. Tkačev, P. I. Vecnyj boj: Pamfletnoe nasledie Ja.
Galana i tradicii M. Gor'kogo. Minsk: Izd. Belorussek
University, 1970.

2611. Vorob'ev, V. F. A. M. Gor'kijo socialisticeskom
ralizme. Kiev: Izd. Kievsk University, 1968.

2612. Weil, Irwin. Gorky: His Literary Development and Influence on Soviet Intellectual Life. New York: Random House,
1966.

2613. Wolfe, Bertram D. The Bridge and the Abyss: The
Troubled Friendship of Maxim Gorky and V. I. Lenin. New
York: Praeger, 1967.

2614. Yershov, Peter. Letters of Gorki and Andreev, 1899-1912. New York: Columbia University Press, 1958.

Articles

2615. Abusch, Alexander. "Maxim Gorki: Wegebahner der sozialistischen Weltliterature." Neue Deutsche Literatur. Vol. 16 (August, 1968), pp. 3-12.

2616. Adling, Wilfred. "Gorkis Weg zu dramatischer Meisterschaft und das sozialistische-humanistische Menschenbild." in Rolf Rohmer, ed. Theater hier und heute. Berlin.

2617. _____. "Gorki und Shakespeare: Zur Shapespeare-Rezeption im dramatischen Spätwerk Maxim Gorkis." Shakespeare-Jahrbuch. Vol. 105 (1969), pp. 89-103.

2618. Bjalick, Boris. "Maxim Gorki über Probleme der Literatur." Kunst und Literatur. Vol. 16 (1968), pp. 171-80.

2619. Blair, Kitty Hunter. "Gorky on Gorky." Theatre Quarterly. Vol. 3, no. 9 (January-March, 1973), pp. 27-30.

2620. Borew, J. "Maxim Gorki und einige aktuelle Probleme der Ästhetik." Kunst und Literatur. Vol. 16 (1968), pp. 561-67.

2621. Brian-Chaninov, N. "Maxim Gorky, 1869-1936, un aperçu sur sa vie et sur son oeuvre." Mercure de France. Vol. 269 (july 15, 1936), pp. 426-9.

2622. Bunin, I. "Appreciation of Maxim Gorki." Yale Review. Vol. 26 (March, 1937), pp. 533-42.

2623. Carr, E. H. "Appreciation of Maxim Gorki." Spectator. Vol. 156 (June 26, 1936), pp. 1178.

2624. Desnizki, W. "Gorki und Majakowski zum gleichen Thema." Kunst und Literatur. Vol. 16 (1968), pp. 244-53.

2625. Eventov, I. S. "O nekotoryx osobennostjax dramaturgii M. Gor'kogo (Komičeskoe i tragičeskoe)." Russkaja Literatura. Vol. 12, no. 4 (1969), pp. 57-74.

2626. _____. "Tragikomedija uxodjascego Mira: O drammaturg ičeskoj ēpopee M. Gor'Kogo." Russkaja Literatura. Vol. 14, no. 2 (1971), pp. 36-52.

2627. Gordon, Manqa. "Sketch of Maxim Gorky." Saturday Review of Literature. Vol. 14 (August 1, 1936), pp. 3-4.

2628. Grouzdev, I. "Gorki et son époque: résumé." Annales Politiques et Littéraires. Vol. 113 (April 10, 1939), pp. 382-4.

2629. Gužieva, H. W. "Russkaja realističeskaja dramaturgija 1910-x godoy." Russkaja Literatura. Vol. 12, no. 3 (1969), pp. 36-54.

2630. Katschalow, W. L. "Meine Begegnungen mit Maxim Gorki." Kunst und Literatur. Vol. 16 (1968), pp. 227-36.

2631. Kaun, Alexander S. "Glimpses of Gorki." Bookman. Vol. 65 (July, 1927), pp. 506-10.

2632. _____. "Gorki on Literature." Books Abroad. Vol. 16 (October, 1942), pp. 395-7.

2633. _____. "Maxim Gorki: A Challenge." Nation. Vol. 143 (July 11, 1936), pp. 48-9.

2634. _____. "Maxim Gorky and the Bolsheviks." Slavonic Review. Vol. 8 (March, 1930), pp. 432-48.

2635. _____. "Maxim Gorky: In Search of a Synthesis." Slavonic Review. Vol. 17 (January, 1939), pp. 429-44.

2636. _____. "Maxim Gorky's Militant Optimism." American Review. Vol. 4 (July, 1976), pp. 395-9.

2637. _____. "Some of Maxim Gorky's Untranslated Plays." Slavia. Vol. 15 (1940), pp. 10-13.

2638. Lee, R. "Maxim Gorky Emerges." World Today. Vol. 56 (June, 1930), pp. 32-8.

2639. Lisenko, Sofija. "Gorki i ukrainskata saevtska dramaturgija of 30-te godini." Ezik i Literatura. Vol. 25, no. 4 (1970), pp. 27-40.

2640. Makarenko, A. "Maxim Gorki in meinem Leben." Kunst und Literatur. Vol. 16 (1968), pp. 274-81.

2641. Manning, C. A. Maxim Gorky." South Atlantic Quarterly. Vol. 33 (July, 1934), pp. 219-228.

2642. Mjasnikov, A. S. "Maxim Gorki und Fragen der modernen Asthetik." Kunst und Literatur. Vol. 16 (1968), pp. 883-909.

2643. Moravcevich, Nicholas. "Gorky and the Western Naturalists: Anatomy of a Misalliance." Comparative Literature. Vol. 21 (1969), pp. 63-75.

2644. Pertsov, Victor. "The Pioneers: Notes on the Creative Method of Gorky and Mayakovsky." Soviet Literature. Vol. 10 (1968), pp. 136-41.

2645. Pérus, J. "Les Débuts de Gorki en France et l'influence de Nietzsche." Revue de Littérature Comparée. Vol. 27 (April, 1953), pp. 160-8.

2646. Poggioli, R. "Massimo Gorkij, 1868-1936." Nuova
Antologia. Vol. 386 (July 16, 1936), pp. 234-8.

2647. Posener, S. "Le 60e Anniversaire de Maxim Gorki."
Mercure de France. Vol. 203 (April 15, 1928), pp. 480-5.

2648. Roberts, R. E. "Maxim Gorki." New Statesman and
Nation. Vol. II (June 27, 1936), pp. 1025.

2649. Ryurikov, Boris. "The Maxim Gorky Tradition and Contemporary Literature." Soviet Literature. Vol. 2 (1968),
pp. 138-56.

2650. Verax, J. "Maxime Gorky et la guerre." Journal des
Débats. Vol. 38, Part 1 (March 6, 1931), pp. 406-8.

2651. Weil, Irwin. "Gor'kij's Relations with the Bolsheviks
and Symbolists." Slavic and East European Journal. Vol. 4
(1960), pp. 201-19.

2652. Yarmolinsky, Avraham. "Maxim Gorky." American
Scholar. Vol. 11 (1941), pp. 89-98.

2653. Youzovsky, J. "The Work of Maxim Gorky." Theatre
Arts Monthly. Vol. 20 (September, 1936), pp. 718-25.

2654. Zweig, S. "Maxim Gorky." Virginia Quarterly Review.
Vol. 5 (October, 1929), pp. 492-501.

Theses and Dissertations

2655. Rempel, Margareta. "Leo Tolstoy, Gerhart Hauptmann
and Maxim Gorky. A Comparative Study." Ph.D. Dissertation.
University of Iowa, 1959.

[COUNT] LEO [LEV NIKOLAEVICH] TOLSTOY

(1828-1910)

Selected Full-length Plays:

> Zarazhemnoe semeistvo (The Contaminated
>   Family, 1864)
> Nigilist (The Nihilist, 1866)
> Peter Khlebnik (1886)
> Dramaticheskaia obrabotka legendy ob
>   Aggee (Dramatic Adaptation of the
>   Legend of King Aggee, 1886)
> Vlast tmy, illi Kogutok uryaz, vsey
>   ptichke propast (The Power of Dark-
>   ness, or If a Claw is Caught, the
>   Bird is Lost; The Dominion of
>   Darkness, 1886)

Plody proveshcheniva (The Fruits of
   Enlightenment, The Fruits of Culture,
   1886)
Zhivoi Trup (The Living Corpse, Redemp-
   tion, The Man Who Was Dead, 1900)
Ot nei vse kachestra (The Cause of It All,
   Everything Stems from It, 1910)
Pervyi Vinokur (The First Distiller, 1910)
Svyet ro Tmye Svyettit (The Light That
   Shines in Darkness, 1912)

Books

2656. Chertkov, Vladimir Grigor'evich. Last Days of Tolstoy.
London: Heinemann, 1922.

2657. Christian, R. R. Tolstoy: A Critical Introduction.
London: Cambridge University Press, 1969.

2658. Fausset, Hugh I'Anson. Tolstoy: the Inner Drama.
London: J. Cape, 1927. New York: Harcourt & Brace & Co.,
1928.

2659. Gibian, George. Tolstoi and Shakespeare. The Hague:
Mouton, 1957.

2660. Gifford, Henry. Leo Tolstoy. A Critical Anthology.
Hammondsworth, England: Penguin Books, 1971.

2661. Keim, Albert. Tolstoi. Paris: P. Lafitte, 1913.

2662. Knight, George Wilson. Shakespeare and Tolstoy. London: H. Milford, Oxford University Press, 1934.

2663. Kuzminskaya, Mrs. Tatyana Andreyevna. Tolstoy as I
Knew Him: My Life at Home and at Yasnaya Polyana. New York:
Macmillan, 1948.

2664. Larvin, Janko. Tolstoy: An Approach. New York: Macmillan Company, 1946.

2665. Lloyd, John Arthur. Two Russian Reformers: Ivan
Turgenev, Leo Tolstoy. London: Lane, 1911.

2666. Lukács, György. Tolstoi und die westliche Literatur.
Düsseldorf: Progress Verlag J. Fladung, 1954.

2667. Matlaw, Ralph E. Tolstoy. A Collection of Critical
Essays. New Jersey: Prentice-Hall, 1967.

2668. Maude, Aylmer. Family Views of Tolstoy. London:
Allen and Unwin, 1926.

2669. _____. Leo Tolstoy. New York: Dodd, 1918.

2670. _____. Leo Tolstoy and His Works. London:
Oxford, 1931.

2671. Maude, Aylmer. Life of Tolstoy. New York: Dodd, 1910.

2672. Nazarov, Alexsandr Ivanovich. Tolstoy, the Inconstant Genius. New York: Stokes, 1929.

2673. Noyes, George Rapall. Tolstoy. New York: Duffield & Co., 1918.

2674. Polner, Tikhon Ivanovich. Tolstoy and His Wife. New York: Norton, 1945.

2675. Rempel, Maragreta. Leo Tolstoy, Gerhart Hauptmann and Maxim Gorky: A Comparative Study. Ames, Iowa: University of Iowa Press, 1959.

2676. Rolland, Romain. Tolstoy.. New York: E. P. Dutton, 1911.

2677. Shestov, Lev. Doestoevsky, Tolstoy and Nietzsche. Athens, Ohio: Ohio University Press, 1969.

2678. Simmons, Ernest Joseph. Introduction to Tolstoy's Writing. Chicago: University of Chicago Press, 1968.

2679. _____. Leo Tolstoy. New York: Vintage Books, 1946.

2680. Spiers, Logan. Tolstoy and Chekhov. Cambridge: Cambridge University Press, 1971.

2681. Spence, Gordon W. Tolstoy the Ascetic. New York: Barnes and Noble, 1968.

2682. Steiner, E. A. Tolstoy, The Man and His Message. New York: Fleming H. Revell Co., 1914.

2683. Steiner, George. Tolstoy or Dostoevsky. An Essay In the Old Criticism. New York: Knopf, 1959.

2684. Tolstoy, Leo. Private Diary of Leo Tolstoy, 1853-1857. London: Heinemann, 1927.

2685. _____. Tolstoy: Literary Fragments, Letters and Reminiscences Not Previously Published. New York: Dial Press, 1931.

2686. Troyat, Henri. Tolstoy. Garden City, New York: Doubleday, 1967.

2687. Zweig, Stefan. Adepts in Self Portraiture. New York: Viking Press, 1928.

In Russian:

2688. Bychkov, Leo Nikolaevich. L. N. Tolstoy. Ocherk tvor-
chestva. Moscow: 1954.

2689. Gudzii, Nikolai K. Lev Nikolaevich Tolstoy. Moscow:
1959.

2690. Gusev, Nikolai N. Lev Nikolaevich Tolstoy. Materialy
y biografii. Three Volumes. Moscow, 1954-63.

2691. Khrapchenko, Mikhail B. Lev Tolstoy kak khudozhnik.
Moscow: Khudozhestvennaia literatura, 1971.

2692. Saburov, Aleksandr. 'Voyna i mir' L. N. Tolstogo.
Problematika i poetika. Moscow: 1959.

Theses and Dissertations

2693. Freling, Roger N. "A Critical Study of Two Tolstoi
Plays: The Power of Darkness and The Live Corpse." Ph.D.
Dissertation. University of Washington, 1972.

2694. Korman, William R. "Tolstoi and the Drama." Ph.D.
Dissertation. Stanford University, 1973.

2695. Moore, Arthur U. "Art, Community and Theatre, A Study
of the Theories of Five Nineteenth Century Artists: Tolstoy,
Wagner, Nietzsche, Appia, Rolland." Ph.D. Dissertation.
Cornell University, 1936.

Articles

2696. Abraham, J. H. "The Religious Ideas and Social Philosophy of Tolstoy." International Journal of Ethics. Vol.
40 (October, 1929), pp. 105-20.

2697. Benson, Ruth C. "Women in Tolstoy: The Ideal and the
Erotic." Urbana: University of Illinois Press, 1973, n. pag.

2698. Bernstein, E. "Turgenev and the Tolstoys." New
Statesman. Vol. 7 (March 10, 1934), pp. 349-50.

2699. Bonnaud-Lamotte, B. "Tolstoï et le théâtre révolu-
tionnaire selon l'équipe des Cahiers de la Quinzaine et autre
revues," in Travaux de linguistique et de Littérature publiés
par le Centre de Philologie et de littératures romanes de
l'Université de Strasbourg. Paris: Libr. C. Klincksieck,
1971, pp. 139-144.

2700. De Casseres, B. "Idealism of Lyof Tolstoi." International. Vol. 8 (April, 1914), pp. 129-30.

2701. Flew, A. "Tolstoi and the Meaning of Life." Ethics.
Vol. 73 (January, 1963), pp. 110-18.

2702. Gorky, M. "Reminiscences of Leo Tolstoy." Nation. Vol. 112 (March 9, 1921), pp. 379-80.

2703. Nag, Martin. "Tolstoj og Ibsen." Ibsenforbundet: Arbok. (1972), pp. 78-82.

2704. Nazaroff, A. I. "Tolstoy: A Centenary Study." Bookman. (September, 1928), pp. 28-35.

2705. Philonenko, A. "Histoire et religion chez Tolstoi." Revue de Théologie et de Philosophie. Vol. 3 (1968), pp. 65-87.

2706. Roberts, R. E. "Analysis of Leo Tolstoy." Bookman. Vol. 74 (August, 1928), pp. 239-43.

2707. Shaw, George Bernard. "Dramatist, Tragedian or Comedian?" Mercury (London). Vol. 4 (May, 1921), pp. 31-4.

2708. Simmons, E. J. "Recent Publications on L. N. Tolstoi." Slavonic Review. Vol. 20 (1941), pp. 338-46.

2709. Tiander, K. "Tolstojs Lebenstragödie." Deutsche Rundschau. Vol. 204 (September, 1925), pp. 271-7.

2710. Vladesco, T. "Entre Ibsen et Tolstoi: réflexions sur l'archisme." Mercure de France. Vol. 206 (September 15, 1928), pp. 5669-87.

2711. Williams, R. "Tolstoy, Lawrence and Tragedy." Kenyon Review. Vol. 25 (Autumn, 1963), pp. 633-50.

2712. Woolf, L. "Tolstoi's Plays." Nation (London). Vol. 34 (March 1, 1924), p. 766.

IVAN [SERGEIVICH] TURGENEV

(1818-1883)

Selected Full-length Plays:

> Bezdenezhye (Penniless, Broke, 1845)
> Nakhlebnik (The Family Charge, A Poor
>   Gentleman, 1849)
> Zavtrak u predvoditelya (An Amicable
>   Settlement, 1849)
> Mesyats v devevne (A Month in the
>   Country, 1850)
> Razgovor na bolshoy doroge (A Conver-
>   sation on the Highway, 1850)
> Provintsialka (A Provincial Lady,
>   The Lady from the Provinces, The
>   Country Woman, 1851)

Gdne tonko, tam i ruvotsya (Where It
   Is Thin, There It Breaks; One May
   Spin a Thread Too Finely, 1851)
Vecher v Sorrenk (An Evening in
   Sorrento, 1852)

Books

2713. Bonetsky, K. I., ed. Turgenev v russkoy kritike,
Sbornik statey. Moscow, 1953.

2714. Efimova, Evgeniia M. I. S. Turgenev. Seminariy. Lon-
ingrad, 1958.

2715. Garnett, Edward William. Turgenev: A Study. London:
Collins, 1917.

2716. Gottlieb, Nora and Raymond Chapman, ed. & trans.
Letters to an Actress: The Story of Turgenev and Savina.
Athens, Ohio: Ohio University Press, 1974.

2717. Granjard, Henri. Ivan Tourguénev et les courants
politiques et sociaux de son temps. Paris: Institut d'études
slaves de l'Université de Paris, 1954.

2718. Lloyd, John Arthur Thomas. Ivan Turgenev. London:
R. Hale, 1942.

2719. _____ . Two Russian Reformers: Ivan Turgenev,
Leo Tolstoy. London: Lane, 1911.

2720. Magarshack, David. Turgenev: A Life. New York: Grove
Press, 1954.

2721. Moser, Charles A. Ivan Turgenev. New York: Columbia
University Press, 1972.

2722. Nazarova, L. N. and A. D. Alkseev, eds. Bibliografija
literatury o I. S. Turgeneve, 1918-1967. Leningrad: Nauka,
1970.

2723. Yachnin, Rissa and David H. Stam. Turgenev in English:
A Checklist of Works by and about Him. New York: New York
Public Library, 1962.

2724. Yarmolinsky, Avrahm. Turgenev, the Man, His Art and
His Age. New York: The Century Company, 1926.

Theses and Dissertations

2725. Gettmann, Royal A. "Turgenev in England and America."
Ph.D. Dissertation. University of Illinois, 1938.

2726. Hershkowitz, Harry. "Democratic Ideas in Turgenev's
Works." Ph.D. Dissertation. Columbia University, 1932.

2727. Kappler, Richard Georges. "Turgenev and the French." Ph.D. Dissertation. Columbia University, 1961.

2728. Maurer, Sigred Helga. "Schopenhauer in Russia: His Influence on Turgenev, Fet and Tolstoy. Ph.D. Dissertation. University of California, 1967.

2729. Ozdrovsky, Marina. "The Plays of Turgenev in Relation to Nineteenth Century European and Russian Drama." Ph.D. Dissertation. Columbia University, 1972.

2730. Sly, Gerlinde H. "The Role of Social Consciousness and Fatalism in the Works of Georg Büchner and the Younger Ivan Sergevevich Turgenev." Ph.D. Dissertation. New York University, 1966.

Articles

2731. Carr, E. H. "Turgenev and Dostoyevsky." Slavonic Review. Vol. 8 (June, 1929), pp. 156-63.

2732. Cross, A. G. "The Breaking Strings of Chekhov and Turgenev." Slavonic and East European Review. Vol. 47 (1970), pp. 510-13.

2733. Howe, I. "Turgenev: The Virtues of Hesitation." Hudson Review. Vol. 8 (Winter, 1956), pp. 533-51.

2734. Korn, David. "Turgenev in Nineteenth Century America." Russian Review. Vol. 27 (1968), pp. 461-67.

2735. Maurois, André. "Le théâtre de Tourguéniev." Cahiers de la Compagnie Madeleine Renaud-Jean Louis Barrault. Vol. 52 (1965), pp. 91-96.

2736. Montreynaud, Florence. "Les Relations de Zola et de Tourguéniev: Documents inédits." Cahiers Naturalistes. Vol. 43 (1972), pp. 55-82.

2737. Kappler, Richard G. "Ivan S. Turgenev as a Critic of French Literature." Comparative Literature. Vol. 20 (1968), pp. 133-41.

2738. Pritchett, V. S. "Hero of Our Time?" London Mercury. Vol. 36 (August, 1937), pp. 359-64.

2739. Sayler, O. M. "Turgenieff as a Playwright." North American Review. Vol. 214 (September, 1921), pp. 293-400.

2740. Squire, J. "Ivan Turgenev: An Appreciation." Illustrated London News. Vol. 202 (April 10, 1943), p. 404.

2741. Terras, Victor. "Turgenev's Aesthetic and Western Realism." Comparative Literature. Vol. 22 (1970), pp. 19-35.

2742. Waddington, Patrick. "Two Months in the Country: A Critical Episode in the Life and Career of Turgenev." New Zealand Slavonic Journal. Vol. 2 (Winter, 1973), pp. 29-50.

2743. Woodcock, G. "Elusive Ideal: Notes on Turgenev." Sewanee Review. Vol. 69 (Winter, 1961), pp. 34-47.

2744. Zviguilsky, Alexandre. "Tourgéniev et Galdós." Revue de Littérature Comparée. Vol. 41 (1967), pp. 117-120.

XI SPAIN

General Commentaries

Books

2745. Bell, Aubrey FitzGerald. Contemporary Spanish Literature. New York: Knopf, 1933.

2746. Benedikt, Michael and George E. Wellworth. Modern Spanish Theatre. New York: Dutton, 1968.

2747. Blanco García, Francisco. La literatura española en el siglo XIX. Three Volumes. Madrid: Sáenz de Jubera Hermanos, 1894-1912.

2748. Bueno, Manuel. Teatro español contemporanéo. Madrid: Edit. V. Prieto y Cía, 1910.

2749. Chaytor, H. J. Dramatic Theory in Spain. Cambridge, England: The University Press, 1925.

2750. Curzon, Henri de. Un théâtre d'idées en Espagne: Etude analytique. Paris, 1911.

2751. _____. Le théâtre espagnol. Versailles: Cerf, 1898.

2752. Díaz de Escova, Narciso, and Francisco de P. de la Vega. Historia del teatro español. Two Volumes. Barcelona: Montaner y Simon, 1924.

2753. Fitzmaurice-Kelly, James. New History of Spanish Literature. London: Oxford University Press, 1926.

2754. Gassier, Alfred. Le Théâtre espagnol. Paris: n.p., 1898.

2755. Gonzáles--Blanco, Andres. Los dramaturgos españoles contemporáneos. Valencia: Editorial, 1917.

2756. Gregersen, Halfden A. I. Ibsen and Spain, A Study In Comparative Drama. Cambridge: Harvard University Press, 1936.

2757. Hormigón, Juan A. Teatro, realismo y cultura de masas. Madrid: Edicusa, 1974.

2758. Julia Martinez, Eduardo. Teatro moderno. Madrid: Instituto Antonio de Nebrija, 1947.

2759. León, Pagano, José. Al través de la España litereria. Barcelona: n.p., 1904.

2760. Mérimée, Ernest. History of Spanish Literature. New York: Holt, 1930.

2761. Rebello, Luiz F. Teatro moderno: caminhos e figuras. Lisbon: Sociedade Gráfica Editorial, 1964.

2762. Ruiz Ramon, Francisco. Historia del teatro español Siglo XX. Madrid: Alianza, 1971.

2763. Sainz de Robles, Federico C. El teatro español, historia y antologia. Madrid: M. Aguilar, 1942-43.

2764. Turrell, Charles A. Contemporary Spanish Dramatists. Boston: Badger, 1919.

2765. Valbuena Prat, Angel. Teatro moderno español. Zaragoza: Ediciones Partenon, 1944.

2766. Yxart, José. El arte escénico en Espana. Two Volumes. Barcelona: Imp. de la Vanguardia, 1894-96.

Articles

2767. Ayer, Charles C. "Foreign Drama on the English and American Stage." Colorado Studies. Vol. 10, no. 3 (1913), 149-61.

2768. Bahr, Hermann. "Notizen zur neueren spanischen Literatur." Preussische Jahrbücher. Vol. 200 (April-May, 1925), pp. 13-22, 136-67.

2769. Curzon, Henri de. "Le théâtre de l'Espagne." Revue de France Moderne. 1899, n. pag.

2770. Davis, G. "The Critical Reception of Naturalism in Spain before La cuestión palpitante." Hispanic Review. Vol. 22 (April, 1954), pp. 165-74.

2771. Gregersen, Halfden. "Visiting Italian Interpreters of Ibsen in Barcelona and Madrid." Hispanic Review. Vol. 3, no. 2 (1935), pp. 166-9.

2772. Hutton, E. "The Real Drama in Spain." Mask. Vol. 1
(March, 1908), pp. 5-8.

2773. Lott, Robert E. "On Mannerism and Mannered Approaches
in Un Drama Nuevo, Consuelo and Earlier Nineteenth-Century
Spanish Plays." Hispania. Vol. 54 (1971), pp. 844-55.

2774. Pérez de la Dehesa, Lily L. "Naturalismo y teatro
social en cataluña." Comparative Literature Studies. Vol.
5 (1968), pp. 279-302.

2775. Turrell, C. A. "Some Aspects of Contemporary Spanish
Drama." Poet Lore. Vol. 29 (May-June, 1918), pp. 319-30.

2776. Unamuno, Miguel de. La regeneración del teatro español." España Moderna. Vol. 91 (1896), pp. 5-36.

2777. Wallace, Elizabeth. "Spanish Drama of Today." Atlantic Monthly. Vol. 102 (September, 1908), pp. 357-66.

Theses and Dissertations

2778. Brown, James R. "An Aspect of Realism in Modern Spanish Drama. The Concept of Society." Ph.D. Dissertation.
University of Chicago, 1941.

2779. Gregersen, Halfdan I. "Ibsen and Spain. A Study in
Comparative Drama." Ph.D. Dissertation. Columbia University,
1936.

2780. Klein, Richard B. "The Development of Realism in Late
Nineteenth-Century Spanish Drama." Ph.D. Dissertation. University of Illinois, 1971.

2781. Noble, Judith A. "Development of the Theme of Materialism in the Social Thesis Drama of Nineteenth Century
Spain." Ph.D. Dissertation. Louisiana State University,
1969.

2782. Rozentals, Gunta. "Realism in Alta Comedia." Ph.D.
Dissertation. University of Minnesota, 1969.

JOAQUIN DICENTA Y BENEDICTO

(1863-1917)

Selected Full-length Plays:

>
> Los Irresponsables (The Irresponsible
>   Ones, 1892)
> Juan José (1895)
> Aurora (Dawn, 1899)
> Daniel (1906)
> Luciano (1907)
> El Crimen de Ayer (Yesterday's Crime,
>   1908)
> Sobre vivirse (To Stay Alive, 1911)
> El Señor Feudal (The Feudal Master,
>   1913)
> El lobo (The Wolf, 1913)

Books

2783. Gonzáles-Blanco, Andrés. Los dramaturgos españoles contemporáneos. Valencia: Edit. Cervantes, 1917.

Articles

2784. Hall, H. B. "Joaquin Dicenta and the Drama of Social Criticism." Hispanic Review. Vol. 20 (January, 1952), pp. 44-66.

2785. Morby, E. S. "Notes on Dicenta's Material and Method: Repetition as Self-plagiarism." Hispanic Review. Vol. 9 (July, 1941), pp. 383-93.

JOSÉ ECHEGARAY [Y EIZAGUIRRE]

(1832-1916)

Selected Full-length Plays:

>
> Lo que no puede decirse (That Which Can't
>   Be Uttered, 1877)
> La muerte en los labios (Death on the
>   Lips, 1880)
> O locura o santidad (Madman or Saint, Folly
>   or Saintliness, 1881)
> El gran Galeoto (The Great Galeoto, The
>   Great Go-Between, The World and His
>   Wife, 1881)
> El bandido Lisandro (Lisandro the Bandit,
>   1886)
> De mala raza (The Evil Race, 1886)
> Los fantasmos (Ghosts, 1887)

La realidad y el delirio (Reality and
    Delirium, 1887)
El hijo de hierro y el hijo de carne
    (The Son of Iron and the Son of
    Flesh, 1888)
Siempre en ridículo (Always Ridiculous,
    1890)
Comedia sin desenlace (Play Without a
    Catastrophe, 1891)
Mariana (1892)
El hijo de Don Juan (The Son of Don
    Juan, 1892)
El poder de la impotencia (The Power of
    Weakness, 1893)
Maria Rosa (1894)
Mancha que limpia (The Cleansing Stain,
    1895)
El salvaje (Savage Love, 1896)
La calumnia por castigo (The Lies for
    Punishment, 1897)
La duda (The Doubt, 1898)
El hombre negro (The Man in Black, 1898)
Silencio de muerte (The Silence of Death,
    1898)

Books

2786. Curzon, Henri de. Le théâtre de José Echegaray.
Paris: Fischbacher, 1912.

2787. Gallego y Burin, Antonio. Echegaray: Su obra dramát-
ica. Granada: Tip. Lit. P. V. Traveset, 1917.

2788. Herrán, Fermín. Echegaray: Su tiempo y su teatro.
Madrid: Imp. de Fortanet, 1880.

2789. Leal, José R. Teatro nuevo. Juicio crítico de las
obras de José Echegaray. Havana: La Propaganda Literaria,
1880.

2790. Olmet, Luis A. de, and A. García Carrafa. Echegaray.
Madrid: n. p., 1912.

Theses and Dissertations

2791. Berkowitz, H. C. "José Echegaray: His Life and Dramatic Works." M.A. Thesis. Cornell University, 1918.

2792. Bowen, Edwin DuBose. "The Influence of Ibsen Upon
Echegaray as a Dramatist." Ph.D. Dissertation. Southern
Methodist University, 1941.

2793. Goldberg, Isaac. "Don José Echegaray. A Study in
Modern Spanish Drama." Ph.D. Dissertation. Harvard University, 1912.

2794. Kalil, Mary. "The Treatment of Social Problems in the Works of José Echegaray." Ph.D. Dissertation. University of Arizona, 1933.

2795. Mercer, Lucille E. "The Dramatic Art of José Echegaray. M.A. Thesis. The Ohio State University, 1928.

2796. Young, John R. "José Echegaray. A Study of His Dramatic Technique." Ph.D. Dissertation. Illinois University, 1938.

Articles

2797. Alas, L. "Ibsen y Echegaray." Correspondencia de España. Vol. 4 (1892), pp. 23-8.

2798. Curzon, Henri. "Le théâtre d'Echegaray." Nouvelle Revue. Vols. 25, 26 (1912), p. 180.

2799. Gardiner, Fanny Hale. "Echegaray: Spanish Statesman, Dramatist, Poet." Poet Lore. Vol. 12 (1900), pp. 405-16.

2800. Gregersen, Halfden. "Ibsen and Echegaray." Hispanic Review. Vol. 1 (1933), pp. 338-40.

2801. Kennedy, Ruth Lee. "The Indebtedness of Echegaray to Ibsen." Sewanee Review. Vol. 34 (October, 1926), pp. 402-15.

2802. Lynch, Hannah. "José Echegaray." Contemporary Review. Vol. 64 (October, 1893), pp. 576-95.

2803. Newberry, Wilma. "Echegaray and Pirandello." PMLA. Vol. 8 (March, 1966), pp. 123-29.

2804. Mérimée, Ernest. "José Echegaray et son oeuvre dramatique." Bulletin Hispanique. Vol. 18 (October-December, 1916), pp. 247-78.

2805. Pitollet, Camille. "Echegaray et Ibsen." Bulletin de la Société Études des Professeurs de Langues Méridionales. Vol. 29, no. 80 (1934), pp. 158-64.

2806. Smith, Nora Archibald. "José Echegaray." Poet Lore. Vol. 20 (May-June, 1909), pp. 218-28.

2807. "Spain's Homage to Echegaray." Review of Reviews. Vol. 31 (May, 1905), pp. 613-14.

BENITO PÉREZ GALDÓS

(1843-1920)

Selected Full-length Plays:

La loca de la casa (The Madwoman of the
    House, 1893)
Los Condenados (The Condemned, 1894)
Voluntad (Will Power, 1895)
El Abuelo (The Grandfather, 1897)
Electra (1901)
Alma y vida (Soul and Life, 1902)
Mariucha (1903)
Bárbara (1905)
Gerona (1905)
Amor y ciencia (Love and Science, 1905)
Casandra (1910)
Celia en los infiernos (Celia in the
    Slums, 1913)
Sor Simona (Sister Simona, 1915)
El Tacaño Salomon (Solomor the Miser,
    1916)

Books

2808. Berkowitz, Hyman C. Pérez Galdós, Spanish Liberal
Crusader. Madison, Wisconsin: University of Wisconsin Press,
1948.

2809. Casalduero, Joaquin. Vida y obra de Galdós (1843-
1920). Madrid: Editorial Gredos, 1970.

2810. Dennis, Ward H. Pérez Galdós: A Study in Characterization. Madrid: "Episodios Nacionales," 1968.

2811. Faus Sevilla, Pilar. La sociedad española del siglo
XIX en la obra de Pérez Galdós. Valencia: Nacher, 1972.

2812. Gutierrez-Gamero y Romante, Emilio. Galdós y su obra.
Madrid: Impr. Ruiz, 1935.

2813. Montesinos, José F. Galdós. Madrid: Castalia, 1968.

2814. Sackett, Theodore A. Pérez Galdós: An Annotated Bibliography. Albuquerque: University of New Mexico Press, 1968.

2815. Varey, J. E., ed. Galdós Studies. London: Tamesis,
1970.

2816. Walton, Leslie B. Pérez Galdós and the Spanish Novel
of the Nineteenth Century. London: J. M. Dent & Sons, 1927.

Theses and Dissertations

2817. Carney, Hal. "The Dramatic Technique of Benito Pérez Galdós." Ph.D. Dissertation. University of Nebraska, 1957.

2818. Davis, John Frank. "The Proletarian Elements in the Works of Pérez Galdós." Ph.D. Dissertation. University of Missouri (Columbia), 1939.

2819. Finkenthal, Stanley M. "The Theatre of Pérez Galdós: The Artist as Social Critic." Ph.D. Dissertation. New York University, 1972.

2820. Gallagher, Mary L. "Galdós as a Dramatist." Ph.D. Dissertation. University of Pittsburgh, 1935.

2821. Goodale, Hope K. "Pérez Galdós, Dramatic Critic and Dramatist." Ph.D. Dissertation. Bryn Mawr University, 1966.

2822. Orsag, Shirley A. "Galdós' Presentation of Women in the Light of Naturalism." Ph.D. Dissertation. University of Pittsburgh, 1972.

Articles

2823. Altamira y Crevea, Rafael. "El teatro de Galdós," in De Historia y de arte. Madrid: n.p., 1898.

2824. Anderson Imbert, Enrique. "Un drama ibseniano de Galdós. Sur. Vol. 16, no. 167 (1948), pp. 26-31.

2825. Berkowitz, H. C. "Galdós and the Generation of 1898." Philological Quarterly. Vol. 21 (January, 1942), pp. 107-20.

2826. Casalduero, J. "El Desarrollo de la Obra de Galdós." Hispanic Review. Vol. 10 (July, 1942), pp. 244-50.

2827. Doménech, Ricardo. "En busca del teatro de Galdós." Etudios Escénicos. Vol. 18 (1974), pp. 11-12.

2828. Elton, Willa S. "Autocensura en el drama galdósiano." Estudios Escénicos. Vol. 18 (1974), pp. 139-54.

2829. Gil, Alfonso M. "Notas e impresiones acerca del teatro de Benito Pérez Galdós." Estudios Escénicos. Vol. 18 (1974), pp. 155-64.

2830. Gonzales Lopez, Emilio. "El drama social contemporáneo: Pérez Galdós y Gomez de la Serna." Estudios Escénicos. Vol. 18 (1974), pp. 203-14.

2831. Goodale, Hope K. "Allusions to Shakespeare in Galdós." Hispanic Review. Vol. 39 (1971), pp. 249-60.

2832. Machado y Ruiz, Manuel. "Galdós, dramaturgo." Lectura. Vol. 20 (1920), pp. 208-21.

2833. Madariaga, S. de. "Work of Pérez Galdós." Contemporary Review. Vol. 117 (April, 1929), pp. 508-16.

2834. Monterde Garcia Icazbalcetam, Francisco. "Don Benito Peréz Galdos y el teatro de su época." Filosofía y Letras. Vol. 17 (1949), pp. 287-300.

2835. Pérez Minik, Domingo. "Galdós, ese dramaturgo recobrado." Estudios Escénicos. Vol. 18 (1974), pp. 13-24.

2836. Vazquez Maldonado, F. "El teatro de Galdós," in Pareceres. Almería: Tip. del diario de Almería, 1930, n. pag.

2837. Waldeck, R. W. "Benito Pérez Galdós, Novelist, Dramatist and Reformer." The Critic. Vol. 45 (1904), pp. 447-9.

2838. Warshaw, J. "Galdós' Apprenticeship in the Drama." Modern Language Notes. Vol. 44 (November, 1929), pp. 459-63.

ENRIQUE GASPAR [Y RIMBAU *OR* Y PALENCIA]

(1842-1902)

Selected Full-length Plays:

> Las circumstancias (The Circumstances, 1867)
> La levita (The Frockcoat, 1868)
> Don Ramon y el senor Ramon (1868)
> El estómago (The Stomach, 1871)
> Los Niños grandes (The Childish Grandees, 1871)
> La lengua (The Tongue, 1882)
> Lola (1885)
> Las personas decentes (Decent People, 1890)
> La huelga de hijos (The Strike of Sons, 1893)
> La eterna cuestión (The Eternal Question, 1895)

Books

2839. Hurtado y González Palencia. Historia de la literatura española. Madrid: Tip. de la Revista de Archives, 1922.

2840. Kirschenbaum, Leo. Enrique Gaspar and the Social Drama in Spain. Berkeley: University of Southern California Press, 1944.

2841. Poyán, Díaz Danuel. Enrique Gaspar. Medio siglo de teatro español. Two Volumes. Madrid: Editorial Gredos.

Articles

2842. Alsina, José. "Un autor olvidado, Enrique Gaspar."
Blanco y Negro. June 28, 1925, n. pag.

2843. Cabello y Lapiedra. "La escena española en el siglo
XX--Enrique Gaspar." Gente Conocida. July 31, 1902, p. 61-3.

2844. Canals, Salvador. "Enrique Gaspar." Nuestro Tiempo.
September, 1902, pp. 377-92.

2845. Deleite y Piñuela, J. "Del Madrid teatral fines del
siglo XIX--el realismo de Enrique Gaspar." El Mercantil
Valenciano. December 13, 1931, n. pag.

2846. López Núñez, Juan. "Dramaturgos olvidados." La Voz.
September 15, 1930, n. pag.

2847. Pardo Bazán, Emilia. "Un ibseniano español," in Obras
Completas. Vol. 47. Madrid: n.p., 1893, pp. 250-4.

ANGEL GUIMERÁ

(1845-1924)

Selected Full-length Plays:

>   Maria Rosa (1890)
>   En Pólvora (Gunpowder, The Laborer,
>   1893)
>   La Pecadora (The Prostitute, Daniela,
>   1893)
>   Terra baixa (The Lowlands, Marta of
>   the Lowlands, 1896)
>   La Festa del Blat (The Festival of
>   Wheat, Harvest Home, 1896)
>   Mossín Janot (1898)
>   La filla del mar (The Daughter of the
>   Sea, 1900)
>   Arrán de Terra (Poor of the Earth,
>   1901)
>   La Miralta (1905)
>   Jesús que torna (Jesus Returns, 1917)

Books

2848. Cruset, José. Angel Guimerá: universalidad y grandeza
en el teatro catalan. Barcelona: La Vanguardia española,
1971.

2849. Guimerá, Angel. Angel Guimerá en els seus millors
escrits. Barcelona: Editorial Miquel Arimany, 1974.

2850. Miracle, Josep. Guimerá. Barcelona: Editorial Aedos,
1958.

2851. Miracle, Josep. La leyenda y la historia en la bio-
grafia de Angel Guimerá. Barcelona: La Laguna de Tenerife,
1952.

Articles

2852. "Portrait." New York Dramatic Mirror. Vol. 61 (June
19, 1909), p. 6.

INDEX TO AUTHORS CITED

ABOUT THE COMPILER

Robert D. Boyer is assistant professor in the Division of Comparative Studies in the Humanities at Ohio State University in Columbus. His articles have appeared in such journals as *Theatre Studies* and *Speech Journal.*